THE *InterActive* READER™ PLUS

TEACHER'S GUIDE

Active Reading Strategies for All Students

Grade 6

McDougal Littell
A HOUGHTON MIFFLIN COMPANY
Evanston, Illinois   Boston   Dallas

McDougal Littell Inc. grants permission to the classroom teacher to reproduce copymasters as needed.

Copyright © 2003 by McDougal Littell Inc.
Box 1667, Evanston, Illinois 60204
All rights reserved. Printed in the United States of America.

ISBN-13: 978-0-618-31024-1   ISBN-10: 0-618-31024-X

6 7 8 9 – PBO– 08 07 06

Table of Contents

What Is *The InterActive Reader™ Plus*?

A book that allows students with different abilities to develop stronger reading skills by encouraging the use of a variety of comprehension strategies.

Every student is on the same page, but strategic help varies across three levels:

The InterActive Reader™ Plus

Includes

- Literature selections from the Grade 6 *Language of Literature* broken into short, manageable sections
- Reading support throughout
- A consumable format that allows students to mark the text with their notes and questions
- In-book activity sheets

The InterActive Reader™ Plus with Additional Support

Includes

- All of the features of *The InterActive Reader™ Plus*
- Special reading support for your struggling readers, including
  - a brief summary with every section
  - more contextual background information
  - extra reading checks
- Page layouts that are the same across all books

The InterActive Reader™ Plus for English Learners

Includes

- All the features of *The InterActive Reader™ Plus*
- Special support for English Learners, including
  - a brief summary with every section
  - more contextual background information
  - special language and culture notes
  - extra reading checks
- Page layouts that are the same across all books

The InterActive Reading Process

The InterActive Reader™ _Plus_ encourages students to write in their books!

All levels of _The InterActive Reader_™ _Plus_ provide students and teachers with a unique resource that fosters reading comprehension. _The InterActive Reader_™ _Plus_ encourages students to engage or _interact_ with the text. Activities before, during, and after reading a selection prompt students to make personal connections; ask themselves questions; clarify their ideas; and visualize objects, persons, and places—all thinking processes performed by proficient readers.

The following features help students interact with the text:

Before Reading

Connect to Your Life and **Key to the Selection** give students concrete ways to begin thinking about the selection they will read.

FOCUS Appearing before each "chunk" of text, the Focus serves as a mini-preview and sets the purpose for reading.

Additional Support for Struggling Readers and English Learners

As the story begins... Every chunk of text begins with a brief summary of the section.

During Reading

MARK IT UP **KEEP TRACK** Using a system of stars, question marks, and exclamation marks, students monitor their understanding as they read.

Pause & Reflect Students read until the Pause & Reflect symbol appears, signaling them to stop and answer the questions in the margins. These questions allow students to follow up on the purpose-setting statement in the Focus and to learn and practice a variety of reading skills and strategies, including

- summarizing
- inferring
- questioning
- predicting
- visualizing
- connecting
- clarifying
- evaluating

- drawing conclusions
- stating opinions
- locating main ideas
- making judgments
- analyzing
- identifying cause-and-effect relationships
- understanding an author's purpose
- distinguishing fact from opinion

MARK IT UP This activity invites students to underline, circle, or highlight key words or passages that help clarify meaning.

 Frequently, students are told to reread a key passage aloud to themselves or to a partner to focus on a particular idea, author's intent, or author's use of language.

 Often, students are told to reread a key passage and then given a question that checks their comprehension.

Additional Support for Struggling Readers and English Learners

 Reading Check These questions at key points in the text help students clarify what is happening in a selection.

MORE ABOUT . . . These notes provide key background information, such as historical context, political situations, and scientific background, needed for understanding the selection.

WHAT DOES IT MEAN? Possibly confusing words, phrases, references, and other constructions are clearly explained in these notes.

 Reader's Success Strategy Specifically for struggling readers, these notes give useful and fun tips and strategies for comprehending the selection.

English Learner Support **Language** Support for English Learners involves a wide range of vocabulary, language, and culture issues that are covered in these special notes.

After Reading

 Challenge At the end of most selections, a Challenge activity requires students to reenter the selection to analyze a key idea and to answer a higher-level question.

SkillBuilder Pages During and after reading a selection, students are encouraged to complete the SkillBuilder pages that follow each lesson. The three SkillBuilder pages help students practice and apply important skills.

• **Active Reading SkillBuilder** Comprehension skills are reinforced through graphics and other visual representations, requiring students to use their understanding of the selection to extend their reading skills.

• **Literary Analysis SkillBuilder** Literary elements are reinforced through graphics and other visual representations, requiring students to use their understanding of the selection to extend their literary skills.

• **Words to Know SkillBuilder** (for most selections) Words underlined and defined in the selection are reviewed, requiring students to use the words contextually and in original sentences.

Ongoing Assessment In addition to increasing students' involvement in the reading process, *The InterActive Reader™ Plus* offers you, the teacher, a window on students' progress and problems. Students' notes, responses, and other markings should be looked at regularly as part of the ongoing informal assessment process.

Who Will Benefit?

The InterActive Reader™ Plus helps students with differing abilities to access authentic text.

The InterActive Reader™ Plus
(for on-level and above-level students)

- On-level students will find appropriate support or scaffolding to hone their reading process strategies and skills. The interactive activities enable students to construct meaning and to recognize *how* that meaning was constructed.

- Above-level students will be able to sharpen their analytical reading skills using this level. Being able to write in the book allows these students to annotate authors' use of tone, mood, symbols, and other literary concepts addressed by the College Board.

The InterActive Reader™ Plus with Additional Support
(for below-level readers)

Struggling readers will achieve best in this level. Summaries, additional background information, extra vocabulary support, and extra interactive activities will provide the necessary help for these students. Allowing students to work in pairs or small groups and partner-reading followed by talking through their answers to questions in the side columns will not only build reading competence but also reading confidence!

Three levels of books . . . yet the SAME text on the SAME page . . . and *all* students receive the differentiated support they need for their reading abilities.

The InterActive Reader™ Plus for English Learners
(for students learning English)

Students learning English will achieve best in this level. Extra assistance to meet their specific needs will allow these students to break through the word-level barrier to focus on the meaning and ideas of the selection.

How is *The InterActive Reader™ Plus* best used in the classroom?

Because all three levels contain the *same* literary selections with the *same* page numbers, you can easily use them in a single classroom. As you introduce a selection or discuss a "chunk" of text, there will never be any confusion by students, for they will have their own customized side-column activities based on their reading abilities. *The InterActive Reader™ Plus* changes the level of support, not the literature.

Lesson Planning

You may wish to use the following sequence for a lesson using all levels of *The InterActive Reader™ Plus*:

Before Reading

- Assign the **Connect to Your Life** and **Key to the Story** activities for the whole class. Students may complete them independently or with partners before sharing their answers with the group.

During Reading

- Read aloud the **Focus** and **Mark It Up** to clarify the "reading with pen in hand" activity that is suggested.

- Read aloud or think aloud or model the thinking strategy required to complete the **Mark It Up** task for the first section.

- Encourage all students to read through the side-column notes and to answer questions and mark anything that puzzles or confuses them. Struggling readers and English learners will find summaries and notes especially for them.

- At the Pause & Reflect, discuss as a group the questions listed in the side column or have students work with partners to answer the questions.

- Beginning with the next section, again read the **Focus** and **Mark It Up.** At this point you may have some students working independently while you assist others with think-alouds or other strategies.

- Use the SkillBuilder pages along with the reading if appropriate. For example, an Active Reading SkillBuilder on predicting is best filled out while students read. They can then check the accuracy of their predictions as they finish the selection.

After Reading

- You may wish to work together as a whole class on the **Challenge** activity, or you may find pairs or small groups most effective.

- Use the SkillBuilder pages as an effective review and reinforcement of the vocabulary, reading, and literary skills covered.

Suggested Reading Options

A variety of methods can be used with *The InterActive Reader™ Plus*.

The InterActive Reader™ Plus allows you to choose from a number of different reading options as you assign students work. Each Lesson Plan in this Guide suggests one of the following options, the suggestion being based on the nature of the selection itself. However, any reading options may be used at any time. Options marked with an asterisk (*) are especially effective with Students Acquiring English.

Independent Reading

Students can read independently, using the questions in the margins of their books for guidance and focus. Though most often this option is used with students who need little support, all students should have some opportunities to read independently. In this situation, *The InterActive Reader™ Plus* may be used as a take-home text.

Note: If *The InterActive Reader™ Plus* is being used in conjunction with *The Language of Literature*, you may wish to begin the prereading activities, such as Connect to Your Life and Build Background, in class; the main anthology can then be left at school while students carry home their smaller and less cumbersome readers.

Partner/Cooperative Reading*

Students can read in pairs, pausing at the indicated places to discuss the questions, write answers, and compare notations and highlighted passages. Alternatively, students can read in small groups, pausing in the same manner to discuss the selection and respond to prompts. In either setting, encourage students to discuss the strategies they use as they read.

Teacher Modeling*

Read aloud the first part of a selection, discuss key events or concepts that are important for comprehension, and then have students continue reading on their own. For particularly challenging selections, reading aloud can continue further into the selection, or there could be an alternating of silent reading and teacher read-aloud.

Oral Reading*

This option works well for plays, speeches, or selections that contain an abundance of dialogue. It can also work well with narrative passages, providing an aural dimension to the comprehension process.

Audio Library*

Recordings of almost all selections in *The InterActive Reader™ Plus* are provided as part of the *Language of Literature* core program. You may find it useful to have students read along with these recordings.

Note: In order to familiarize students with the lesson structure and format of *The InterActive Reader™ Plus*, you might consider reading aloud the beginning of each selection and modeling the Focus and Pause & Reflect activities provided.

Reciprocal Teaching

Reciprocal teaching refers to an instructional activity that teaches students concrete, specific, "comprehension-fostering" strategies they will need whenever they approach the reading of a new text. The activity consists of a dialogue between students and teacher, with each taking a turn in the role of the teacher or leader. Classroom use of this activity has been found to improve the reading comprehension of both good and struggling readers.

Step 1: Have everyone silently read a short passage (one or several paragraphs) of a new text. Model the following four thinking strategies using only the part of the reading that has been read.

- **Questioning** – Ask the class to think of a question that everyone can answer because everyone has read the same text. Model by generating a question for the class. Call on a student to answer your question. Ask that student to then generate a question for the class and to call on another student to answer her question. Repeat this procedure until you think all students are thoroughly familiar with the facts and details of the passage. (If students do not ask a question beginning with *why*, model one for them to move their thinking from literal to inferential comprehension.)

- **Clarifying** – Model for the class a confusion you need to clarify; for example, a word or a phrase that caused you to pause as you initially read the passage. Think aloud as you discuss your mental engagement with this section, explaining to the class how you figured it out. Ask students if they found any confusing parts when they read the passage. Have a dialogue about the problem-solving methods used by students to make sense of confusing parts.

- **Summarizing** – After students have comprehended the passage as a result of the reciprocal questioning and clarifying strategies, ask them to think of a one-sentence summary for the passage. Ask a volunteer to share his summary statement. Encourage others to revise, if needed, the shared summary by elaborating and embellishing its content. Identify the best summary through a dialogue with class members.

- **Predicting** – Now that students know what the first passage in the reading means, ask them to predict what the author will discuss next.

Step 2: Ask everyone to silently read another portion of text. Have a student volunteer repeat Step 1, serving as the teacher/leader, over this new portion.

Step 3: In groups of four, have students silently read the next portion of text, taking turns role-playing the leader and following the 4-step procedure.

Teacher's Role: Guide students' practice by monitoring the student dialogue in each group during steps 2 and 3. Remind students of the procedure and give additional modeling of the steps.

Reciprocal Teaching training provides students with explicit ways to interact with new text. *The InterActive Reader™ Plus* extends this powerful technique by focusing on additional strategies: connecting, visualizing, and evaluating. You will notice that students connect and visualize while clarifying and evaluate in order to predict.

For each Lesson Plan in *The InterActive Reader™ Plus,* one of the above comprehension strategies is modeled. An ongoing review of all of the strategies provides a helpful reminder to students and encourages their pursuit of independent reading.

Strategies for Reading

These strategies can help you gain a better understanding of what you read. Whenever you find yourself having difficulty making sense of what you're reading, choose and use the strategy that seems most likely to help.

PREDICT   Try to figure out what will happen next and how the selection might end. Then read on to see how accurate your guesses are.

VISUALIZE   Visualize characters, events, and setting to help you understand what's happening. When you read nonfiction, pay attention to the images that form in your mind as you read.

CONNECT   Connect personally with what you're reading. Think of similarities between the descriptions in the selection and what you have personally experienced, heard about, or read about.

QUESTION   Question what happens while you read. Searching for reasons behind events and characters' feelings can help you feel closer to what you are reading.

CLARIFY   Stop occasionally to review your understanding of what you read. You can do this by **summarizing** what you have read, identifying the **main idea,** and **making inferences**—drawing conclusions from the information you are given. Reread passages you don't understand.

EVALUATE   Form opinions about what you read, both while you're reading and after you've finished. Develop your own ideas about characters and events.

Reaching Middle School Readers

One of the many challenges of middle school teaching is accommodating the wide range of reading abilities and interests among students. For those students who are hooked on reading, the challenge is to provide a steady diet of rich materials. But for many students, reading is a chore that requires enormous effort and yields little success.

Students who are not able to read at grade level often do not succeed in school. While much of the focus of the early grades is on learning to read, the focus shifts in the middle grades to reading to learn. Students who do not have a strong foundation in basic decoding and comprehension skills become struggling readers. Their poor reading ability denies them access to the content of the textbooks; as a result, they fall behind in almost every subject area. Below-level reading ability most often is the result of inadequate decoding skills, poor comprehension, or a combination of both.

Decoding skills provide readers with strategies for determining the pronunciation of the written word. Basic decoding skills involve matching letters and letter combinations with spoken sounds and blending those sounds into words. As students encounter longer—multisyllabic—words, they need to divide these words into manageable chunks or syllables.

Decoding is an enabling skill for comprehension. Comprehension is a process of constructing meaning from text. Readers integrate the information in the text with their prior knowledge to make sense of what they read. Specific comprehension skills and strategies, such as main idea, sequence, and visualizing can help students recognize the relationships among ideas, figure out text structures, and create pictures of what they read.

This book provides some basic tools and strategies that will help you help your students to become readers. The lessons and articles can be used as needed, or they can be organized into mini-units of instruction.

Developing Fluency in All Readers

Reading fluency is the ability to automatically recognize words so that attention can be focused on the meaning of the written material. Fluency involves both decoding and comprehension skills; fluent readers decode text with little or no effort as they construct meaning from that text. Teachers can usually spot readers who struggle with decoding the text. Other readers, however, may be able to say the words and sound as though they are reading, but they have little or no understanding of what they read. These readers often go unnoticed, especially in the content areas.

Fluency is a developmental skill that improves with practice. The more students read, the better readers they become. The reading level at which a student is fluent is called his or her *independent reading level*. However, a student's independent reading level may vary with the type of material he or she is reading. For example, reading a short story is often easier than reading a textbook.

A key part in developing reading fluency is determining a student's independent reading level and then providing a range of materials at that level. Developing Fluent Readers on pages 14–16 offers diagnostic tools for determining reading levels and tips for improving fluency.

Helping All Readers Break the Code

There are many reasons that some students struggle with reading. Often poor readers spend most of their mental energy trying to figure out, or decode, the words. With their brains focused on the letters and corresponding sounds, there is little attention left to think about what the words mean. Until readers achieve a basic level of automaticity in word recognition, they are not reading for meaning.

Although most middle school students do have a knowledge of basic phonics, some students fail to develop strategies for using the letter-sound correspondences. They often have difficulty decoding new words, and multisyllabic words are especially problematic. As students encounter longer words they need to be able to break these words into parts.

The lessons on applying multisyllabic rules in Teaching Decoding Strategies on pages 107–117 provide students with strategies for tackling longer words. These lessons also provide a basic review of phonics within a model of direct instruction. You can expand this review for students who need more intensive work in this area. You can also skip the basic phonics instruction and focus on multisyllabic word attack strategies.

Using the Most Effective Teaching Strategies

Choosing *how* to teach something is as important as deciding *what* to teach. While a variety of methods are sound, some methods are more effective in teaching specific skills and strategies than others.

Decoding skills need to be taught explicitly and systematically through direct instruction. These skills can be taught to mastery. The lessons in Teaching Decoding Strategies offer an efficient set of steps and teaching script for short but effective lessons in these skills.

Comprehension skills, however, are developmental skills that are not easily mastered. Students will continue to grow in their understanding of increasingly difficult reading materials throughout life.

Comprehension skills can be modeled so that students are shown the thinking processes behind these skills. The Comprehension Mini-Lessons provide passages and teaching script to model basic comprehension skills.

Establishing a Reading Process

Good readers are strategic in how they approach reading. They consciously or unconsciously do certain things before, during, and after reading. Poor readers, however, often possess few or none of the strategies required for proficient reading. To help struggling readers, establish a routine for reading that involves strategies before, during, and after reading.

- **Before Reading** New ideas presented in reading materials need to be integrated with the reader's **prior knowledge** for understanding to occur. Have students preview the material to see what it is about. Discuss what they already know about the topic and have them **predict** new information they might learn about it. Talk about a **purpose** for reading and have students think about reading strategies they might use with the material.

- **During Reading** Good readers keep track of their understanding as they read. They recognize important or interesting information, know when they don't understand something, and figure out what to do to adjust their understanding. Poor readers are often unaware of these **self-monitoring strategies**. To help these readers become more involved in their reading, suggest that they read with a pencil in hand to jot down notes and questions as they read. If students own the reading materials, they can mark the text as they read. *The InterActive Readers*™ that accompany *The Language of Literature* are ideal for this type of work.

- **After Reading** Provide opportunities for readers to reflect on what they have read. These can involve group or class discussion and writing in journals and logs.

Creating Independent Readers

As you work to give students the skills they need to read for themselves, you can also incorporate some basic routines into your classroom that will help your students extend their understanding.

- **Read aloud.** People of all ages love a good story. Read aloud to your students and hook them on some authors and genres they might not have tackled themselves. For most material, students' listening comprehension is more advanced than their comprehension of written material. Listening helps them develop the thinking skills needed to understand complex text.

- **Write daily.** Writing is a powerful tool to understanding. Encourage students to use writing to work through problems, explore new ideas, or respond to the literature they read. Encourage students to keep journals and learning logs.

- **Read daily.** Allow time for sustained silent reading. Set aside classroom time for students to read self-selected materials. Students who read become better readers, and students are more likely to choose to read if they can pursue ideas they find interesting.

- **Build a classroom library.** If possible, provide a wide range of reading materials so that students are exposed to diverse topics and genres. Respect students' reading choices. Struggling readers need first to view themselves as readers.

- **Promote discussion.** Set ground rules for discussion so that all opinions are heard. Model good discussion behaviors by asking follow-up questions, expanding on ideas presented, and offering alternate ways of viewing topics.

When teachers allocate time to these experiences, students see literacy as possible.

Developing Fluent Readers

Good readers are fluent readers. They recognize words automatically, group individual words into meaningful phrases, and apply phonic, morphemic, and contextual clues when confronted with a new word. Fluency is a combination of accuracy (number of words identified correctly) and rate (number of words per minute) of reading. Fluency can be taught directly, and it improves as a consequence of students' reading a lot of materials that are within their instructional range.

Understanding Reading Levels

Every student reads at a specific level regardless of the grade in which he or she is placed. Reading level in this context is concerned with the relationship between a specific selection or book and a student's ability to read that selection. The following are common terms used to describe these levels:

- **independent level**—The student reads material in which no more than 1 in 20 words is difficult. The material can be read without teacher involvement and is likely to be material students would choose to read on their own.

- **instructional level**—The student reads material in which no more than 2 in 20 words are difficult. The material is most likely found in school and read with teacher involvement.

- **frustration level**—The student reads material in which significantly more than 2 in 20 (or 89%) of the words are difficult. Students will probably get little out of reading the material.

If students read only material that's too easy, growth in skill, vocabulary, and understanding is too slow. If students read only difficult material, they may give up in frustration much too early.

Providing Reading Materials in the Student's Instructional Range

Most states have testing programs that provide information about each student's reading ability. Once you determine a student's general reading level, you can work with the library media teacher to identify reading materials that will be within the student's instructional level. To develop fluency, students should read materials that contain a high proportion of words that they know already or can easily decode. Work with each student to develop a list of books to read, and have students record their progress on a Reading Log.

Repeated Oral Readings

Repeated oral readings of passages is a strategy that improves fluency. Oral reading also improves prosody, which is the art of sounding natural when you read, or reading with appropriate intonation, expression, and rhythm.

Beginning readers sound awkward when they read aloud. They pause and halt at the wrong places; they emphasize the wrong syllables; they may read in a monotone. Repeated oral readings can increase fluency and prosody as students 1) identify words faster and faster each time they read; 2) correctly identify a larger percentage of words; 3) segment text into appropriate phrases; 4) change pitch and emphasis to fit the meaning of the text.

To improve fluency and prosody, select passages that are brief, thought provoking, and at the student's current independent level of reading. You may choose narrative or expository text, or have the student choose something he or she enjoys. Performing a play, practicing to give a speech, reading to younger students, and rereading a passage to find evidence in support of an argument are all activities that provide opportunities to reread. For the following exercise, you may choose to pair students together and have them read to each other, or use this as a one-on-one teacher-student or tutor-student activity.

1. Select an excerpt within the student's reading level that ranges from 50–200 words in length.

2. Have the student read the passage aloud to a partner. The partner records the number of seconds it takes to read the whole passage, and notes the number of errors. Reverse roles so that each student has a chance to read to the other.

3. Read the passage aloud to the students so that students can hear it read correctly.

4. As homework, or as an in-class assignment, have students practice reading the passage out loud on their own.

5. After practice, have each student read aloud again to his or her partner, who records the time and the number of errors.

6. After repeated practice and readings the student will read the passage fluently, that is, with a moderate rate and near 100% accuracy.

Example Excerpt

I have a little dream
For the flying of a plane.
I have a little scheme,
I'll follow yet again.

There is a little heaven,
Just around the hill.
I haven't seen it for a long time,
But I know it's waiting still.

from Dragonwings
by Laurence Yep

Repeated Silent Readings

Having students silently read and reread passages that are at their instructional level also improves fluency. As they practice, students will recognize words more quickly each time, will group words into meaningful phrases more quickly, and will increase their reading rate. One nice thing about repeated silent reading is that a student can do it individually. Many students enjoy timing themselves when they read and seeing improvement over time. Have them keep a record on a piece of graph paper.

Modeling

Students benefit from repeated opportunities to hear English spoken fluently. By listening to live models or tapes, listeners can understand the rhythm of the language and the pitch and pronunciation of particular words and phrases. They can hear when to pause, when to speed up, and what words to emphasize. In addition, you can model

or ask an experienced reader to read passages aloud. At most advanced levels, this technique is particularly useful to introduce students to various forms of dialect. As you play the tapes aloud, have students read along silently or chorally, or pause the tapes after each paragraph and have the students try reading the same passage aloud.

Phrase-Cued Text

Less proficient readers may not know when to pause in text. They may pause in the middle of a phrase, or run through a comma or period. They may not recognize verb phrases, prepositional phases, or even phrases marked by parentheses or brackets as words that "go together." This makes their reading disjointed and choppy, or gives it a monotone quality. Some poems have essentially one phrase per line and can be used to demonstrate to students how to phrase text. Or, you may take a passage and have students rewrite it with one phrase per line, so that they pause at the end of each line. Alternatively, you can show them how a passage should be read by inserting slash marks or blank spaces at appropriate places to pause. Choose passages of about 50–100 words in length from fiction or nonfiction selections. For example, you can take a passage like the following:

Example Modeling

When the man entered the room, he failed to notice the trembling brown fox crouching in the corner next to the refrigerator. When the man opened the door of the refrigerator to grab a cold soda, the fox leapt between his feet and the door and scrambled for a hiding place on the shelf behind the lettuce.

And present it to students in this way:

When the man entered the room,/he failed to notice/ the trembling brown fox/ crouching in the corner/ next to the refrigerator. When the man opened the door of the refrigerator/ to grab a cold soda,/ the fox leapt between his feet and the door/ and scrambled for a hiding place/ on the shelf /behind the lettuce.

Have students read and then reread the passage, stopping to pause at each slash mark.

Informal Reading Inventory

An informal inventory can give an initial idea of a student's reading level. Teachers often use an Informal Reading Inventory (IRI) to place students in the appropriate textbook.

To conduct an IRI, you need at least one 100-word passage from the material in question and 10 comprehension questions about the material. If you want more than one passage, select them randomly from every 30th page or so. Have the student read the same passage twice—the first time orally to assess oral reading skills. The student should read the passage a second time silently, after which he or she answers questions for assessment of reading comprehension.

Suggestions for administering an IRI:

1. Tell the student he or she will read the passage out loud and then again silently, and then you will ask some questions.

2. Give the student a copy of the passage and keep one for yourself. Have the student read the passage. As the student reads out loud, note on your copy the number of errors he or she makes:

   Mispronunciations: Words that are mispronounced, with the exception of proper nouns.
   Omissions: Words left out that are crucial to understanding a sentence or a concept.
   Additions: Words inserted in a sentence that change the meaning of the text.
   Substitutions: Words substituted for actual words in the text that change the meaning of a sentence.

Use these criteria for assessing reading levels after oral reading:

- Fewer than 3 errors—The student is unlikely to have difficulty decoding text.

- Between 4 and 9 errors—The student is likely to have some difficulty and may need special attention.

- More than 10 errors—The student is likely to have great difficulty and may need placement in less challenging material.

3. Have the student read the passage again, silently.

4. When the student finishes, ask the comprehension questions you have prepared ahead of time. Tell the student that he or she can look back at the passage before answering a question.

5. Note the number of correct responses. Use these criteria for assessing reading level after silent reading:

   - Eight or more—The student should be able to interpret the selections effectively.

   - Five to seven—The student is likely to have difficulty.

   - Fewer than five—The student needs individual help or alternate placement.

6. Evaluate results from oral and silent reading to decide how good a match the material is for a student's independent or instructional level.

Another approach allows you to assess the student's choice for independent reading. Have the student independently select a book he or she would like to read. The student should open to a random page in the middle of the book (that has not been read before) and begin reading silently from the top of the page. Ask the student to extend one finger for each time he or she comes across an unfamiliar word. If, by the end of that page, the student has five or more fingers extended, the book is probably too difficult for that student. You may want to suggest that the student find a book more suitable to his or her reading level.

Research/Related Readings

The following research supports the philosophy and pedagogical design of *The InterActive Reader™ Plus*:

Beck, I., et al. "Getting at the Meaning: How to Help Students Unpack Difficult Text." *American Educator: The Unique Power of Reading and How to Unleash It* 22.1–2 (1996): 66–71, 85.

California Reading Initiative and Special Education in California: Critical Ideas Focusing on Meaningful Reform. Sacramento: California Special Education Reading Task Force, California Department of Education and California State Board of Education, 1999.

Carnine, D., J. Silbert, and E. J. Kame'enui. *Direction Instruction Reading.* Columbus: Merrill, 1990.

Honig, B., L. Diamond, and L. Gutlohn. *Teaching Reading Sourcebook.* Novato, CA: Arena, 2000.

Irvin, Judith L. *Reading and the Middle School Student.* 2nd ed. Boston: Allyn & Bacon, 1998.

Langer, J. A., and A. N. Applebee. "Reading and Writing Instruction: Toward a Theory of Teaching and Learning." *Review of Research in Education.* Ed. E. Rothkopf. Washington, D.C.: American Educational Research Association, 1986.

Lapp, D., J. Flood, and N. Farnan. *Content Area Reading and Learning: Instructional Strategies.* 2nd ed. Boston: Allyn & Bacon, 1996.

Lyon, G. Reid. "Learning to Read: A Call from Research to Action." *National Center for Learning Disabilities.* 9 Nov. 1999 <http://www.ncld.org/theirworld/lyon98.html>

Palinscar, A. S., and A. L. Brown. "Interactive Teaching to Promote Independent Learning from Text." *The Reading Teacher* 39.8 (1986): 771–777.

Palinscar, A. S., and A. L. Brown. "Reciprocal Teaching of Comprehension-Fostering and Comprehension-Monitoring Activities." *Cognition and Instruction* 1.2: 117–175.

Pearson, P. D., et al. "Developing Expertise in Reading Comprehension." *What Research Says to the Teacher.* Ed. S. J. Samuels and A. E. Farstrip. Newark: International Reading Association, 1992.

Rosenshine, B., and C. Meister. "Reciprocal Teaching: A Review of the Research." *Review of Educational Research* 64.4 (1994): 479–530.

Simmons, D. C., and E. J. Kame'enui, eds. *What Reading Research Tells Us About Children with Diverse Needs: Bases and Basics.* Mahwah: Lawrence Erlbaum, 1998.

Tierney, R. J., J. E. Readence, and E. K. Dishner. *Reading Strategies and Practices: A Compendium.* 4th ed. Boston: Allyn & Bacon, 1995.

Tompkins, Gail. *50 Literacy Strategies: Step by Step.* Upper Saddle River: Merrill, 1998.

Lesson Plans

Before Reading

Direct students' attention to the **Connect to Your Life** and **Key to the Story** activities on page 2 of *The InterActive Reader.*™ Use the following suggestions to prepare students to read the story.

Connect to Your Life
Guide students in a discussion about how they felt when they turned 11—or how they think they will feel. Encourage students to think about the new privileges and responsibilities they hoped to be entrusted with. What new possibilities did turning 11 seem to promise? After students fill out the word web, let them share their thoughts.

Key to the Story
Ask students to remember a time when they felt that time was passing too slowly or when they wished they could grow up more quickly. Why did they feel this way? Then read aloud the statement from "Eleven." Ask students if they have ever felt younger than their age on their birthday. Tell them to draw on their own experiences as they write a response to Rachel.

BUILD BACKGROUND **The Child Inside** When she was interviewed about this story in 1986, Sandra Cisneros commented that she sometimes feels 11 years old inside, even as an adult: "When I think how I see myself, I would have to be at age eleven. I know I'm thirty-two on the outside, but inside I'm eleven. I'm the girl in the picture with skinny arms and a crumpled shirt and crooked hair. I didn't like school because all they saw was the outside me."

WORDS TO KNOW

except
expect
invisible
sudden

Additional Words to Know

rattling
  page 5, line 33
raggedy
  page 5, line 56
shove
  page 6, line 91
hiccups
  page 7, line 119
pretend
  page 7, line 125

VOCABULARY PREVIEW: Words to Know in Context

You can help students learn the Words to Know by reading aloud the following sentences or writing them on the board. Then show students how to use context clues to help them figure out the meaning.

except: *Except* for Mario, all of the children got permission to go on the field trip.

expect: When I go ice skating, I *expect* to see my friends, skate until I'm exhausted, and drink lots of hot chocolate.

invisible: The *invisible* man in the story could go anywhere he pleased and not worry about being seen.

sudden: We were quietly reading our books when all of a *sudden* the terrible screams shattered the silence.

rattling: When I shook my piggy bank, I heard the coins *rattling* around inside.

raggedy: After being dragged all around the house for five years, the *raggedy* old blanket was torn and full of holes.

shove: They kept pushing us so we finally decided to *shove* them back.

hiccups: I tried to get rid of my *hiccups* by holding my breath, but those embarrassing sounds kept escaping from my closed lips.

pretend: Even though the news upsets us all, we *pretend* that nothing is wrong.

VOCABULARY FOCUS: Using Words with Multiple Meanings

Teacher Modeling Remind students that they will encounter many words with more than one meaning when they read. Tell students that they can often use context clues to figure out which meaning of the word the writer intended. Then use the following modeling suggestions to determine the correct meaning of **mad.** (page 6, line 96)

You could say I know that mad *can mean "crazy or insane" and it can also mean "angry." I can look for context clues in the surrounding sentences to figure out the correct meaning. Phrases like "put that sweater on right now" and "no more nonsense" suggest that Mrs. Price has lost her patience with Rachel. In this case, then,* mad *probably means "angry."*

Student Modeling Now have students follow your example. Ask a volunteer to model using context to determine the correct meaning of **bury.** (page 7, line 114)

A student might say Bury *can mean "to place in the ground" and it can also mean "to hide or conceal." In this scene, Rachel puts her head down on her desk and cries. Since she covers her face with the arms of the sweater, I think* bury *must mean "to hide."*

Mini-Lesson See pages 104–105 of this Guide for additional work on **Using Words with Multiple Meanings.**

During Reading

COMPREHENSION FOCUS

Key Points	Strategies for Success
Target Skill → Making Inferences Rachel doesn't explicitly state that she feels embarrassed or frustrated in the story. Students must be able to use clues from the story and their own prior knowledge to make inferences about her emotions.	**Mini-Lesson** Before students read "Eleven," you may want to teach the **Making Inferences** lesson on pages 134–136 of this Guide. • As students read, have them stop after the *Pause & Reflect* on page 5 and discuss the clues that show how Rachel feels at this point in the story. • Have students use the **Inference Chart** on page 135 of this Guide to help them make their inferences.
Figurative Language The author uses a number of similes to make her descriptions of objects, events, and feelings more vivid. Some students may need help understanding these comparisons.	Explain that a simile is a comparison that uses the words *like* or *as.* Then direct students' attention to the simile "like a waterfall," which is used to describe how the sweater is hanging off Rachel's desk (page 6, line 93). Tell students that creating a mental picture of a waterfall can help them imagine how the sweater looks. Encourage students to identify other similes in the story and to think of the images they create.

Suggested Reading Options

• An oral reading of "Eleven" is available in *The Language of Literature* Audio Library. ◠
• Partner/Cooperative Reading (See page 8 of this Guide.)
• Additional options are described on page 8 of this Guide.

RECIPROCAL TEACHING SUGGESTION ➡ Connecting

Teacher Modeling *Pause & Reflect, page 4* Model for students how to connect what they are reading to their own experiences.

You could say *Rachel has just turned 11, but she says that she doesn't feel that old yet. I can remember times when I knew I wasn't really "acting my age." When I was 11 and used to fight with my little brother, for example, I knew I should be the more mature one, but I wasn't always. My own memories of feeling younger than I was help me relate to what Rachel is saying.*

Student Modeling *Pause & Reflect, page 5* Have several students model connecting their own experiences with what they are reading. Offer this prompt: *When have you been treated unfairly? When did you have trouble speaking up for yourself? How did the experience make you feel?* Students can also use the **Active Reading SkillBuilder** on page 9 to connect Rachel's feelings on her birthday to their own memories and experiences.

Encourage students to use the other five reading strategies when appropriate as they proceed through the rest of this selection. (See page 10 of this Guide.)

ENGLISH LEARNERS

1. Be sure students understand that when Rachel uses the subject pronoun *you,* she is referring to herself, the reader, and people in general. For example, when Rachel says "And you don't feel smart eleven, not until you're almost twelve," she means that most people feel this way.

2. Students might benefit from reading along with the recording of "Eleven" provided in *The Language of Literature* Audio Library. ◯

After Reading

Recommended Follow-Up

- Thinking Through the Literature, page 31, *The Language of Literature*
- Choices & Challenges, pages 32–33, *The Language of Literature*
- SkillBuilders, pages 9–11, *The InterActive Reader*™

Informal Assessment Options

Retell Assign these roles to different students: Mrs. Price and one or two of Rachel's classmates. Then call on students and ask them to retell the story from the point of view of these characters. Students role-playing Mrs. Price should explain why she gave the sweater to Rachel. Students role-playing Rachel's classmates should tell how they felt when the girl began to cry.

Spot Check Read the notes students made in the margins, paying particular attention to their responses to the *Pause & Reflect* and *Mark It Up* prompts. Invite them to explain their answers and discuss any questions they still have about the story.

Formal Assessment Options in *The Language of Literature*

Selection Quiz, page 13, Unit One Resource Book

Selection Test, pages 5–6, Formal Assessment Book

For more teaching options, see pages 26–33 in *The Language of Literature* Teacher's Edition.

Additional Challenge

1. Write Dialogue
Point out that Mrs. Price talks to Rachel but refuses to listen to the girl. Have students write a dialogue in which Rachel finally gets a chance to talk to Mrs. Price. Students should have Rachel tell about her birthday and explain how she felt about the sweater. To help students write the dialogue, ask: *How does Rachel feel when Mrs. Price places the sweater on her desk? How does Rachel feel when she's forced to wear the sweater? How does Rachel feel when Phyllis Lopez claims the sweater? Why does the fact that it is Rachel's birthday make the situation even worse?*

2. [||| MARK IT UP ⟩ Note Sensory Details
Tell students that sensory details appeal to the senses of sight, sound, touch, smell, and taste. Explain that these kinds of details help bring a subject to life. Then ask students to use the sensory details in "Eleven" to write a brief description of the sweater. Have students mark details in the story that support their description. Encourage students to use their description to make a drawing of the sweater.

Before Reading

Have students do the Connect to Your Life and Key to the Biography activities on page 12 of *The InterActive Reader.*™ Use the following suggestions to prepare students to read the story.

Connect to Your Life
Once students have finished the chart, ask for volunteers to call out items from their lists. You may want to list the items on the board in more specific categories, such as Survival, Safety, Communication, and Comfort. Ask: *Which items would be most important? Least important? Which would not have been available at the time of Henson's journey in 1908?*

Key to the Biography
Have students read the Key to the Biography. Then write the following anticipation guide on the board. Tell students that it is designed to get them thinking about the literature, and that answers on an anticipation guide are never graded.

1. It took the Peary expedition two years to reach the North Pole.

2. One member of the expedition died on the journey.

3. Henson became a famous writer and lecturer.

Ask students whether they agree with the statements. Then write "Agree" or "Disagree" next to each. Review the guide after students finish the biography.

Build Background
Explain that, in 1908, Matthew Henson joined Commander Robert E. Peary's expedition. Their goal was to be the first people in history to reach the North Pole. Many previous polar explorers died of exposure to cold; some of their ships became trapped in ice and were crushed or forced far off course. The members of Peary's expedition knew that the history of polar exploration was one of danger and frustration.

WORDS TO KNOW

- apt
- ardent
- deprivation
- menial
- proposition
- resentful
- stamina
- surveyor
- tyranny
- validate

VOCABULARY PREVIEW: Words to Know in Context

You can help students learn the Words to Know by reading aloud the following sentences or writing them on the board. Then show students how to use context clues to help them figure out the meaning.

apt: Eileen is *apt* at dividing fractions. Her teacher is always praising her skill.

ardent: Jon gets bored watching sports on television, but he is *ardent* about playing sports himself.

deprivation: Most of our plants died of water *deprivation* while we were on vacation.

menial: My chores are nothing but *menial,* unskilled work—sweeping the floors and taking out the garbage.

proposition: What do you think of Aisha's *proposition* that we have pizza for lunch?

resentful: Al felt *resentful* when his sister forgot to feed the cats and then blamed him.

stamina: It takes strength to lift weights, but it also takes *stamina* to lift them for hours at a time.

surveyor: A *surveyor,* someone who determines where one person's land ends and another person's begins, is what we need to end this dispute.

tyranny: The people accused the queen of *tyranny* when she announced that she would raise taxes, take villagers' land, and force people to join her army.

validate: Joan claims she made 47 jump shots in a row, but she has no witness to *validate* her feat.

VOCABULARY FOCUS Word Parts: Prefixes

Teacher Modeling Remind students that a prefix is a word part attached to the beginning of a base word or root. Then use the modeling suggestions below to understand the word *unthinking.* (page 17, line 98)

You could say I'm not sure what the writer means by "unthinking cruelty." When I look at the word unthinking, I see that it has the word thinking in it. That's probably the base word, since it can stand on its own. I think the un- part is a prefix, because I've seen it in other words: unusual, unreal, undone. I know that unusual means "not usual," so I bet unthinking means "not thinking" or "without thinking."

Student Modeling Ask for a volunteer to follow your lead. Have the student model his or her analysis of prefixes when determining the meaning of *discomforts.* (page 18, line 128)

A student might say The word discomforts has the word comfort in it, so I think that's the base word. I think the dis- part is a prefix because I have seen it in other words, such as dislike and disobey. I know that disobey is the opposite of obey, so I think that discomfort is the opposite of comfort.

Mini-Lesson See pages 96–97 of this Guide for additional work on **Word Parts: Prefixes.**

During Reading

COMPREHENSION FOCUS

Key Points	Strategies for Success

Target Skill ➡ **Compare and Contrast**

One of the key points in "Matthew Henson at the Top of the World" is that Henson was treated differently from other members of the North Pole expedition simply because of his race. Comparing and contrasting Henson's treatment with that of the others can help students better understand the biography.

Mini-Lesson Before students read "Matthew Henson at the Top of the World," you may want to teach or review the **Compare and Contrast** Lesson on pages 131–133 of this Guide.

- Have students stop after the *Pause & Reflect* on page 26 and discuss how Henson was treated differently from his fellow explorers for many years. Ask: *What steps were taken in an attempt to make up for that discrimination?*
- After reading, you may want to have students use the Venn diagram on page 132 to show similarities and differences between Henson and Admiral Peary.

Main Idea and Details

Jim Haskins's biography of Matthew Henson chronicles Henson's entire life and describes a number of expeditions in which he took part. Students may have difficulty determining the most important points in the biography and sorting out the many details.

As students read, have them fill out the **Active Reading SkillBuilder** on page 27. Students can stop at each of the five *Pause & Reflect* notations and think about whether the section they have just read contains a main idea that should be included in the graphic organizer. When the class has finished the entire selection, discuss which ideas in the biography are the most important.

Suggested Reading Options

- An oral reading of "Matthew Henson at the Top of the World" is available in *The Language of Literature* Audio Library. ◯
- Partner/Cooperative Reading (See page 8 of this Guide.)
- Additional options are described on page 8 of this Guide.

RECIPROCAL TEACHING SUGGESTION ➡ Questioning

Teacher Modeling *Pause & Reflect, page 17* Model for students how they can develop their own questions about events in the biography as they read.

You could say *I already know from reading the Preview that Matthew Henson became a famous explorer. I wonder what there was in his personality that made him so successful? I can tell that he had a difficult life, but there were people who cared about him. His uncle helped him get an education, Janey Moore helped him find work, and Captain Childs helped him with both of those things. The biography also says that Henson was smart and worked hard. I think intelligence, hard work, and help from others made Henson a success.*

Student Modeling *Lines 321–338* Have students reread these lines. Ask them to model their own question-asking strategies about Peary's feelings and behavior. Offer these prompts: *How do you think Peary felt after reaching the Pole? Why do you think he was so quiet during the return trip? How do you think he felt about Dr. Cook's claim to be the first to reach the Pole?*

Encourage students to use the other five reading strategies when appropriate as they proceed through the rest of the selection. (See page 10 of this Guide.)

ENGLISH LEARNERS

1. Ask students to look at pages 17–18, lines 106–118. Explain that Reconstruction (1865–1877) was the attempt to make the South part of the United States again after the Civil War. The period was marked by bitterness. Many Northerners wanted to punish white Southerners by taking their land. The Ku Klux Klan used violence against African Americans. Reconstruction made Henson's life even more difficult.

2. Students might benefit from reading along with the recording of "Matthew Henson at the Top of the World" provided in *The Language of Literature* Audio Library. ◯

After Reading

Recommended Follow-Up
- Thinking Through the Literature, page 111, *The Language of Literature*
- Choices & Challenges, pages 112–113, *The Language of Literature*
- SkillBuilders, pages 27–29, *The InterActive Reader*™

Informal Assessment Options

Retell Divide students into small groups and have each group retell the story from Henson's point of view. Encourage group members to skim the biography and reread quotations from Henson. Each group should choose one person to play Henson; the other group members should coach that person.

Spot Check Look at the notes students made on page 19 in answer to the question "What is your opinion of Henson and Peary?" Discuss their answers and the reasons behind them. Have students' opinions changed now that they have finished the biography?

Formal Assessment Options in *The Language of Literature*

Selection Quiz, page 51, Unit One Resource Book

Selection Test, pages 15–16, Formal Assessment Book

For more teaching options, see pages 100–113 in *The Language of Literature* Teacher's Edition.

Additional Challenge

1. Create a Talk Show
Divide the class into small groups and have each group create its own talk show about the polar expedition. In each group, one student can play Henson, one can play Peary, one can be the show's host, and the rest can be audience members. The hosts should summarize the challenges and results of the expedition, the audience members should think of questions for the explorers, and the explorers should think about what they have read in the biography as they answer the questions.

2. ⌁‖ MARK IT UP ⧁ Examine the Main Character
Have students look at pages 15–16, lines 37–72. Direct them to mark words and phrases in this section of the biography that describe Henson. Offer this prompt: *What words does the biographer use to tell you what Henson was like—not just his age or what he looked like, but his attitude and personality?*

Before Reading

Direct students' attention to the Connect to Your Life and Key to the Informative Article activities on page 30 of *The InterActive Reader*™. Use the following suggestions to prepare students to read the selection.

Connect to Your Life
Ask students to share what they know about forest fires. Record their responses on the board and have them write the same information in the first column of their K-W-L charts. Next, have students list what they want to learn in the second column. Remind students that thinking about what they know and want to learn about a topic can help them set a purpose for reading an article about that topic.

Key to the Informative Article
Have students use the information in this section to add to their K-W-L charts. Ask: *In what ways can a forest fire actually be beneficial?*

BUILD BACKGROUND Connect to Biology Explain to students that when fires begin in wilderness areas, park managers are faced with a difficult decision. Sometimes managers let the fires burn to clear away dead trees and to encourage new plant growth by allowing sunlight to reach the ground. Rain can extinguish the fires. However, if rain does not come and wilderness fires grow too large, they can destroy huge areas of mature forest and threaten people who live or work nearby. This selection tells about fires that started small but quickly grew out of control.

WORDS TO KNOW

- bear
- canopy
- ember
- geyser
- merge
- oxygen
- threaten
- tinder
- veer
- withering

Additional Words to Know

- dwindle
  page 32, line 11
- churning
  page 35, line 98

VOCABULARY PREVIEW: Words to Know in Context

You can help students learn the Words to Know by reading aloud the following sentences or writing them on the board. Then show students how to use context clues to help them figure out the meaning of the boldfaced words.

bear: If we all *bear* down on the boulder, maybe we can push it off the road.

canopy: High overhead, the *canopy* of tree leaves was so thick that it protected us from feeling a drop of rain.

ember: After a few hours, there was nothing left of the logs in the fireplace except a pile of small, glowing *embers*.

geyser: Tourists gather around the hot spring every hour to see the *geyser* spray hot water and steam into the air.

merge: At the point where the two medium-size streams *merge,* the waters combine to form a full, rushing river.

oxygen: The fire sucked much of the *oxygen* out of the air, making it difficult to breathe.

threaten: After the storm, the raging river *threatened* the lives of the townspeople.

tinder: We gathered dry twigs and other *tinder* to start the campfire.

veer: The stunt planes dive toward the ground, but at the last minute they *veer* back upward.

withering: The hot summer sun was so *withering* that all the flowers turned brown and brittle.

dwindle: We ate so much cereal last week that now our supplies of the food are beginning to *dwindle*.

churning: A strong wind began *churning* the pile of leaves, turning them over and over.

VOCABULARY FOCUS: Using Context Clues

Teacher Modeling Tell students that sometimes writers explain an unusual or difficult word by providing an explanation of it, or by restating it in different words. A dash or a colon often signals an explanation or restatement. Model using the term *park communities.* (page 34, line 79)

You could say I'm not sure what the term park communities *means, but I see a dash after it. I read the explanation that follows: "the information centers and the buildings where people slept, ate, and shopped." This definition of* park communities *makes sense here.*

Student Modeling Now have students follow your example. Call on a volunteer to model figuring out the word *snags* by looking for this type of context clue. (page 34, lines 63–64)

A student might say I know one meaning of snags, *"catches on something." But here I see a dash after the word, followed by a definition: "dead trees that are still standing." This restatement helps me understand what the author means by* snags *in this sentence.*

Mini-Lesson See pages 92–95 of this Guide for additional work on **Using Context Clues.**

During Reading

COMPREHENSION FOCUS

Key Points	Strategies for Success
Target Skill ➡ Main Idea and Details Some students may have difficulty noting and making sense of the many important details in this selection. An ability to identify and remember main ideas and key details is crucial to understanding the events in "Summer of Fire."	**Mini-Lesson** Before students read "Summer of Fire," you may want to teach or review the **Main Idea and Details** lesson on pages 119–122 of this Guide. • As students read, have them complete the **Active Reading SkillBuilder** on page 37, which focuses on the chronological order of important events in the story.
Multiple Causes To understand why the 1988 fires in Yellowstone were so severe, students must recognize the multiple causes of the huge fires and the effects of each cause.	• Read aloud the opening paragraph (page 32). Discuss how the dry conditions the author describes could contribute to the number and the seriousness of the wildfires. Have students read the third paragraph (lines 25–31) silently. Ask why Yellowstone officials would not rush to put out a fire started by lightning. Ask students to work with a partner at each *Pause & Reflect* to list other factors that caused the 1988 fires to be so serious.

Suggested Reading Options

• An oral reading of "Summer of Fire" is available in *The Language of Literature* Audio Library. ◠
• Partner/Cooperative Reading (See page 8 of this Guide.)
• Additional options are described on page 8 of this Guide.

RECIPROCAL TEACHING SUGGESTION ➡ Visualizing

Teacher Modeling *Pause & Reflect, page 33* Model for students how to use sensory details to visualize what is happening in the selection.

You could say When I read "forests were tinder dry . . . skies grew dark with storm clouds . . . Thunder growled and lightning crackled" (page 32, lines 12–14), I picture in my mind the heat and dryness of Yellowstone. This helps me understand how a forest fire could start and grow there.

Student Modeling *Pause & Reflect, page 35* Have students model visualizing the scene in the last paragraph on page 33 through the first full paragraph on page 34. Offer these prompts: *What do you think it looks like when flames "gallop" or fire "jumps"? What do you think flames sound like when they "roar"?*

Encourage students to use the other five reading strategies when appropriate as they proceed through the rest of this selection. (See page 10 of this Guide.)

ENGLISH LEARNERS

1. Because this selection requires students to keep track of many details, you may wish to have them work with a partner to summarize what they've learned at each *Pause & Reflect*. They can record this information in their K-W-L charts.

2. Students might benefit from reading along with the recording of "Summer of Fire" provided in *The Language of Literature* Audio Library. ◯

After Reading

Recommended Follow-Up

- Thinking Through the Literature, page 121, *The Language of Literature*
- Choices & Challenges, pages 122–123, *The Language of Literature*
- SkillBuilders, pages 37–39, *The InterActive Reader*™

Informal Assessment Options

Group Retelling Have students work in groups of three to retell the story orally. One student might describe the dry conditions that made the park vulnerable to fire. Another student might describe how the fires spread, and the third student might explain the outcome.

Spot Check Look at the notes students made in the margins of the selection. Invite them to explain their answers and discuss any questions they still have about the selection.

Formal Assessment Options in *The Language of Literature*

Selection Quiz, page 58, Unit One Resource Book

Selection Test, pages 17–18, Formal Assessment Book

For more teaching options, see pages 114–123 in *The Language of Literature* Teacher's Edition.

Additional Challenge

1. Role-Play an Interview
Have partners present mock news interviews about the fire. One partner should play the interviewer, and the other can play a firefighter or a witness to events. Encourage both partners to skim the article for details and to think about what it must have been like to witness such severe fires. Offer this prompt: *Based on what you have read, what did the firefighters and other witnesses see, hear, and feel?*

2. ▐▌▌ MARK IT UP ⟩ Vivid Verbs
The author helps readers visualize the events in the selection by using precise language, including vivid verbs. Direct students to circle verbs that convey strong visual images, such as *galloped* (line 62) and *leaped* (line 65). Discuss why these verbs are more effective than *went* or *moved*. Encourage students to use strong verbs in their own writing and speaking.

Before Reading

Have students do the Connect to Your Life and Key to the Story activities on page 40 of *The InterActive Reader.*™ Use the following suggestions to prepare students to read the story.

Connect to Your Life
Guide students in a discussion about the word *courage.* You might ask: *What does the word* courage *mean to you? What are some examples of courageous behavior?* Then have students fill in their charts. You may wish to invite students to share their examples of courageous acts.

Key to the Story
Ask students to name words that are related to *danger.* Record their responses in a web on the board. For example, some students might say *battle, dare, courage, risk, harm, disaster, accident,* and so forth. Once students understand how these words relate to *danger* have them do the activity on page 40.

BUILD BACKGROUND Connect to Geography
Explain to students that this story is set in a small village on Bora Bora, an island in the southern Pacific Ocean. Ask a volunteer to locate this island on a map. The Polynesians who live there grow coconuts, sugar cane, rice, and tropical fruits. Because it is faster to travel by canoe than it is to walk, the islanders often use canoes to travel from one part of the island to another. Point out that Bora Bora is surrounded by reefs, underwater ridges made of rock or coral that provide a home for many kinds of ocean life, including sharks. Sharks play an important role, eating small animals and plants, and leaving behind food scraps that nourish other reef life.

WORDS TO KNOW

expedition

harpoon

lagoon

phosphorus

reef

Additional Words to Know

crag
  page 42, line 11

slay
  page 44, line 93

pursuit
  page 48, line 194

glisten
  page 49, line 241

dismay
  page 50, line 268

VOCABULARY PREVIEW: Words to Know in Context

You can help students learn the Words to Know by reading aloud the following sentences or writing them on the board. Then show students how to use context clues to help them figure out the meaning.

expedition: With our backpacks filled with food and supplies, we set out on an *expedition* to find the cave.

harpoon: Holding the *harpoon* by its long wooden handle, she stabbed the spear end into the large fish.

lagoon: He sailed his boat on the *lagoon,* passing close by the sandbar that separated the shallow body of water from the sea.

phosphorus: In the dark, moonless night, the yellow glow from the *phosphorus* floating on the water guided our boat.

reef: The *reef* was so close to the surface of the water that the raft got stuck on the white coral ridge.

crag: The mountain goat balanced on the tip of a *crag* and then leapt to another steep rock.

slay: After the knights in the tale *slay* the dragon, they proudly carry its body through the kingdom.

pursuit: When the squirrel hopped across the park, the dog dashed after it in *pursuit.*

glisten: In the morning light, the drops of dew *glisten* brightly on the grass.

dismay: The children cried out in *dismay* when they realized their dog was missing.

VOCABULARY FOCUS Word Parts: Compound Words

Teacher Modeling Remind students that sometimes they can figure out the meaning of an unfamiliar compound word by thinking about the two words that make it up. Use the following modeling suggestion for the word **outstretched.** (page 42, line 15)

You could say *I see that the two words* out *and* stretched *make up the compound word* outstretched. *Something that is stretched is pulled or spread so its length is extended. The parts of an island that are outstretched must extend from the main body of the island like arms. This meaning makes sense in the sentence.*

Student Modeling Now have students follow your lead. Ask a volunteer to use the modeling strategy to figure out the meaning of the word **undergrowth.** (page 48, line 194)

A student might say *I see that the two words* under *and* growth *make up the compound word* undergrowth. *Growth can name things that grow, such as plants and trees. I can guess that undergrowth means "plants that grow under trees, low to the ground." This makes sense in the sentence.*

Mini-Lesson
See pages 96–99 of this Guide for additional work on **Compound Words.**

During Reading

COMPREHENSION FOCUS

Key Points	Strategies for Success
Target Skill ➡ Narrative Elements The interplay between characters, setting, and events helps make this a very suspenseful story. In order to appreciate the story to its fullest, students need to understand the story's cultural setting and the importance of the ocean in the lives of the villagers.	**Mini-Lesson** Before students read "Ghost of the Lagoon," teach the **Narrative Elements** lesson on pages 143–146 of this Guide. • Read aloud the first two paragraphs of the story and discuss its setting. Guide students to identify details that reveal the way of life in the village and the importance of the ocean. • As students read, have them fill in the **Story Map** on page 144 of this Guide.
Inferring a Character's Motivations The author gives many clues for why Mako wants, and later chooses, to fight Tupa without explicitly stating what his motivations are. Students' ability to infer Mako's motivations is crucial to their understanding of the story.	At the *Pause & Reflect* on page 45, work with students to identify the two reasons Mako has for wanting to kill the shark. Then, after students read page 50, ask them what additional reason Mako has for fighting Tupa.

Suggested Reading Options

• An oral reading of "Ghost of the Lagoon" is available in *The Language of Literature* Audio Library. ◯
• Partner/Cooperative Reading (See page 8 of this Guide.)
• Additional options are described on page 8 of this Guide.

RECIPROCAL TEACHING SUGGESTION ➡ Making Predictions

Teacher Modeling *Pause & Reflect, page 45* Model making a prediction about what might happen next in the story once Mako resolves to kill the shark.

You could say *The scene ends with a restless Mako. Mako's grandfather has just told him that Tupa is responsible for his father's death. I think Mako will find a way to confront the shark, but I'm not sure he has enough courage. Perhaps he'll wait a while until he can plan a way to kill the shark. However, at the end of this scene, Mako seems very determined to avenge his father's death. Something tells me that he will have a chance to go against the shark.*

Student Modeling *Pause & Reflect, page 50* Have a volunteer model making a prediction about what might happen to Mako and his dog Afa. Offer these prompts: *What do you think will happen to Afa? What actions do you think Mako will take to save his dog? Do you think Mako will kill the shark?*

Encourage students to use the other five reading strategies when appropriate as they proceed through the rest of the selection. (See page 10 of this Guide.)

ENGLISH LEARNERS

1. Make sure that students understand the meanings of these phrases:

   squared his shoulders, page 44, line 92

   caught his breath, page 46, line 156

   "I'll make short work of you!" page 47, lines 175–176

   shake him soundly, page 50, line 261

   found its mark, page 51, line 296

2. Students might benefit from reading along with the recording of "Ghost of the Lagoon" provided in *The Language of Literature* Audio Library. 🎧

After Reading

Recommended Follow-Up

- Thinking Through the Literature, page 132, *The Language of Literature*
- Choices & Challenges, pages 133–134, *The Language of Literature*
- SkillBuilders, pages 53–55, *The InterActive Reader*™

Informal Assessment Options

Retell Have small groups of students retell the story as if they are villagers who have heard of Mako's great courage. They can take turns retelling as many details as they can to present a vivid picture of the story's setting and plot.

Spot Check Look at the notes students wrote in the margins to make sure they understood the story. Invite them to ask any questions they still have about parts that confused them.

Formal Assessment Options in *The Language of Literature*

Selection Quiz, page 65, Unit One Resource Book

Selection Test, pages 19–20, Formal Assessment Book

For more teaching options, see pages 124–134 in *The Language of Literature* Teacher's Edition.

Additional Challenge

1. Write a Sequel
Have students write a prediction about how life might change in the village now that Tupa is dead. Ask students to consider how Mako's life will change when he wins the king's reward.

2. Examine Figurative Language
Point out the use of simile and personification on page 42, lines 8–10. Then have students look for other examples of figurative language in the text. Write these examples on the board and discuss how each is used.

3. ▐▌▌ MARK IT UP ▷ Visualize Setting
Have students circle as many details about the setting as possible. Then have them draw a picture of the island, representing some of the details Armstrong Sperry uses to describe the setting.

Before Reading

Direct students' attention to the Connect to Your Life and Key to the Memoir activities on page 56 of *The InterActive Reader.*™ Use the following suggestions to prepare students to read the memoir.

Connect to Your Life
Discuss with students the importance of using caution around wild or unfamiliar animals. Brainstorm with them a list of tips for dealing with such animals. Record students' responses on the board and have them select a tip from the list to write on their signs.

Key to the Memoir
Explain to students that the memoir tells about an encounter the author had with a wild animal that taught him an important lesson. Have students answer the question on page 56 of *The InterActive Reader*™; invite volunteers to share their responses. Then discuss possible consequences of treating a wild animal like a pet.

BUILD BACKGROUND **Connect to Geography** Thick forests once covered 70 percent of Minnesota. Today, forests cover only about 35 percent of the state. Minnesota's most spectacular woods can be found in the 3-million-acre Superior National Forest, north of Lake Superior. The northern and northeastern sections of the state are the most rugged. In this region, people are scarce, but wild animals are plentiful. One of the few states where timber wolves still roam free, Minnesota is also home to white-tailed deer, beavers, and black bears.

Make sure students understand that bears are incredibly strong, and that they generally show no fear of people. Explain that problems sometimes arise when humans live or camp near areas where bears roam because the animals are drawn to the smells of food and garbage; people need to use great caution around bears, who can attack quickly when they feel threatened.

WORDS TO KNOW

menace
novelty
predator
rummaging
scavenging

Additional Words to Know

abound
page 58, line 12

hibernation
page 58, line 23

accustomed
page 59, line 51

truce
page 60, line 68

VOCABULARY PREVIEW: Words to Know in Context

You can help students learn the Words to Know by reading aloud the following sentences or writing them on the board. Then show students how to use context clues to help them figure out the meaning.

menace: The hungry coyotes that lived in the nearby hills were a terrible *menace* to the neighborhood cats and small dogs.

novelty: The first time she heard the seals, Sarah was charmed, but the *novelty* wore off after their barking had kept her awake for two nights.

predator: The wolf, a tireless *predator,* caught the rabbit and ate it on the spot.

rummaging: Tossing clothing on the floor, we went *rummaging* through the drawer until we found the key.

scavenging: The lost dog was *scavenging* in the garbage can, looking for scraps of food.

---

abound: Wild deer *abound* in the area; there are so many that we have to fence in our vegetable garden.

hibernation: Bears coming out of *hibernation* are very hungry and sometimes grumpy after a whole winter's sleep.

accustomed: At first we were surprised when the bird landed on our heads, but now we are *accustomed* to it.

truce: The war finally ended when the two sides agreed to a *truce* and set down their weapons.

VOCABULARY FOCUS: Understanding Idioms

Teacher Modeling Remind students that an *idiom* is an expression whose meaning is different from the literal meanings of its individual words. Let them know that they can use context clues to understand the meaning of an unfamiliar idiom. Then use the following modeling suggestions for the idiom ***trade on this fear*** (page 58, line 31):

You might say I've never heard the expression trade on this fear. *Paulsen says that the dogs are afraid of the bears, and that the bears often frighten the dogs away and eat the food they leave behind. The dogs' fear of the bears is a good thing for the bears, and the bears know it. I think that* trade on this fear *must mean "take advantage of this fear" or "use this fear for their own benefit."*

Student Modeling Next, ask a volunteer to use context clues to determine the meaning of ***when it is all boiled down*** (page 62, lines 156–157):

A student could say I don't know the expression when it is all boiled down. *The author is reflecting on the lesson he learned from the bear when he says, "when it is all boiled down, I am nothing more and nothing less than any other animal in the woods." It sounds like he means "in the end, I have learned that I am nothing more and nothing less than any other animal in the woods." This is his way of summing up what he has learned. I think that* boiled down *means "simplified or summed up."*

> **Mini-Lesson**
> See pages 102–103 of this Guide for additional work on **Understanding Idioms.**

During Reading

COMPREHENSION FOCUS

Key Points	Strategies for Success
Target Skill → Cause and Effect In "Woodsong," Gary Paulsen describes several decisions and actions that had major consequences for him. Students must be able to recognize cause-and-effect relationships in order to understand why events unfold as they do in this memoir.	**Mini-Lesson** Before students read "Woodsong," you may wish to teach the **Cause-and-Effect** lesson on pages 126–130 of this Guide. • As students read, have them stop after the *Pause & Reflect* on page 59 to identify the cause-and-effect relationships they've read about so far. • During or after their reading, have students complete the **Cause-and-Effect Chain** on page 129 of this Guide.
Setting This memoir is set in the wilderness around Paulsen's family home. Their unusual living conditions and circumstances may confuse some students. Students need to understand that Gary Paulsen and his family had chosen to live in a wilderness area, where they had to grow their own food and take care of their other needs themselves.	Read aloud the first paragraph on page 58. Ask students to identify the setting ("the edge of wilderness"). Point out that in many wilderness areas there are no stores, no services, and no gas, electricity, or running water. Ask students to name some things the narrator and his family might have to do for themselves in this setting. As students read the selection, have them identify examples of self-sufficiency that the narrator describes (growing food in a garden, disposing of trash by burning it).

Suggested Reading Options

• An oral reading of "Woodsong" is available in *The Language of Literature* Audio Library. ◠
• Partner/Cooperative Reading (See page 8 of this Guide.)
• Additional options are described on page 8 of this Guide.

RECIPROCAL TEACHING SUGGESTION ➡ Questioning

Teacher Modeling *Pause & Reflect, page 60* Have students read the paragraph from lines 59–68. Model using the questioning strategy to clear up confusion.

You could say *I don't understand the line "the goats never really believed in the truce" (line 68). I ask myself: What is the author trying to say about the goats and the bears? When I reread the paragraph I see that the bears always left the goats alone, as if there was an agreement, or truce, between them. However, the goats still act frightened of the bears. This must be what the author means—the goats don't trust the bears not to attack them, even though the bears have never done so.*

Student Modeling *Pause & Reflect, page 60* Have several students model how to ask questions about the author's explanation of why they would wait for a northerly breeze before they would burn their garbage. Offer this prompt: *Where was the Paulsen home located relative to the rest of the wilderness area? What might happen if the wind blew smoke from the burning garbage toward the wilderness area? Would a northerly breeze always solve the problem? Why or why not?*

Students can use the question frame in the **Active Reading SkillBuilder** on page 63 to organize their questions and answers.

Encourage students to use the other five reading strategies when appropriate as they proceed through the rest of the memoir. (See page 10 of this Guide.)

ENGLISH LEARNERS

1. Make sure students understand these idioms:
   taken over (assumed control of), page 58, line 16
   deal with it ourselves (handle it ourselves, dispose of it ourselves), page 60, lines 70–71
2. Students might benefit from reading along with the recording of the memoir provided in *The Language of Literature* Audio Library. ◖

After Reading

Recommended Follow-Up

- Thinking Through the Literature, page 170, *The Language of Literature*
- Choices & Challenges, pages 171–173, *The Language of Literature*
- SkillBuilders, pages 63–65, *The InterActive Reader*™

Informal Assessment Options

Retell Have students work in groups of three to retell the memoir. Each group member should be responsible for retelling one section. Groups can present their retellings to the class using pantomimed actions and props to dramatize events.

Spot Check Check the notes students made in the margins to see if they reveal a basic understanding of the memoir. Invite them to discuss any questions they still have.

Formal Assessment Options in *The Language of Literature*

Selection Quiz, page 87, Unit One Resource Book

Selection Test, pages 25–26, Formal Assessment Book

For more teaching options, see pages 165–173 in *The Language of Literature* Teacher's Edition

Additional Challenge

1. Compare and Contrast

Have students compare and contrast Gary Paulsen's decision not to kill Scarhead with Mako's decision to kill Tupa in "Ghost of the Lagoon." Ask: *Are Scarhead and Tupa equally dangerous? Why does Mako decide to kill Tupa? How are the events leading up to Tupa's death different from the confrontation between Paulsen and Scarhead?*

2. ⦚MARK IT UP⟩ Cause and Effect

Ask: *What cause-and-effect chain in the last section of the memoir leads to an important lesson for the author?* Beginning at the top of page 61, have students draw an arrow between each pair of events that are a cause and effect. Have them write *C* next to each cause and *E* next to each effect in this chain of events. Remind students that in some cases, an event is both the effect of a preceding event and the cause of a following event.

Before Reading

Have students do the Connect to Your Life and Key to the Story activities on page 66 of *The InterActive Reader.*™ Use the following suggestions to prepare students to read the story.

Connect to Your Life
Guide students in a discussion about how the weather affects them. To jog their memories, encourage students to recall specific days when they experienced rainy and sunny weather. Before they fill in the third sentence in the diagram, have students brainstorm to name different types of weather. After students complete the diagram, let them share their thoughts.

Key to the Story
The story is about a girl who is mistreated because she is perceived by others as different. Ask volunteers to read the reasons they listed to explain why some people avoid those who seem different. Then have a brief discussion about the word *different.* You might ask: *Why are people sometimes fearful of those who appear to be different?*

BUILD BACKGROUND
Connect to Science Tell students that "All Summer in a Day" is set on Venus, the second planet from the sun. Explain to them that, thanks to advances in space exploration technology, we now know far more about Venus than we did in 1954, when Ray Bradbury's story was first published. For one thing, scientists have determined that Venus is a hot, dry planet. There is no liquid water on its surface.

WORDS TO KNOW

apparatus
concussion
resilient
savor
tumultuously

Additional Words to Know

slackening
   page 69, line 56
vital
   page 71, line 112
suspended
   page 74, line 198
solemn
   page 75, line 244

VOCABULARY PREVIEW: Words to Know in Context

You can help students learn the Words to Know by reading aloud the following sentences or writing them on the board. Then show students how to use context clues to help them figure out the meaning.

apparatus: No one else in the drama club knew how to repair the *apparatus* that was used to produce sound effects.

concussion: Even though we were across the street, the *concussion* caused by the explosion knocked us to the ground.

resilient: My sister proved how *resilient* she was during the game when she recovered from a rough fall and immediately got ready for the next play.

savor: Because I like to *savor* my food, I eat slowly and appreciate every bite.

tumultuously: The assembly began *tumultuously,* with the children running up and down the aisles and refusing to keep still.

---

slackening: Once they knew the rain was *slackening,* the children put away their umbrellas and began to plan the picnic.

vital: Sarah knew it was *vital* that she take her medicine every day.

suspended: The balloon seemed to be *suspended* in the air as it floated over the town.

solemn: Her *solemn* expression told me that something was terribly wrong.

VOCABULARY FOCUS Word Parts: Suffixes

Teacher Modeling Tell students that they can sometimes figure out the meaning of an unfamiliar word by thinking about the word parts it contains. Then use the following modeling suggestions to use the base word and suffix to figure out the meaning of *remembrance.* (page 69, line 34)

You could say I'm not sure what remembrance *means, but I can try breaking the word into parts. I see the suffix* -ance, *which means "action or condition." I also see the base word* remember, *which means "to think of again." By combining the meanings of these word parts, I can figure out that* remembrance *must mean "the act of recalling something."*

Student Modeling Now have students follow your lead. Ask a volunteer to model using the base word and suffix to figure out the meaning of *fleshlike.* (page 73, line 186)

A student might say I'm not familiar with the word fleshlike. *However, I do know that the base word* flesh *means "meat," and the suffix* -like *means "characteristic of." Therefore, I think that* fleshlike *must mean "having the characteristics of meat."*

Mini-Lesson
See pages 96 and 98 of this Guide for additional work on **Word Parts: Suffixes.**

During Reading

COMPREHENSION FOCUS

Key Points	Strategies for Success
Target Skill ➡ Predicting Tell students that when they make a prediction while reading, they make a guess about what will happen next. They use clues from the story and their own prior knowledge to make a prediction. In "All Summer in a Day," it is important that students make predictions about what will happen to the main character.	**Mini-Lesson** Before students read "All Summer in a Day," you may want to teach the **Predicting** lesson on pages 137–139 of this Guide. • As students read, have them stop after the *Pause & Reflect* on page 72 and discuss their predictions about what will happen to Margot. You may want to have students use the **Predicting Chart** on page 138 of this Guide to list their predictions. • After students finish the story, ask them whether their predictions were correct.
Figurative Language The author uses figurative language to create vivid images in readers' minds. However, some of the similes and metaphors used throughout this story may be difficult for students to understand.	Encourage students to think of the images created by the similes and metaphors in the story. For example, in the simile "like a feverish wheel, all tumbling spokes" (page 69, lines 61–62), students might imagine a wheel spinning so quickly and wildly that its spokes fall all over each other. In the metaphor "she was an old photograph dusted from an album, whitened away" (page 70, lines 70–72), students might visualize a faded, old photo of someone long dead.

Suggested Reading Options

• An oral reading of "All Summer in a Day" is available in *The Language of Literature* Audio Library. ○
• Partner/Cooperative Reading (See page 8 of this Guide.)
• Additional options are described on page8 of this Guide.

RECIPROCAL TEACHING SUGGESTION ➡ Clarifying

Teacher Modeling *Pause & Reflect, page 69* Model for students how to clarify and understand what they have read.

You could say *I know the children are waiting for something. However, I don't think they are waiting for a spaceship, recess, or their parents. The children arrived on a spaceship with their parents, but they don't seem to be thinking about them right now. They want to go outside, but recess doesn't fully explain what they are waiting for. They become very excited when the rain begins to stop, and they spent the day before talking about the sun. I think the children must be waiting for the sun to come out.*

Student Modeling *Pause & Reflect, page 72* Have several students model clarifying why the children dislike Margot. Offer these prompts: *What do the children say when Margot remembers what the sun looked like? How does Margot act when the other children want to play? Why might Margot return to Earth?*

Encourage students to use the other five reading strategies when appropriate as they proceed through the rest of the selection. (See page 10 of this Guide.)

ENGLISH LEARNERS

1. Students may have trouble understanding some of the long sentences in the story. Tell them that they should break the sentences into smaller sentences or parts. For instance, the long sentence on pages 72–73, lines 153–160, can be broken into two parts. The first part describes what happens when the film of the violent event is halted. The second part describes the contrast when the still image is projected instead.

2. Students might benefit from reading along with the recording of "All Summer in a Day" provided in *The Language of Literature* Audio Library. ◯

After Reading

Recommended Follow-Up

- Thinking Through the Literature, page 216, *The Language of Literature*
- Choices & Challenges, page 217, *The Language of Literature*
- SkillBuilders, pages 77–79, *The InterActive Reader*™

Informal Assessment Options

Retell Have students retell the story from Margot's point of view. Offer these prompts:
- *Tell what it's like to live on a planet where it always rains.*
- *Describe how you felt when you were locked in the closet.*

Spot Check Read the notes students wrote in the margins, paying particular attention to their responses to the *Pause & Reflect* questions. Have them share their written answers and discuss any questions they still have about the story.

Formal Assessment Options in *The Language of Literature*

Selection Quiz, page 14, Unit Two Resource Book

Selection Test, pages 33–34, Formal Assessment Book

For more teaching options, see pages 209–218 in *The Language of Literature* Teacher's Edition.

Additional Challenge

1. Write a New Ending
Point out that the story ends with the children letting Margot out of the closet. However, the reader doesn't learn what happens next. Have students discuss what Margot might say or do when she emerges from the closet. Remind students that Margot loves the sun and was greatly looking forward to seeing it again. Then ask students to write a new ending for the story telling what happens after the children unlock the door.

2. ⌗ MARK IT UP ⟩ Evaluate Characters
Tell students that characters' attitudes and feelings often change during a story as a result of specific events. Then have students mark the places that indicate how the children's attitude toward Margot and the sun change. Ask: *How do the children feel about Margot when they lock her in the closet? How do they feel when the sun comes out? How do they feel when the rain begins again? How do the children feel when they let Margot out?*

Before Reading

Have students do the Connect to Your Life and Key to the Memoir activities on page 80 of *The InterActive Reader.*™ Use the following suggestions to prepare students to read the memoir.

Connect to Your Life
Bring in street maps for students to look at. Draw their attention to how the street names are shown and how important landmarks are indicated. Then have students complete their own maps.

Key to the Memoir
Have students read the Key to the Memoir. Ask students to think about how "Chinatown" might have been like and unlike other neighborhoods in a big city. You might ask: *Why would the people in "Chinatown" teach their children the Chinese language?*

BUILD BACKGROUND Connect to Social Studies Explain that immigrants from all over the world have been drawn to San Francisco and other large cities because of the promise of jobs. Then point out that immigrants often formed smaller communities within big cities, sometimes as a result of laws that restricted them from buying property elsewhere. Finally, explain that today, ethnic neighborhoods such as Chinatown, Greektown, Little Italy, and Little Havana thrive in some American cities. These communities add to the rich diversity of city life and provide a haven of support for new immigrants.

WORDS TO KNOW

entice
gaudy
immensely
palatial
remotely
shunned
stereotype
taboo
tenement
vulgar

Additional Words to Know

forbade
　page 85, line 126
disgrace
　page 87, line 189
gulf
　page 88, line 217

VOCABULARY PREVIEW: Words to Know in Context

You can help students learn the Words to Know by reading aloud the following sentences or writing them on the board. Then show students how to use context clues to help them figure out the meaning.

entice: The baby sitter tried to *entice* the children to eat their dinner by promising them ice cream for dessert.

gaudy: She wore a large, *gaudy* ring to show off her wealth.

immensely: He was *immensely* strong and he lifted the car all by himself.

palatial: The *palatial* home had huge rooms with rich furniture and thick carpet.

remotely: I'm very good at basketball, but I'm not even *remotely* good at baseball.

shunned: The new student was *shunned,* or avoided, by the rest of the class.

stereotype: It is a *stereotype* that all lifeguards are tanned, blonde, and athletic.

taboo: Since the committee felt the subject was *taboo,* no one mentioned it at the meeting.

tenement: The family lived in a *tenement,* a rundown building for the very poor.

vulgar: The neighbor showed no respect when she called my aunt a *vulgar* name.

---

forbade: Her parents *forbade* us to go near the slippery, dangerous rocks.

disgrace: He is in *disgrace* for cheating on the test.

gulf: The argument created a *gulf* of misunderstanding that kept them apart.

VOCABULARY FOCUS: Using Context Clues

Teacher Modeling Remind students that sometimes they can use context clues to figure out the meaning of unfamiliar words. Model using context clues to figure out the meaning of the word *boundaries* (page 82, line 13).

Mini-Lesson
See pages 92–95 of this Guide for additional work on **Using Context Clues.**

You could say *I'm not sure what* boundaries *means, so I look for context clues. The author is describing a place that is set within certain streets and neighborhoods.* Boundaries *seems to mean "borders" or "limits."*

Student Modeling Ask a volunteer to model how to use context clues to determine the meaning of the word *reinforced* (page 87, line 170).

A student might say *The author says he believed he was terrible at sports. He also says that hitting Sister Bridget with the ball* reinforced *that belief. That experience made him feel even worse about his athletic ability.* Reinforced *must mean "made stronger."*

During Reading

COMPREHENSION FOCUS

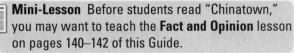

Key Points	Strategies for Success
Target Skill ➡ Fact and Opinion Laurence Yep presents both facts and opinions in this memoir. Students must be able to identify his opinions about himself, his family, and his community, as well as supporting the facts in order to understand how his childhood experiences helped shape his identity.	**Mini-Lesson** Before students read "Chinatown," you may want to teach the **Fact and Opinion** lesson on pages 140–142 of this Guide. • Read Aloud lines 69–75 on page 84. Then ask students to identify Yep's opinion about the Chinatown housing projects (bleak) and the detail that supports it. • After reading, have students complete the **Active Reading SkillBuilder** on page 91 of *The InterActive Reader.*™
The Author's Self-Image Yep does not present his childhood memories in sequential order. Rather, they are linked by the fact that each experience contributed to his sense of himself as an outsider. Students must understand the author's view of himself in order to fully appreciate the memoir.	At the *Pause & Reflect* on page 83, ask: *How does Yep say he was different from his classmates?* At the *Pause & Reflect* on page 84, ask: *In what way did Yep's Chinese heritage make him an outsider in San Francisco?* As students continue to read, tell them to note other examples that reflect the author's view of himself as being an outsider within one's own community.

Suggested Reading Options

• Partner/Cooperative Reading (See page 8 of this Guide.)
• Additional options are described on page 8 of this Guide.

RECIPROCAL TEACHING SUGGESTION ➡ Questioning

Teacher Modeling *Pause & Reflect, page 83* Model using the questioning strategy to understand the author's meaning.

You could say When I read lines 21–34 on pages 82–83, I ask myself: Why is this memory important to him? What does the cottage represent, or stand for, at this point in his life? Yep mentions that there was very little plant life in Chinatown. The only green he saw was the paint on his school. I think the cottage represents a world that was not his own. This world did not welcome him, yet he admired it greatly.

Student Modeling *Pause & Reflect, page 84* Ask a student to model the strategy to figure out what Yep means by "invisible barriers." Offer this prompt: A barrier can be anything physical, mental, or emotional that blocks or prevents a person from doing something. Ask: *What did many white San Franciscans have that many Chinese did not? (wealth) How was this a "barrier" for Chinatown's residents?*

Encourage students to use the other five reading strategies when appropriate as they proceed through the rest of the memoir. (See page 10 of this Guide.)

ENGLISH LEARNERS

Make sure students understand the following terms:

physical area, page 82, line 12
was charm itself, page 82, line 30
rolled foul, page 87, line 161
as fate would have it, page 87, lines 162–163

After Reading

Recommended Follow-Up

- Thinking Through the Literature, page 227, *The Language of Literature*
- Choices & Challenges, pages 228–229, *The Language of Literature*
- SkillBuilders, pages 91–93, *The InterActive Reader*™

Informal Assessment Options

Retell Have students work in groups of four to retell the memoir. Each group member can tell about one of the following topics: What Chinatown was like in Yep's childhood; Yep's schoolmate Paul; Yep's experiences playing sports; Yep's feelings as an outsider.

Spot Check Read the notations students made in the margins. Ask students who used the **?** notation whether they were able to clear up their confusion, and if so, how.

Formal Assessment Options in *The Language of Literature*

Selection Quiz, page 21, Unit Two Resource Book

Selection Test, pages 35–36, Formal Assessment Book

For more teaching options, see pages 219–229 in *The Language of Literature* Teacher's Edition.

Additional Challenge

1. Comparing Characters
Ask: *How would you compare the author with Paul and Harold, the two boys in this memoir who live in Chinatown?* Have students support their answers with details from the memoir.

2. MARK IT UP ⟩ Figurative Language
Briefly review similes and metaphors with students. Then have them underline examples of these figures of speech in "Chinatown." [Examples: "pieces of the puzzle" (line 8); "like a living sea" (line 29)]. Then discuss with students what makes each example so effective.

Before Reading

Direct students' attention to the Connect to Your Life and Key to the Short Story activities on page 94 of *The InterActive Reader.*™ Use the following suggestions to prepare students to read the story.

Connect to Your Life

Invite students to describe their own experiences during a move. Guide students by asking them to tell what steps were involved in the move, including packing, traveling to the new place, and adjusting to the new home. Then ask students what they found most difficult about the move. *What parts did they enjoy?* After the discussion, have students complete the chart.

Key to the Short Story

Point out that when the children of migrant farmers move from place to place, they must change schools. Also, many children miss months of school at a time because they must help with the harvest. Ask students how these moves probably affect the children's education. *Why might the children's lack of education force them to remain migrant farmers when they grow up?*

BUILD BACKGROUND

Connect to Social Studies Tell students that this story is about the problems faced by Panchito, a young Mexican-American boy in a family of migrant farm workers in California. Explain that migrant farm workers are laborers who migrate, or move, from one agricultural area to another in search of work. The workers often move in a circuit—a regular route of travel—that follows the harvest seasons in different places.

WORDS TO KNOW

hesitantly
instinct
jalopy
surplus
vineyard

Additional Words to Know

peak
  page 96, line 4
thoroughly
  page 97, line 56
drone
  page 100, line 138
startled
  page 102, line 212
enthusiastically
  page 103, line 227

VOCABULARY PREVIEW: Words to Know in Context

You can help students learn the Words to Know by reading aloud the following sentences or writing them on the board. Then show students how to use context clues to help them figure out the meaning.

hesitantly: The student answered the question slowly and *hesitantly* because he wasn't sure of the answer.

instinct: When the thunderstorm began, the dog's first *instinct* was to run and hide.

jalopy: We locked our rusty old *jalopy* in the garage with the other cars.

surplus: Since no one ate anything at the party, a *surplus* of food was left over.

vineyard: I walked slowly through the *vineyard,* looking at the full bunches of grapes on the vines.

---

peak: Strawberries at their *peak* are fat, deep red, and sweet.

thoroughly: I cleaned my room *thoroughly,* removing every speck of dust.

drone: The steady *drone* of the bees as they buzzed around the flowers made me sleepy.

startled: A sudden noise in the library *startled* me and made me jump out of my chair.

enthusiastically: The children jumped up and down *enthusiastically* when I offered to take them to the amusement park.

VOCABULARY FOCUS Word Parts: Suffixes

Teacher Modeling Tell students that they can sometimes figure out the meaning of an unfamiliar word by thinking about the word parts it contains. Then use the following modeling suggestions for the word **wearily** (page 98, line 87).

You could say *I'm not sure what* wearily *means, but I can try breaking the word into parts. I see the suffix -ly, which means "in a particular way or manner." I also see the base word* weary, *which means "tired." I can figure out from these word parts that* wearily *is an adverb. It must mean "in a tired way."*

Student Modeling Now have students follow your lead. Ask a volunteer to model using the base word and suffix to figure out the meaning of **speechless** (page 102, line 213).

A student might say *I'm not familiar with the word* speechless. *However, I do know that the base word* speech *means "speaking" or "language," and the suffix -less means "without." So* speechless *must mean "unable to speak."*

Mini-Lesson
See pages 96 and 98 of this Guide for additional work on **Word Parts: Suffixes.**

During Reading

COMPREHENSION FOCUS

Key Points	Strategies for Success

Target Skill ➡ Making Inferences

The writer does not explain everything that happens in this story. It is crucial that students be able to make inferences in order to understand the key events.

Mini-Lesson Before students read "The Circuit," you may want to teach or review the **Making Inferences** lesson on pages 134–136 of this Guide.

- Read aloud lines 263–269 on page 104. Ask students what they can infer from the fact that the family's things are packed. Ask: *What clues from the story helped you make your inference?*

- Have students complete the **Active Reading SkillBuilder** on page 105, which will help them make inferences about the story's characters.

Characterization

It is essential for students to put together details to draw conclusions about the character of Mr. Lema.

After the *Pause & Reflect* on page 104, have students discuss Mr. Lema's personality. Ask: *What clues tell you what kind of teacher Mr. Lema is?*

Suggested Reading Options

- An oral reading of "The Circuit" is available in *The Language of Literature* Audio Library. 🎧
- Partner/Cooperative Reading (See page 8 of this Guide.)
- Additional options are described on page 8 of this Guide.

RECIPROCAL TEACHING SUGGESTION ➡ Visualizing

Teacher Modeling *Pause & Reflect, page 99* Model for students how to use details to form a mental picture of the garage where Panchito's family will live.

You could say *I can picture the garage in lines 107–111. The walls have been eaten by termites, the roof has lots of holes, and the floor is made of loose dirt. From this description, I can visualize a dirty, broken-down garage with sagging walls and a decaying roof.*

Student Modeling *Pause & Reflect, page 101* Have several students model visualizing the vineyard where Panchito is working. Offer this prompt: *What details describe the heat? What details describe the insects and the ground?*

Encourage students to use the other five reading strategies when appropriate as they proceed through the rest of the story. (See page 10 of this Guide.)

ENGLISH LEARNERS

1. Make sure students understand that *since* can mean both "from the time" and "because." (page 98, line 92) Help students understand that the word means "because" in this sentence. Papa's inability to speak English is the reason that Mama speaks to the foreman.

2. Students might benefit from reading along with the recording of "The Circuit" provided in *The Language of Literature* Audio Library. ◯

After Reading

Recommended Follow-Up

• Thinking Through the Literature, page 272, *The Language of Literature*

• Choices & Challenges, pages 273–274, *The Language of Literature*

• SkillBuilders, pages 105–107, *The InterActive Reader™*

Informal Assessment Options

Retell Write each of the following phrases on cards: *packing up the car; finding work in Fresno; working in the vineyard; going to school; finding that the boxes have been packed once again.* Distribute the cards in random order to a small group of students. Have them place the cards in the correct order. Then have them use the cards as prompts to retell the story. Encourage students to add a few details to explain each phrase.

Spot Check Read the notations students made in the margins. Ask students who used the **?** symbol if they still have questions about the story.

Formal Assessment Options in *The Language of Literature*

Selection Quiz, page 45, Unit Two Resource Book

Selection Test, pages 41–42, Formal Assessment Book

For more teaching options, see pages 264–274 in *The Language of Literature* Teacher's Edition.

Additional Challenge

1. **Describe a Character's Feelings**
   Point out that at the end of the story, Panchito says that the family's boxes are packed, but he doesn't tell how he feels about moving again. Have students write a brief paragraph in which they describe what Panchito must be feeling. To help students get started, ask: *How did Panchito feel about moving to Fresno? How does he feel about the school in Fresno? Why might he want to keep going to that school?*

2. **▐▌▌ MARK IT UP ⟩ Identify Details**
   Remind students that the story describes the family's two special possessions: Papa's car and Mama's cooking pot. Have students underline details in the story that tell about these possessions. Then have students discuss what the car and cooking pot represent to the family. Ask: *How does Papa feel about his car? How do Mama and the rest of the family treat the cooking pot? Why might these possessions be important to a family that must move from one broken-down shack to another?*

Before Reading

Direct students' attention to the Connect to Your Life and Key to the Poems activities on page 108 of *The InterActive Reader.*™ Use the following suggestions to prepare students to read the poems.

Connect to Your Life
Have students fill out the graphic organizer and discuss their responses. Ask: *Why did you choose the place and the type of transportation you did? What is it that interests you about them?* Explain that in the two poems the students will read, making the trip itself is as important as reaching the destination.

Key to the Poems
Ask a volunteer to read aloud the excerpt from "Night Journey" while you clap out the rhythm. Help students notice that the lines have a regular beat. Then explain the symbols used to mark light and heavy stresses.

BUILD BACKGROUND Connect to Social Studies Explain to students that both "Western Wagons" and "Night Journey" are about people traveling across the American West.

"Western Wagons" describes the experiences of settlers who traveled west in horse-drawn or ox-drawn covered wagons in the early to mid-1800s. These wagons were sometimes called *prairie schooners* because their white canvas tops made them look a little like sailing ships. A journey west in a prairie schooner took months of grueling travel, often through deserts and rugged terrain. One of the most heavily used western routes was the Oregon Trail. Between 1835 and 1855, approximately 10,000 deaths occurred on the Oregon Trail, mostly from accidents and disease. People made the dangerous journey west in search of gold or rich farmland or to avoid religious persecution.

"Night Journey" is set many years later, when locomotive trains had made the trip safer, faster, and more comfortable. A coast-to-coast trip by train took less than a week. You might ask students to discuss how each method of travel might have affected the experiences of the travelers.

Strategies for Reading Poetry:

- Notice the form of the poem: the number of lines and their shape on the page.
- Read the poem aloud a few times. Listen for rhymes and rhythms.
- Visualize the images and comparisons.
- Mark words or phrases that appeal to you.
- Ask yourself what message the poet is trying to send.
- Think about what the poem is saying to you.

FOCUS ON POETRY

Before students read "Western Wagons" and "Night Journey," you may want to have them read the feature "Poetry" on pages 189–193 of *The Language of Literature.* That lesson shows how key elements in a poem work together to stir emotion and create meaning. It also suggests some strategies students can use when reading poetry; these are summarized in the column at the left. The activities below will help prepare students for reading "Western Wagons" and "Night Journey."

- **Sound** Help students identify the rhythm pattern in the four lines from "Night Journey" on page 108. Then ask for a volunteer to read the first two lines of "Western Wagons." Have students compare the rhythms. Students may mention that "Night Journey" has short, clipped lines whose rhythm imitates the chugging of a train, while "Western Wagons" has long, musical-sounding lines like those in traditional songs.

- **Theme** Both poems explore the nature of the American West and Americans' relationship to it. After students have read the Preview, work with them to list some of the things the American West symbolizes for Americans, such as freedom, opportunity, wilderness, beauty, and the courageous spirit of exploration.

VOCABULARY FOCUS: Using Words with Multiple Meanings

Teacher Modeling Remind students that many words have more than one meaning and that sometimes they can use the context to help them figure out which meaning applies in a particular sentence or line. Model the strategy using the word *blaze* (page 110, line 1).

You could say Blaze *can mean "burn brightly" or "mark a trail or path." I can check the context for a clue as to which of these meanings is used here. The words "the trail" help me figure out that blaze must mean "mark a trail."*

Student Modeling Ask a student volunteer to use the context to figure out the meaning of *rocks* (page 112, line 2).

A student might say *I know the word* rocks *has several meanings, including "more than one stone" and "moves back and forth." In this line the word seems to tell about an action, something that the movement of a train does to the earth. The meaning that makes sense here is "moves back and forth."*

> **Mini-Lesson**
> See pages 104–105 of this Guide for additional work on **Using Words with Multiple Meanings.**

During Reading

COMPREHENSION FOCUS

Key Points	Strategies for Success
Target Skill ➡ Compare and Contrast It is crucial for students to understand and compare the ideas about traveling west expressed in these poems.	**Mini-Lesson** Before students read the poems, you might teach or review the **Compare and Contrast** lesson on pages 131–133 of this Guide. • After reading, have students fill in the Venn diagram on page 132 of this Guide.
Sound Devices To appreciate the poems fully, students must notice that the writers use rhyme and rhythm to support their ideas about traveling west.	• Read aloud lines 1–4 of "Western Wagons." Help students notice that each pair of lines rhymes. Point out that each of the first three lines contains 14 syllables and that the fourth line contains 15. Mention that the rhythm is regular, with a heavy stress following a light one. • Have a volunteer read aloud lines 1–5 of "Night Journey." Help students notice that each line contains six syllables, that the rhythm is regular, and that lines 1 and 5 rhyme, as do lines 2 and 3. • Have students complete both the **Active Reading SkillBuilder** and the **Literary Analysis SkillBuilder** on pages 114–115 of *The InterActive Reader.*™

Suggested Reading Options

• Oral readings of "Western Wagons" and "Night Journey" are available in *The Language of Literature* Audio Library. ◯
• Oral Reading (See page 8 of this Guide.)
• Additional options are described on page 8 of this Guide.

RECIPROCAL TEACHING SUGGESTION ➡ Visualizing

Teacher Modeling *Pause & Reflect, page 111* Model for students how to visualize the setting of "Western Wagons."

You could say *As I read the poem, I try to picture in my mind what it was like to travel across the country by covered wagon. When I read the line "all across the continent the endless campfires glowed," I get an image of a nighttime scene with the lights of many small fires dotting the prairie.*

Student Modeling *Pause & Reflect, page 113* Have several students model visualizing the images in "Night Journey." Offer these prompts: *What images do you see as you read the poet's description of the train trip? What words does the poet use to help you imagine the view at night?*

Encourage students to use the other five reading strategies when appropriate as they proceed through the poems. (See page 10 of this Guide.)

ENGLISH LEARNERS

1. Help students understand the following expressions: "Western Wagons" (pages 110–111): "the trail was still to blaze"; "We've broken land and cleared it"; "tame the land"; "Night Journey"(pages 112–113): "the train bears west"; "line of sight"; "thunder through ravines"; "washed with light."

2. Students might benefit from reading along with the recordings of the poems provided in *The Language of Literature* Audio Library. ◯

After Reading

Recommended Follow-Up

- Thinking Through the Literature, page 287, *The Language of Literature*
- Choices & Challenges, page 288, *The Language of Literature*
- SkillBuilders, pages 114–115, *The InterActive Reader*™

Informal Assessment Options

Retell Have students work in pairs to retell the two poems together as a dialogue between the settlers in the first poem and the traveler in the second. Each partner should review one poem and note the most important details to share. Encourage students to think about how the settlers and traveler are alike and how they are different. Students may mention that while both the settlers and the traveler love the land and love travel, the traveler is calm and does not want to tame the land the way the settlers do.

Spot Check Look at the notes students made in the margins. Make sure their answers show an understanding of what they have read.

Formal Assessment Options in *The Language of Literature*

Selection Test, pages 45–46, Formal Assessment Book

For more teaching options, see pages 284–288 in *The Language of Literature* Teacher's Edition.

Additional Challenge

1. **Explain an Opinion**
   Ask: *Do you think the pioneers described in "Western Wagons" were wise or foolish to travel west?* Have students support their views with details from the poem.

2. **‖‖MARK IT UP ⬗ Examine Alliteration**
   Review with students what alliteration is—the repetition of consonant sounds at the beginning of two or more words (**n**ervous **n**ight; **m**assive, **m**urky **m**ountain). Discuss what alliteration adds to a poem. Students may say that alliteration can make a poem more musical-sounding and easier to remember. Then have them circle examples of alliteration in "Night Journey," such as "We **r**ush into a **r**ain/That **r**attles double glass."

Before Reading

Direct students' attention to the Connect to Your Life and Key to the Biography activities on page 116 of *The InterActive Reader.*™ Use the following suggestions to prepare students to read the biography.

Connect to Your Life
Lead students in a general discussion of ways in which people commonly identify themselves, such as by name, family background, skills and talents, occupation, ethnicity, and cultural heritage. After students fill out the chart on page 116, let them share their responses.

Key to the Biography
Have students locate Africa on a world map and describe its location in relation to North America. Then have a volunteer read aloud the information about the Songhai Empire. Ask: *What do you think might have made this empire powerful? What resources do you think the people of Songhai might have had to trade?*

BUILD BACKGROUND **Connect to History** After students have read the Preview on page 117, explain that the selection takes place long ago, in the ruins of the Songhai Empire. Large and powerful, the Songhai Empire dominated West Africa for hundreds of years, reaching its peak in the 1500s. Most of its great wealth came from gold. From the 1500s to the 1800s, Europeans regularly traded with Africans to acquire captives to be sold into slavery. Africans captured by enemy tribes were often marched to coastal slave markets, traded to Europeans for a variety of goods, and taken across the sea to be sold as slaves in the Americas.

WORDS TO KNOW

bondage

chaos

dynasty

inhabitant

premise

procedure

prosper

reservation

status

trek

Additional Words to Know

captives
  page 124, line 187
ransom
  page 126, line 252

VOCABULARY PREVIEW: Words to Know in Context

You can help students learn the Words to Know by reading aloud the following sentences or writing them on the board. Then show students how to use context clues to help them figure out the meaning.

bondage: Many Africans lost their freedom when they were captured and sold into *bondage.*

chaos: There was *chaos* when the teacher left the classroom: the children began throwing books on the floor, jumping on the desks, and shouting at each other.

dynasty: The family's *dynasty* continued when the old man died and his young son became the new ruler.

inhabitant: After everyone else moved away, he was the only *inhabitant* left in the town.

premise: Our country was founded on the principle, or *premise,* that all people are equal.

procedure: To check out a library book, please follow the *procedure* written on the poster.

prosper: Our business will *prosper,* and then we will be able to buy anything we want.

reservation: When the father told his small daughter about the tooth fairy, she believed him completely and without any *reservation.*

status: His high *status* in society was reflected by his fine clothes and proud bearing.

trek: After the hikers completed their *trek* to the top of the mountain, they were hungry and exhausted.

captives: The *captives* tried to escape from prison, but the guards blocked their way.

ransom: In the movie, the frightened parents agree to pay the kidnapper a *ransom* in order to get their son back.

VOCABULARY FOCUS: Using Prefixes

Teacher Modeling Remind students that they can use their knowledge of prefixes to help them figure out the meaning of an unfamiliar word. Model using the word *enslave* (page 130, line 397).

You could say I've seen the prefix en- in words like enable. I know that enable means "to make or cause to be able." I also know that a slave is someone who is forced to work for and obey another. Enslave *is a verb. It probably means "to cause to become a slave" or "to put into slavery."*

Student Modeling Have students model using their knowledge of prefixes to help them figure out the meaning of the word *unfortunate* (page 118, line 18).

A student might say I recognize the prefix un- *from words like* unhappy, *and I know it usually means "not." The word* fortunate *means "lucky," so* unfortunate *must mean "not lucky." This meaning makes sense in the sentence.*

Mini-Lesson
See pages 96–97 of this Guide for additional work on **Word Parts: Using Prefixes.**

During Reading

COMPREHENSION FOCUS

Key Points	Strategies for Success
Target Skill ➡ Sequence This biography covers a long period of time and describes many events in one man's life. Students must follow the sequence of events carefully in order to understand why, how, and when events happen.	**Mini-Lesson** Before students read "Abd al-Rahman Ibrahima," you may want to teach the **Sequence** lesson on pages 123–125 of this Guide. • Have pairs of students stop after each *Pause & Reflect* to list the important events and the order in which they occur. • Each time they pause, students can add events and dates to the time line provided in the **Active Reading SkillBuilder** on page 133.
Author's Purpose Students will better appreciate the biography if they understand that the author's purpose for writing is not only to inform, but also to persuade readers to think about the injustices of slavery.	After students read the last paragraph of the biography and complete the Reread activity in the margin, ask them to restate the author's opinion of slavery in their own words. Also have students explain how they can tell what the author thinks. Then guide them in a discussion about why they think Myers wrote this piece.

Suggested Reading Options

• An oral reading of "Abd al-Rahman Ibrahima" is available in *The Language of Literature* Audio Library. ◯
• Partner/Cooperative Reading (See page 8 of this Guide.)
• Additional options are described on page 8 of this Guide.

RECIPROCAL TEACHING SUGGESTION ➡ Evaluating

Teacher Modeling *Pause & Reflect, page 125* Model using the evaluating strategy to help students form opinions about Ibrahima's African and white captors.

You could say *I was surprised to learn that other Africans captured Ibrahima and sold him to the slave traders. Both the African and the European captors seemed brutal and cruel. These people cared only about wealth, not about human life.*

Student Modeling *Pause & Reflect, page 127* Have several students model using the evaluating strategy to form opinions about Ibrahima's decision to return to Mr. Foster. Offer this prompt: *Do you think Ibrahima made the right choice when he returned to Mr. Foster? What else could he have done?*

Encourage students to use the other five reading strategies when appropriate as they proceed through the rest of the biography. (See page 10 of this Guide.)

ENGLISH LEARNERS

1. Make sure students understand the meaning of these idioms:

   eyed each other (looked at each other), page 118, line 15

   came of age (became an adult), page 119, lines 42–43

   speak their native tongues (speak their native languages), page 127, line 293

   of royal blood (from a royal family or heritage), page 129, line 349

2. Students might benefit from reading along with the recording of the biography provided in *The Language of Literature* Audio Library. ○

After Reading

Recommended Follow-Up

- Thinking Through the Literature, page 378, *The Language of Literature*
- Choices & Challenges, pages 379–380, *The Language of Literature*
- SkillBuilders, pages 133–135, *The InterActive Reader™*

Informal Assessment Options

Retell Have students form groups of five. Each group member should describe events from one phase of Ibrahima's life: the early years, the war with the Mandingo, the voyage to America, the years on Foster's farm, and the campaign to free Ibrahima from slavery.

Spot Check Read the notes students wrote in the margins, paying special attention to their responses to the *Pause & Reflect* questions. Invite them to discuss any questions they still have.

Formal Assessment Options in *The Language of Literature*

Selection Quiz, page 33, Unit Three Resource Book

Selection Test, pages 57–58, Formal Assessment Book

For more teaching options, see pages 365–380 in *The Language of Literature* Teacher's Edition.

Additional Challenge

1. Role-Play a Character

Have groups of students enact a court scene in which they role-play lawyers, abolitionists, and friends arguing for Ibrahima's freedom. Students should write a loose script for the enactment, making decisions about who should speak and in what order. Some students will be comfortable improvising their speeches, but others may prefer to write out their testimony and speak from the script.

2. MARK IT UP ⟫ Contrasting Views

Have students contrast Thomas Foster's view of Ibrahima with Ibrahima's understanding of his own identity. Have them underline details in the text that reveal these different perspectives.

Before Reading

Direct students' attention to the Connect to Your Life and Key to the Autobiography activities on page 136 of *The InterActive Reader.*™ Use the following suggestions to prepare students to read the autobiography.

Connect to Your Life
Review the five senses with students. Then ask students to name some things they like to touch, smell, and taste. After the discussion, have students complete their lists.

Key to the Autobiography
Ask students to think about a time when they felt sad and alone. Then invite students to remember what cheered them up. You might ask: *Did someone make you feel better? If so, what did the person say or do?* Tell students that they might draw on their personal experiences as they write to Helen Keller. They could share their experiences or provide words of comfort.

BUILD BACKGROUND **Connect to History** Tell students that the first school for the hearing impaired opened in Hartford, Connecticut, in 1817. It was established by Thomas Gallaudet, a Hartford minister, and Laurent Clerc, a deaf teacher from the Institute of Deaf-Mutes in Paris, France. Clerc brought with him French sign language, which he combined with several visual languages from the United States to create American Sign Language (ASL). Other schools for the hearing impaired followed, including Gallaudet University. Today, many schools offer programs and services to help students learn ASL.

Explain that ASL combines signs, gestures, facial expressions, and a hand alphabet. It is now the fourth most used language in the United States. As more people learn sign language, those with hearing loss face fewer barriers in today's society.

WORDS TO KNOW

- bitterness
- impress
- persist
- prey
- repentance
- reveal
- sentiment
- succeed
- tangible
- vainly

VOCABULARY PREVIEW: Words to Know in Context

You can help students learn the Words to Know by reading aloud the following sentences or writing them on the board. Then show students how to use context clues to help them figure out the meaning.

bitterness: The angry expression on her face showed the *bitterness* she felt at being left out.

impress: Before beginning the sailing lessons, the instructor tried to *impress* upon us the importance of always wearing our life preservers.

persist: Usually my sister will *persist* until she figures out how to solve a math problem; however, this time she just gave up.

prey: In the story, the woman's fears *prey* upon her until she finally goes mad.

repentance: When the boy saw the little girl cry, he felt *repentance* for smashing her doll.

reveal: The magician will *reveal* the secret of the trick only if we promise never to tell it to anyone else.

sentiment: Filled with *sentiment,* the old man cried when he looked at the old photos.

succeed: In this area, days of sunshine always *succeed,* or follow, rainy days.

tangible: When the lights went out, the darkness was almost *tangible*—that is, it seemed as though we could reach out and touch it.

vainly: They tried *vainly* to put the broken toy back together, but it was beyond repair.

VOCABULARY FOCUS: Using Words with Multiple Meanings

Teacher Modeling Remind students that many words have more than one meaning. When they read, students can often use context clues to help them figure out which meaning of the word the writer intended. If students aren't familiar with a word's multiple meanings, encourage them to look the word up in a dictionary. Then use the following modeling suggestions for the word *dashed* (page 140, line 74).

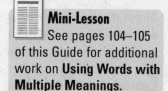

Mini-Lesson
See pages 104–105 of this Guide for additional work on **Using Words with Multiple Meanings**.

You could say I know dashed *can mean "rushed" or "moved quickly," but those meanings don't seem right here. When I look the word up in the dictionary, I see that it can also mean "smashed." The phrase "fragments of the broken doll" is a clue that this meaning is the correct one.*

Student Modeling Now have students follow your lead. Ask a volunteer to model the strategy to determine the meaning of *drawing* (page 141, line 91).

A student might say I know drawing *can mean "sketching," but that doesn't make sense here. The dictionary lists other meanings, including "causing to flow." In this passage, the narrator describes water gushing from a spout, so "causing to flow" must be the right meaning.*

During Reading

COMPREHENSION FOCUS

Key Points	Strategies for Success
It is essential for students to contrast Helen's life before Anne Sullivan became her teacher with her life after she learned the connection between words and objects.	**Mini-Lesson** Before students read "The Story of My Life," you may want to teach or review the **Compare and Contrast** lesson on pages 131–133 of this Guide.
	• Read aloud lines 26–35 on pages 138–139 and lines 99–103 on page 141. Then have students contrast Helen's feelings of being shut up in a fog with her feelings of being set free.
	• Have students fill in the **Venn Diagram** on page 132 of this Guide during or after reading.
Conflict It is important for students to understand Helen's conflicts in this selection.	Help students see that there are two main conflicts in the selection: an external one between Helen and Anne and an internal one within Helen. Then discuss how both conflicts are resolved.

Suggested Reading Options

- An oral reading of "The Story of My Life" is available in *The Language of Literature* Audio Library.
- Partner/Cooperative Reading (See page 8 of this Guide.)
- Additional options are described on page 8 of this Guide.

RECIPROCAL TEACHING SUGGESTION ➡ Clarifying

Teacher Modeling *Pause & Reflect, page 139* Model for students how to use the clarifying strategy to figure out who took Helen's hand.

You could say When I reread lines 36–40 carefully, I see that the person who took Helen's hand was someone "who had come to reveal all things to me." Since Helen's teacher had come to help the girl communicate and understand her own thoughts and feelings, the passage must describe Anne Sullivan. It must be she who took the girl's hand.

Student Modeling *Pause & Reflect, page 142* Ask several volunteers to model using clarifying to understand how Helen felt about the broken doll. Offer these prompts: *How did Helen feel when she broke the doll? Why did she feel this way? How did she feel when she tried to put the doll back together? What had changed for Helen?* Students can also use the **Active Reading SkillBuilder** on page 143 of *The Interactive Reader*™ to clarify other important events in the selection.

Encourage students to use the other five reading strategies when appropriate as they proceed through the rest of the autobiography. (See page 10 of this Guide.)

ENGLISH LEARNERS

1. Be sure students understand that as a little girl, Helen could not read, write, hear, see, or speak. Tell them that she learned to communicate her thoughts as she got older. Encourage students to think about their own experiences and frustrations with learning a second language. Then ask them to think about how difficult it must have been for the young Helen to live in a world without language of any kind.

2. Students might benefit from reading along with the recording of the excerpt from "The Story of My Life" provided in *The Language of Literature* Audio Library. ⌒

After Reading

Recommended Follow-Up

- Thinking Through the Literature, page 385, *The Language of Literature*
- Choices & Challenges, pages 386–387, *The Language of Literature*
- SkillBuilders, pages 143–145, *The InterActive Reader*™

Informal Assessment Options

Retell Have students retell the main events in this autobiography from Anne Sullivan's point of view. Offer these prompts:
- *What did you think of Helen when you first met her?*
- *How did you feel when she broke the doll you gave her?*
- *How did Helen act when she understood what water meant?*
- *How did you feel when you knew that Helen could finally begin to communicate with the world?*

Spot Check Read the notations students made in the margins to see whether they show an understanding of the autobiography. Pay particular attention to their answers to the *Pause & Reflect* questions.

Formal Assessment Options in *The Language of Literature*

Selection Quiz, page 40, Unit Three Resource Book

Selection Test, pages 59–60, Formal Assessment Book

For more teaching options, see pages 381–387 in *The Language of Literature* Teacher's Edition.

Additional Challenge

1. Interpret a Statement
Ask students to write a sentence or two in response to this prompt: *What does Helen mean when she says that she saw everything with the strange, new sight that had come upon her?* Before students begin writing, tell them that the statement does not mean that Helen is no longer blind. Ask students to consider how blind people might "see" or perceive the world.

2. ▐▌▌ MARK IT UP ⧽ Understand Sensory Details
Point out that Helen Keller uses sensory details to describe her thoughts and impressions. Have students reread the selection and underline the words or phrases that appeal to the senses of touch, sight, hearing, taste, and smell. Then ask: *Why do you think Helen Keller uses these details to describe her experiences? How do the sensory details help you understand her world?*

Before Reading

Direct students' attention to the Connect to Your Life and Key to the Story activities on page 146 of *The InterActive Reader.*™ Use the following suggestions to prepare students to read the story.

Connect to Your Life
Ask students who have owned dogs to tell what they like about having them. Then focus the discussion on ways dogs can help people. Have students complete their webs and share their ideas with the class.

Key to the Story
Give students an idea of how long 400 miles is by identifying a place that is about that distance from your school. Then have students read the paragraph and complete the activity.

BUILD BACKGROUND **Connect to Geography** Point out that Cornwall, the story's setting, is a peninsula bordered by the Atlantic Ocean and the English Channel. The coast of Cornwall is characterized by rocky cliffs and small inlets. Farming and fishing are both important industries there, and the harbors are used mainly by fishing boats. A typical village in Cornwall has white cottages lining steep, narrow streets. The region is a popular vacation spot.

WORDS TO KNOW

agitated

assure

atone

coma

conceal

draft

inquire

melancholy

rivet

transfusion

Additional Words to Know

erupt
  page 148, line 32

resolution
  page 151, line 120

VOCABULARY PREVIEW: Words to Know in Context

You can help students learn the Words to Know by reading aloud the following sentences or writing them on the board. Then show students how to use context clues to help them figure out the meaning.

agitated: I *agitated* the water in the still pond by kicking it.

assure: During the lightning storm, we *assured* the frightened child that he was safe inside the house.

atone: She wanted to *atone* for her mistake; that is, she wanted to repair the damage she had done.

coma: When my brother was in a *coma,* he seemed to be in a deep sleep from which no one could wake him.

conceal: We tried to *conceal* the present from the birthday girl by hiding it behind the couch.

draft: After my first day of summer camp, I got out my pen and began to *draft* a letter to my parents.

inquire: If you need directions to the museum, you can *inquire* at the information center.

melancholy: The children felt sad when they returned to school, and their *melancholy* mood lasted for a few days.

rivet: All eyes were *riveted* on stage when the superstar singer made his entrance.

transfusion: The patient needed a *transfusion* to replace some of the lost blood.

---

erupt: I worried that my mother would *erupt,* or explode, in anger when she saw my messy room.

resolution: After I got sick from eating a whole box of chocolates, I made a *resolution* never to eat candy again.

VOCABULARY FOCUS: Using Context Clues

Teacher Modeling Remind students that sometimes they can use context clues to help them figure out the meaning of an unfamiliar word. Model using the word *reluctant* (page 151, line 110).

You could say *I'm not sure what* reluctant *means, so I look for clues in the rest of the sentence. The author says that Lob "had been led whining away." It sounds like Lob didn't want to leave and resisted going. I think that* reluctant *is an adjective that means "unwilling."*

Mini-Lesson See pages 92–95 of this Guide for additional work on **Using Context Clues.**

Student Modeling Have student volunteers model using the strategy to figure out the meaning of *haggard* (page 160, line 382).

A student might say *I've never seen this word before. The author uses it to describe Sandy's parents, who have "sat in the waiting room" of a hospital for hours, not knowing if their injured daughter will live or die. They are probably extremely tired and worried. I think* haggard *probably means "looking completely worn out or exhausted."*

During Reading

COMPREHENSION FOCUS

Key Points	Strategies for Success
Target Skill ➡ Predicting It is important for students to be able to predict where the story is headed.	**Mini-Lesson** Before students read "Lob's Girl," you may want to teach or review the **Predicting** lesson on pages 137–139 of this Guide. • Read aloud lines 114–122 on page 151. Then ask students to predict what may happen because of Lob's unusually strong liking for the Pengellys. Students may answer that Lob may want to live with the Pengellys, or that Lob's owner may become angry with the family. • After reading, students can complete the **Literary Analysis SkillBuilder** on page 166.
Mysterious Ending The story's eerie ending suggests that Lob, who is dead, visits Sandy in the hospital. To make sense of this story, students must grasp the implications of the final scene.	After students finish reading, ask them who they think the dog in the final scene was and why they think so. Have students mention other times in the story when Lob did the seemingly impossible to come back to Sandy. Ask: *Why do you think the author leaves readers with this question?*

Suggested Reading Options

• An oral reading of "Lob's Girl" is available in *The Language of Literature* Audio Library. ⌒
• Independent Reading (See page 8 of this Guide.)
• Additional options are described on page 8 of this Guide.

RECIPROCAL TEACHING SUGGESTION ➡ Connecting

Teacher Modeling *Pause & Reflect, Page 155* Help students identify with Sandy by modeling how they might connect her experience with their own.

You could say *After reading lines 190–199, I remember experiences in my own life that help me understand how unhappy Sandy felt at Lob's departure. I remember how sad I have been when I have had to leave friends and family. The author says that Sandy felt "as if she were bruised all over" and that even a trip to the circus could not cure her "sore heart." Even though Lob doesn't belong to Sandy, she's clearly very attached to him, and so feels miserable.*

Student Modeling *Pause & Reflect, page 155* Have several students model the connecting strategy to understand why the children are "breathless" during Mr. Pengelly's phone conversation (line 220). Offer this prompt: *Have you ever had to wait while an adult decided whether to give you something you wanted very much? How did it feel to wait and wonder?*

Encourage students to use the other five reading strategies when appropriate as they proceed through the rest of the story. (See page 10 of this Guide.)

ENGLISH LEARNERS

1. Help students understand unfamiliar British expressions and other idiomatic words and phrases:

   keeping an eye on, page 148, line 19

   took no notice, page 151, line 118

   in a flash, page 157, line 301

   umpty, page 158, line 348

   he was getting on, page 164, lines 521–522

2. Students might benefit from reading along with the recording of "Lob's Girl" provided in *The Language of Literature* Audio Library. ⌒

After Reading

Recommended Follow-Up

- Thinking Through the Literature, page 459, *The Language of Literature*
- Choices & Challenges, pages 460–461, *The Language of Literature*
- SkillBuilders, pages 165–167, *The InterActive Reader™*

Informal Assessment Options

Retell Ask students to imagine that Sandy recovers from the accident, and that a newspaper reporter interviews her and her family about the strange events at the hospital. Have students retell the story in small groups, with one student in each group playing the role of reporter and other students playing the Pengellys and Granny Pearce.

Spot Check Look at the notes students made in the margins of page 164 in answer to the questions "What happened to Lob?" and "How did you feel about the ending of the story?" Discuss their answers and any questions they still have.

Formal Assessment Options in *The Language of Literature*

Selection Quiz, page 10, Unit Four Resource Book

Selection Test, pages 79–80, Formal Assessment Book

For more teaching options, see pages 447–461 in *The Language of Literature* Teacher's Edition.

Additional Challenge

1. **Lob's Story**
   Ask: *If Lob could talk, how would he tell the story?* Have students write or tell the story from Lob's point of view.

2. **||| MARK IT UP ⟩⟩ Who Belongs to Whom?**
   Point out that the story is titled "Lob's Girl," not "Sandy's Dog." Discuss why Joan Aiken may have chosen the title she did. Students may remark that it is a more interesting and unusual title than "Sandy's Dog." Ask: *What do you think the title expresses about Lob?* Have students mark passages in the story that support their points of view. Students may mention Lob's unshakable devotion. They may underline passages such as the first two sentences of the story.

Before Reading

Direct students' attention to the Connect to Your Life and Key to the Drama activities on page 168 of *The InterActive Reader.*™ Use the following suggestions to prepare students to read the drama.

Connect to Your Life
Ask students to name adventure stories or movies that involve a quest, a journey to reach a particular goal. To get students started, you might identify such adventure movies as *Star Wars* and *Raiders of the Lost Ark*. Discuss how the main characters in these stories change and grow as a result of their journeys. After the discussion, have students fill out the chart.

Key to the Drama
Review homophones with students. Explain what homophones are and provide some examples, such as *here* and *hear, which* and *witch,* and *night* and *knight.* Then ask students to identify pairs of homophones. Tell them that by playing with the sound and meaning of such word pairs, the author creates humorous characters and situations. Finally, have students complete the activity.

BUILD BACKGROUND
Connect to Drama Tell students that they are about to read an excerpt from a dramatization of the novel *The Phantom Tollbooth.* Point out that this play, like any other drama, contains stage directions—instructions to the performers, director, and stage crew. Explain that stage directions are usually italicized and placed within parentheses. If a play is read instead of viewed, the reader must examine the stage directions for important clues to action and character. You might also discuss the following terms: *acts, scenes, cast, sets, props, costumes,* and *lighting.*

WORDS TO KNOW

acknowledge

dejectedly

destination

fanfare

ignorance

leisurely

Additional Words to Know

unethical
   page 178, line 204

banished
   page 184, line 378

steadfast
   page 197, line 774

VOCABULARY PREVIEW: Words to Know in Context

You can help students learn the Words to Know by reading aloud the following sentences or writing them on the board. Then show students how to use context clues to help them figure out the meaning.

acknowledge: She pays attention to Carla, but she doesn't even *acknowledge* anyone else.

dejectedly: Sad after losing the big game, the pitcher walked slowly and *dejectedly* home.

destination: The group has been traveling for two days and should reach its final *destination* tomorrow.

fanfare: A blast of trumpets announced the knight's arrival, and the *fanfare* continued as he marched toward the throne.

ignorance: She tried to hide her *ignorance,* but it was clear that she lacked education.

leisurely: We had extra time and took a slow, *leisurely* stroll through the park.

---

unethical: *Unethical* practices, such as copying homework, are not allowed at our school.

banished: When the prince was *banished,* he was forced to leave the kingdom and was not allowed to return.

steadfast: A *steadfast* friend is loyal and dependable.

VOCABULARY FOCUS: Understanding Idioms

Teacher Modeling Remind students that they can often use the context of an unfamiliar idiom to figure out its meaning. Then use the following modeling suggestions for the idiom *killing time* (page 181, line 271).

You could say *I'm not sure what* killing time *means, but Milo uses the expression to explain what he is doing in the Doldrums. He also answers "Nothing much" when asked what he's doing. The Watchdog thinks that* killing time *is worse than wasting time, so I think the idiom must mean "making time pass in doing unimportant things."*

Student Modeling Now have students follow your lead. Ask a volunteer to model using context clues to figure out the meaning of *see eye to eye* (page 182, line 320).

A student might say *I'm not familiar with the expression* see eye to eye, *but I don't think it has to do with looking into someone's eyes. According to Tock, King Azaz and the Mathemagician argue all the time and never agree on anything. Since they never* see eye to eye, *the idiom must mean "being in complete agreement."*

Mini-Lesson
See pages 102–103 of this Guide for additional work on **Understanding Idioms.**

During Reading

COMPREHENSION FOCUS

Key Points	Strategies for Success
Target Skill ➡ Narrative Elements In order to understand the play, students must keep track of changes in the setting as well as the comings and goings of numerous characters.	**Mini-Lesson** Before students read *The Phantom Tollbooth,* you may want to teach or review the **Narrative Elements** lesson on pages 143–146 of this Guide. • Read aloud lines 377–396 on pages 184–185. Ask students to identify the narrative elements revealed in the passage. Ask: *Which characters speak or are mentioned in the passage? What setting do Tock and Milo find themselves in? What problem has been introduced? How do you think the problem will affect Milo?* • As students read the play, have them use the **Story Map** on page 144 of this Guide to keep track of the narrative elements.
Word Play Students will have problems following the play if they are unable to make sense of the word play that is central to the drama's humor.	After the *Pause & Reflect* on page 197, review with students some of the plays on words in this scene. Ask: *What did the waiters bring when Milo asked for "a light snack"? What did they bring when he asked for "a square meal"? Why is Milo's statement—"I didn't know I was going to have to eat my words"—funny?*

Suggested Reading Options

• An oral reading of the excerpt from *The Phantom Tollbooth* is available in *The Language of Literature* Audio Library. 🎧
• Partner/Cooperative Reading (See page 8 of this Guide.)
• Additional options are described on page 8 of this Guide.

RECIPROCAL TEACHING SUGGESTION ➡ Clarifying

Teacher Modeling *Pause & Reflect, page 185* If students are unsure why the scene on page 183 shifts suddenly, model using the clarifying strategy.

You could say *At first I didn't understand why the kings suddenly appear in the scene. However, when I reread lines 316–331 on pages 182–183, I realize that the writer is introducing a flashback. It shows the reader how the princesses came to be banished. The scene changes to help the reader visualize Tock's story.*

Student Modeling *Pause & Reflect, page 185* Have several students model using the clarifying strategy to figure out why Rhyme and Reason have been banished. Offer this prompt: *What decision does King Azaz expect the princesses to make? What decision does the Mathemagician expect? What do the princesses decide? What do both kings do as a result?*

Encourage students to use the other five reading strategies when appropriate as they proceed through the rest of the drama. **(See page 10 of this Guide.)**

ENGLISH LEARNERS

1. Introduce the characters in the play by reading the names aloud and explaining some of the unfamiliar terms: *Lethargarians*—from *lethargy* meaning "drowsiness"; *Tock*—from the tick, tock sound that a clock makes; *unabridged*—meaning "complete"; *humbug*—meaning "fraud."

2. Students might benefit from reading along with the recording of the excerpt from *The Phantom Tollbooth* provided in *The Language of Literature* Audio Library. ◯

After Reading

Recommended Follow-Up

- Thinking Through the Literature, pages 531 and 552, *The Language of Literature*
- Choices & Challenges, pages 553–554, *The Language of Literature*
- SkillBuilders, pages 201–203, *The InterActive Reader*™

Informal Assessment Options

Retell Have students work in small groups to give oral summaries of the drama. Offer these prompts:

- *What does Milo find in his room?*
- *Who does Milo meet on the road to Dictionopolis?*
- *What do the Lethargarians do all day?*
- *What do King Azaz and the Mathemagician disagree about?*
- *What happened as a result of their disagreement?*
- *What does King Azaz want Milo to do?*

Spot Check Look at the notes students made in the margins. Ask students who used the **?** notation if they were able to clear up their confusion, and if so, how.

Formal Assessment Options in *The Language of Literature*

Selection Test, page 89, Formal Assessment Book

For more teaching options, see pages 512–531 in *The Language of Literature* Teacher's Edition.

Additional Challenge

1. Examine Characters
Tell students that some of the characters in *The Phantom Tollbooth* represent different kinds of people or personalities. Discuss what kinds of people the Lethargarians, the Whether Man, and the Humbug represent. Then have students write a brief paragraph explaining what Tock represents. To get students started, ask: *Why does Tock have the body of a clock? What kind of personality does Tock have?*

2. ⫼ MARK IT UP ⟩ Appreciate Humor
Have students underline and read aloud lines from the play that they find humorous. Then ask: *What did the writer do to create humor in these lines?* Help students realize that writers can create humor through such devices as exaggeration and clever word play.

Before Reading

Direct students' attention to the Connect to Your Life and Key to the Story activities on page 204 of *The InterActive Reader.*™ Use the following suggestions to prepare students to read the story.

Connect to Your Life
Share with students one or two advances in technology that have made your life different from that of your grandparents. Then ask: *What technology do you use that did not exist when your grandparents were young? How does this technology affect your daily life?* After students fill out the web, have them share their examples.

Key to the Story
Ask students how they think schools might be different a hundred years from now. Then have them read the passage from the story on page 204. Explain that the "mechanical teacher" is a computer and that the schoolroom is in Margie's own home. Discuss with students whether they think such a school would be more or less fun than their own school. Finally, have them write their responses on the lines.

BUILD BACKGROUND
Connect to Technology Tell students that Isaac Asimov wrote "The Fun They Had" in 1951. Point out that back then, computers were huge machines that had to be kept in refrigerated buildings. They were not user-friendly, and only a computer expert could operate them. Specialists stored information in computers by punching patterns of holes into cards or tape. Tell students that it was only after the invention of the silicon chip in the 1960s that computers became smaller, easier to use, and less expensive. The first personal computers became available for home use in 1977.

WORDS TO KNOW

dispute

loftily

nonchalantly

scornful

sector

Additional Words to Know

crinkly
   page 206, line 12

sorrowfully
   page 207, line 36

adjusted
   page 209, line 96

insert
   page 209, line 120

VOCABULARY PREVIEW: Words to Know in Context

You can help students learn the Words to Know by reading aloud the following sentences or writing them on the board. Then show students how to use context clues to help them figure out the meaning.

dispute: I didn't want to *dispute* you because I get very upset when I argue.

loftily: We thought he would treat us *loftily,* or in a grand and proud manner, but he was really very modest.

nonchalantly: She looked at her report card *nonchalantly,* as if she didn't care what grades she got.

scornful: Because my sister thought the math problem was very simple, she was *scornful* of those who didn't understand it.

sector: People in this part of town support the candidate, while people in that *sector* do not.

---

crinkly: The shirt, which had been stuffed in a drawer, was *crinkly* and needed to be ironed.

sorrowfully: Saddened by the news, we walked *sorrowfully* home.

adjusted: Joe *adjusted* the computer screen until it was level with his eyes.

insert: First, *insert* your money in the machine's slot and then punch in the number of the snack you want.

VOCABULARY FOCUS: Using Context Clues

Teacher Modeling Remind students that they can often use context clues—the surrounding words in a sentence or passage—to figure out the meaning of an unfamiliar word. Then use the following modeling suggestions for the word *slot* (page 207, line 45).

You could say *I don't know what* slot *means, but I can look for context clues in the sentence this word is in. The phrase "where she had to put homework and test papers" tells me that* slot *must mean "a long, narrow opening."*

Student Modeling Now have students follow your lead. Ask a volunteer to model using context clues to determine the meaning of *geared* (page 207, line 53).

A student might say *I'm not familiar with the word* geared. *In this passage, however, the phrases "a little too quick" and "I've slowed it up" help me figure out that* geared *must mean "set" or "adjusted."*

Mini-Lesson
See pages 92–95 of this Guide for additional work on **Using Context Clues.**

During Reading

COMPREHENSION FOCUS

Key Points	Strategies for Success

Target Skill ➡ Making Inferences

The writer does not explain everything about the characters and setting in this story. It is essential that students make inferences in order to understand what school is like for Margie and Tommy.

Mini-Lesson Before students read "The Fun They Had," you may want to teach or review the **Making Inferences** lesson on pages 134–136 of this Guide.

• Read aloud lines 11–16 on page 206. Ask students what they can infer about the books that Margie and Tommy read. Ask: *What clues from the story helped you make your inference?*

• Have students complete the **Active Reading SkillBuilder** on page 211, which will help them make inferences about the story's characters, plot, setting, and theme.

Flashback

It is very important that students identify the flashback in the story and understand what it reveals about schools and teachers in the year 2157.

After the *Pause & Reflect* on page 207, have students identify the flashback (pages 206–207, lines 32–61). Ask: *What clues tell you what school is like for the children in the story?*

Suggested Reading Options

• An oral reading of "The Fun They Had" is available in *The Language of Literature* Audio Library. ◯
• Partner/Cooperative Reading (See page 8 of this Guide.)
• Additional options are described on page 8 of this Guide.

RECIPROCAL TEACHING SUGGESTION ➡ Questioning

Teacher Modeling *Pause & Reflect, page 210* If students have trouble understanding why Margie doesn't see how a man could be a teacher, model using the following strategy.

You could say *When I read lines 79–85 on page 208, I ask myself why Margie doesn't think a man is smart enough to be a teacher. Then I remember that a computer is her teacher. Even though people must program and fix the computers, Margie is used to thnking of her mechanical teacher as all-knowing.*

Student Modeling *Pause & Reflect, page 210* Have several students model using the questioning strategy to figure out why Margie thinks that schools in the past were more fun than her school. Offer this prompt: *How does she picture schools in the past? What does she imagine the students doing?*

Encourage students to use the other five reading strategies when appropriate as they proceed through the rest of the story. (See page 10 of this Guide.)

ENGLISH LEARNERS

1. Tell students that *betcha* (page 208, line 86) is a slang term that stands for "bet you," which means "I'm so sure of what I said that I will give you something if I'm wrong." Point out that the term is not usually taken literally but used to emphasize how sure one is about something.

2. Students might benefit from reading along with the recording of "The Fun They Had" provided in *The Language of Literature* Audio Library. ○

After Reading

Recommended Follow-Up

- Thinking Through the Literature, page 579, *The Language of Literature*
- Choices & Challenges, page 586, *The Language of Literature*
- SkillBuilders, pages 211–213, *The InterActive Reader™*

Informal Assessment Options

Retell Have students summarize the differences between today's schools and those in the story. Offer these prompts:

- *What are teachers like in the story?*
- *Where are the schools located?*
- *How do students learn?*

Spot Check Look at the notes students made in the margins of the story. Invite them to explain their answers and discuss any questions they still have about the story.

Formal Assessment Options in *The Language of Literature*

Selection Quiz, page 55, Unit Four Resource Book

Selection Test, pages 95–96, Formal Assessment Book

For more teaching options, see pages 574–579 and 586 in *The Language of Literature* Teacher's Edition.

Additional Challenge

1. Write a Response
Point out that at the end of the story, Margie imagines school in the old days and considers "how the kids must have loved it." Have students write a brief paragraph in which they respond to Margie's opinion. To help students get started, ask: *How do you feel about school? Do you think most kids love school? How do you think Margie would feel if she were transported to your school?*

2. ▐▐▐ MARK IT UP ⟩ Express an Opinion
Have students explore the contrast between having a human teacher and being taught by a machine. Which kind of teacher would they prefer? Ask: *What are the advantages of having a human teacher? What are the disadvantages? What might you enjoy about having a machine for a teacher?* Have students underline passages in the story that support their views and use these details to develop their opinions.

Before Reading

Direct students' attention to the Connect to Your Life and Key to the Story activities on page 214 of *The InterActive Reader.*™ Use the following suggestions to prepare students to read the story.

Connect to Your Life
Explain to students that when people lose an important sense, such as sight, they come to rely more heavily on their other senses. Ask: *If you lost your sight, what other senses would you rely on the most? Name some situations in which you would use these other senses.* Then have students complete the Connect to Your Life activity.

Key to the Story
If students have never heard of Pompeii, you may want to share with them some of the Build Background information below. This might help them think of what they want to know about Pompeii. Also, remind students that a K-W-L chart is most effective if they return to it after their reading to fill out the third column.

BUILD BACKGROUND Connect to History Explain to students that in A.D. 79, Mount Vesuvius erupted in what is now southern Italy. Burning lava and ash completely buried the nearby city of Pompeii, killing nearly 2,000 of its estimated 20,000 residents. Many died in their homes, but others died trying to escape by boat. Pompeii remained buried for centuries. Then a farm worker struck a wall of the city in 1748. The excavations that followed uncovered the remains of the city, which were remarkably well preserved by the ashes. These remains present a clear picture of what life was like in the ancient Roman Empire. We now know how people dressed, how children were taught, and even how foods were prepared.

WORDS TO KNOW

dislodging

eruption

restore

shrine

vapor

Additional Words to Know

sham
  page 216, line 13

rival
  page 219, line 127

drowsy
  page 224, line 258

VOCABULARY PREVIEW: Words to Know in Context

You can help students learn the Words to Know by reading aloud the following sentences or writing them on the board. Then show students how to use context clues to help them figure out the meaning.

dislodging: Someone keeps *dislodging* the rock, so I keep putting it back into place.

eruption: The *eruption* of Mount St. Helens caused much damage because the volcano belched hot lava and thick ash for miles around.

restore: The artists plan to *restore* the painting, bringing back its original colors and shapes.

shrine: At the *shrine* by the side of the road, the pilgrims lit a candle and said a prayer before the small statue of the saint.

vapor: As the room filled with *vapor* from the leaking gas stove, the man began to cough loudly.

---

sham: We were not fooled by her *sham* boldness because we knew that she was really very afraid.

rival: Our football team isn't good enough to *rival*, or compete with, your school's team.

drowsy: The warm, dim room and the soft music made him feel so *drowsy* that he fell asleep.

VOCABULARY FOCUS Word Parts: Using Roots

Teacher Modeling Remind students that they can sometimes use familiar roots to figure out the meaning of a word. Model using this strategy for the word *merchants* (page 219, line 122).

You could say *I'm not sure what the word* merchant *means. I know the word* merchandise *means "things to buy or sell." The two words appear to have the same root, so they may have similar meanings.* Merchants *is used in the sentence as a noun. It probably means "people who buy and sell things."*

Student Modeling Ask a volunteer to model using roots to figure out the meaning of *naval* (page 223, line 239).

A student might say *I see the term* naval *and wonder what it means. I notice that* naval *looks similar to* navy, *which means "a nation's warships." I recognize* -al *as an adjective ending.* Naval *must mean "having to do with warships."*

Mini-Lesson See pages 100–101 of this Guide for additional work on **Word Parts: Using Roots.**

During Reading

COMPREHENSION FOCUS

Key Points	Strategies for Success

Target Skill ➡ Predicting

The author uses foreshadowing to build suspense and give hints about what will happen in the story. It is important for students to recognize these clues and use them to make predictions.

Mini-Lesson Before students read "The Dog of Pompeii," you may want to teach the **Predicting** lesson on pages 137–139 of this Guide.

- After the *Pause & Reflect* on page 222, complete the Read Aloud activity as a group. Ask students to explain what they think the stranger's warning foreshadows, and why.

- Have students use the **Predicting Chart** on page 138 of this Guide to record additional predictions.

Story's Ending

To understand the story's ending, students must infer that the dog skeleton the excavators found in the bakery is Bimbo's, and that the dog was in the act of snatching bread for Tito.

After students have read the story, read aloud the boxed text on page 230 and call on several students to respond to the director's question.

Suggested Reading Options

- An oral reading of "The Dog of Pompeii" is available in *The Language of Literature* Audio Library. ♫
- Independent Reading (See page 8 of this Guide.)
- Additional options are described on page 8 of this Guide.

RECIPROCAL TEACHING SUGGESTION ➡ Evaluating

Teacher Modeling *Pause & Reflect, page 219* Model using the evaluating strategy to help students form opinions about how well Tito copes with his blindness.

You could say *There are many things Tito can't do because he's blind, such as play games and see the sights of Pompeii. However, his senses of smell and hearing make him aware of aspects of the city that others do not notice. I don't think his blindness keeps him from enjoying his life.*

Student Modeling *Pause & Reflect, page 222* Have volunteers model using the evaluating strategy to form opinions about the householders' argument about whether or not another earthquake will strike Pompeii. Offer this prompt: *What do you think of Rufus's attitude toward the possibility of another earthquake? What do you think of the stranger's comments? How would you compare what they know to what you know about earthquakes and volcanoes?*

Encourage students to use the other five reading strategies when appropriate as they proceed through the rest of the story. (See page 10 of this Guide.)

ENGLISH LEARNERS

1. Make sure students understand these phrases:

   crying their wares, page 221, line 162

   did not stir, page 228, line 372

   worrying his way, page 228, line 377

2. Students might benefit from reading along with the recording of the story provided in *The Language of Literature* Audio Library. ◯

After Reading

Recommended Follow-Up

- Thinking Through the Literature, page 711, *The Language of Literature*
- Choices & Challenges, pages 712–713, *The Language of Literature*
- SkillBuilders, pages 231–233, *The InterActive Reader™*

Informal Assessment Options

Retell Have students orally retell the story from Bimbo's point of view. Have them work in small groups to retell the narrative in round-robin fashion.

Spot Check Look at the notes students made in the margins. Ask students who used the **?** notation if they were able to clear up their confusion, and if so, how.

Formal Assessment Options in *The Language of Literature*

Selection Quiz, page 57, Unit Five Resource Book

Selection Test, pages 115–116, Formal Assessment Book

For more teaching options, see pages 700–713 in *The Language of Literature* Teacher's Edition.

Additional Challenge

1. **Analyze Relationship**
   Ask students to underline details in the story that show how Bimbo takes care of Tito. Then ask: *How would you describe their relationship?*

2. **MARK IT UP ⟩ "View" Tito's World**
   Have students mark story details that show what Tito hears, smells, tastes, and feels by touch, using a different visual symbol for each sense.

Before Reading

Have students do the Connect to Your Life and Key to the Informative Article activities on page 234 of *The InterActive Reader.*™ Use the following suggestions to prepare students to read the article.

Connect to Your Life
Have students share what they know about Egyptian tombs and kings. Ask them to name the kinds of things they might find in the tomb of an Egyptian king. Then have students complete the Connect to Your Life activity.

Key to the Informative Article
Have students read the paragraph and study the map. Then define the term *archaeology*—the study of ancient times and peoples. Tell students that archaeologists learn about the distant past by digging up what is left of ancient cities, buildings, and tombs.

BUILD BACKGROUND Connect to History Tell students that the ancient Egyptians believed in life after death. As a result, the wealthiest Egyptians, including kings and queens, had their bodies preserved after death through the process of mummification. They also had their tombs provided with food and other items that they planned to use in the afterlife. More than sixty tombs have been discovered in the Valley of the Kings. Some of these contained amazing treasures.

In 1922 archaeologist Howard Carter and his sponsor Lord Carnarvon discovered King Tutankhamen's tomb, which contained more than 5,000 objects. Until their discovery, little was known about Tutankhamen. Archaeologists now believe that Tutankhamen served as king from about 1347 B.C. until his death in 1339 B.C.

WORDS TO KNOW

dissuade

intact

sentinel

systematically

tedious

Additional Words to Know

vicinity
page 236, line 23

refuse
page 237, line 32

conduct
page 239, line 97

barren
page 239, line 120

prominent
page 240, line 148

VOCABULARY PREVIEW: Words to Know in Context

You can help students learn the Words to Know by reading aloud the following sentences or writing them on the board. Then show students how to use context clues to help them figure out the meaning.

dissuade: We could not *dissuade* her from taking sky-diving lessons even though we argued strongly against it.

intact: Since the letter had not been opened, the seal on the envelope remained *intact*.

sentinel: The *sentinel* guarded the camp all night while the other soldiers slept.

systematically: Beginning at the farthest corner and working their way toward the door, the police *systematically* searched the room for evidence.

tedious: The students were hired to file, make photocopies, and do other *tedious* tasks.

---

vicinity: She lives in the *vicinity* of the theater and can walk to it in five minutes.

refuse: Toss the banana peels, apple peels, and other bits of *refuse* in the garbage can.

conduct: The guides will show you the way as they *conduct* you from the hotel to the historic battlefield.

barren: The *barren* room did not contain a single piece of furniture.

prominent: The most *prominent* object was the winner's trophy, which was much taller than the other awards.

VOCABULARY FOCUS Word Parts: Prefixes

Teacher Modeling Remind students that sometimes they can use their knowledge of prefixes to help them figure out the meaning of an unfamiliar word. Then use the following modeling suggestion for the word *extraordinary* (page 238, line 64).

You could say I'm not sure what the word extraordinary *means, but I recognize both the prefix* extra- *and the base word* ordinary. *I know that* extra- *can mean "beyond." Since this paragraph describes an exciting discovery,* extraordinary *must mean "beyond what is usual or ordinary." That makes sense in the sentence.*

Student Modeling Have a volunteer model how to use knowledge of the prefix *re-* to figure out the meaning of *resealed* (page 241, line 181).

A student might say I recognize the prefix re- in resealed. *I know that* re- *can mean "again." Since this sentence tells how the robbers had made a small hole and filled it again,* resealed *must mean "sealed or closed again." This definition makes sense here.*

Mini-Lesson
See pages 96 and 97 of this Guide for additional work on **Word Parts: Prefixes.**

During Reading

COMPREHENSION FOCUS

Key Points	Strategies for Success
Target Skill ➡ Main Ideas and Details This nonfiction article contains a great number of factual details. To understand and retain information, students must be able to identify the main idea and key details of each paragraph.	**Mini-Lesson** Before students read "Tutankhamen," you may want to teach or review the **Main Idea and Details** lesson on page 119 of this Guide. • Read aloud the first paragraph of the article on page 236. Then ask students to go back and circle details that support this main idea: *Lord Carnarvon and Howard Carter believed that King Tutankhamen's tomb had yet to be discovered.* Encourage students to write other main ideas in the margin as they read on. • At the *Pause & Reflect* on page 237, ask students to complete the **Active Reading SkillBuilder** on page 243 and then work in pairs to discuss the main ideas they listed.
Sequence It is important for students to understand the sequence of events as they unfold in this article.	• Review with students their responses to the *Pause & Reflect* questions on page 239. • You may wish to have students use the **Sequence/Flow Chart** on page 124 of this Guide.

Suggested Reading Options

• An oral reading of "Tutankhamen" is available in *The Language of Literature* Audio Library. 🎧
• Independent Reading (See page 8 of this Guide.)
• Additional options are described on page 8 of this Guide.

RECIPROCAL TEACHING SUGGESTION ➡ Predicting

Teacher Modeling *Pause & Reflect, page 237* Model predicting whether Lord Carnarvon and Carter will find King Tutankhamen's tomb.

You could say Both Carter and Lord Carnarvon are determined to find the tomb. They know that it would not have been fitting for King Tutankhamen and his queen to be buried in a small pit-tomb. I have a feeling they think the pit-tomb was a device to lure robbers away from the real tomb. Carter and Carnarvon seem to know what they are doing. I predict they will have success by digging near the huts. I'll read on to find out if I'm correct.

Student Modeling *Pause & Reflect, page 241* Have volunteers predict what Carter and Carnarvon will do after discovering a doorway in the anteroom. Offer these prompts: *What do you think the men will do next? Will they examine the treasures in the anteroom or open the sealed doorway at once?*

Encourage students to use the other five reading strategies when appropriate as they proceed through the rest of the article. (See page 10 of this Guide.)

ENGLISH LEARNERS

1. Students can work with English-fluent partners to summarize the events described in each section of the article.
2. Students might benefit from reading along with the recording of "Tutankhamen" from *Lost Worlds* provided in *The Language of Literature* Audio Library. ◯

After Reading

Recommended Follow-Up

- Thinking Through the Literature, page 725, *The Language of Literature*
- Choices & Challenges, pages 726–727, *The Language of Literature*
- SkillBuilders, pages 243–245, *The InterActive Reader™*

Informal Assessment Options

Retell Have students work in groups of four to prepare an oral summary of the article. Each group member should select a different *Pause & Reflect* section to summarize. Students should present their summaries in proper sequence.

Spot Check Review the notes students made in the margins. Invite them to explain their answers and discuss any questions they still have about the article.

Formal Assessment Options in *The Language of Literature*

Selection Quiz, page 64, Unit Five Resource Book

Selection Test, pages 117–118, Formal Assessment Book

For more teaching options, see pages 718–727 in *The Language of Literature* Teacher's Edition.

Additional Challenge

1. Analyze the Article

Have students use Howard Carter's experiences in the Valley of the Kings to create a list of Five Tips for a Successful Archaeological Expedition. Tell students that some tips are directly stated in the article while others may require students to make an inference based on the text. Students' responses can include the following: *have self-control, be patient, have determination,* and so forth.

2. ⦚ MARK IT UP ⟩ **Identify Character Traits**

Write the words below on the board. Then ask: *Which words best describe Howard Carter?* Have students circle details in the article that reveal each trait.

determined
jealous
stubborn
enthusiastic
confident
patient
bossy
considerate

Before Reading

Direct students' attention to the Connect to Your Life and Key to the Poem activities on page 246 of *The InterActive Reader.*™ Use the following suggestions to prepare students to read the poem.

Connect to Your Life Have students share their ideas about what bravery is. Ask: *What does it mean to be brave? Who are some brave people you know or have heard about? What did they do that shows courage?* Then have students fill in the concept web and provide their own definitions and examples of bravery in the space provided.

Key to the Poem Read aloud the explanation on page 246. Then ask a volunteer to read the couplet aloud as you clap the rhythm. Ask students to paraphrase the couplet. Point out that although the end of a line indicates a pause in reading, it does not necessarily signal the end of a thought or idea.

BUILD BACKGROUND Connect to History Explain that John Greenleaf Whittier was born in Massachusetts in 1807 and began writing poetry at the age of 14. Much of the inspiration for his writing came from his belief that slavery was wrong and should be abolished. In "Barbara Frietchie," the poet recounts events that, according to legend, occurred in 1862 during the Civil War.

Strategies for Reading Poetry:

- Notice the form of the poem: the number of lines and their shape on the page.
- Read the poem aloud a few times. Listen for rhymes and rhythms.
- Visualize the images and comparisons.
- Consider the poet's choice of words.
- Ask yourself what message the poet is trying to send.
- Think about what the poem is saying to you.

FOCUS ON POETRY

Before having students read "Barbara Frietchie," you may want to have them read the feature "Poetry" on pages 189–193 of *The Language of Literature.* That lesson shows how key elements work together in a poem to produce emotion and meaning. It also suggests some strategies students can use when reading poetry; these are summarized in the column at the left. The activities below will help prepare students for reading "Barbara Frietchie."

- **Rhythm** As you read aloud the two lines from "Barbara Frietchie" on page 246, have students clap out the rhythm again while you read aloud the words and stress the beat. Point out that the steady rhythm reinforces the image of marching soldiers and that it makes sense for a narrative poem that takes place during wartime to be set to a marching beat.

- **Imagery** Read aloud the poem's first four lines and ask students to identify sensory details that help them imagine this place. Students may mention the words "rich with corn," "clear," "cool," and "green-walled." Point out that writers use words and phrases that appeal to readers' senses to help them visualize a scene or to establish a mood. Encourage students to note additional sensory details as they read on.

VOCABULARY FOCUS: Using Words with Multiple Meanings

Teacher Modeling Remind students that some words have more than one meaning and that they can use context clues to help them figure out which meaning is intended in a particular line or passage. Model using the word *sweep* (page 248, line 5).

You could say I know that the word sweep *has several meanings, including "to clean or clear with a broom or brush" and "to extend gracefully." This line describes what the orchards do around the hills near Frederick, Maryland, so here* sweep *must mean "to extend gracefully."*

Student Modeling Ask a volunteer to use context clues to figure out the correct meaning of the word *fall* (page 248, line 9).

A student might say Fall *can mean "a sudden drop" or "autumn," among other things. The poet describes the setting of the poem as a "September morn" and a "morn of the early fall." Since September is an autumn month,* fall *must mean "autumn" here.*

Mini-Lesson
See pages 104–105 of this Guide for additional work on **Using Words with Multiple Meanings.**

During Reading

COMPREHENSION FOCUS

Key Points	Strategies for Success
Target Skill ➡ Sequence The presence of rhyming couplets and poetic language may distract students' attention from the sequence of events being described in this narrative poem.	**Mini-Lesson** Before students read "Barbara Frietchie," you may want to teach or review the **Sequence** lesson on pages 123–125 of this Guide. • Read aloud lines 17–32 on page 250. Then ask students to paraphrase the events described in these lines. • During or after reading, have students fill in the **Sequence Flow Chart** on page 124 of this Guide.
The Writer's Style Students may find it difficult to work their way through the long sentences and figure out the unusual word order.	• Read aloud lines 1–4 and help students paraphrase this sentence. Point out that *spires* is the subject and *stand* is the verb. • Suggest to students that when they come across a passage that they find confusing, they should reread it several times. Also point out that paying careful attention to the punctuation will help them figure out where a sentence begins and ends. Model how to use the Guide for Reading for help in understanding difficult passages.

Suggested Reading Options

• An oral reading of "Barbara Frietchie" is available in *The Language of Literature* Audio Library. ◯
• Oral Reading (See page 8 of this Guide.)
• Additional options are described on page 8 of this Guide.

RECIPROCAL TEACHING SUGGESTION ➡ Predicting

Teacher Modeling *Pause & Reflect, page 248* Model using the predicting strategy to help students guess how events in this poem will unfold.

You could say *Since the poet describes the disappearance of all the Union flags in sight, I think Barbara Frietchie's actions will have something to do with one of these flags. Maybe she will stand up to the Confederate army in some way.*

Student Modeling *Pause & Reflect, page 252* Have a volunteer model using the predicting strategy to tell what might happen to the flag Barbara Frietchie displays. Offer this prompt: *All day long Barbara Frietchie's Union flag flies over the passing Confederate army. Do you think any of the Confederate soldiers will disobey Stonewall Jackson's order to leave Frietchie alone?*

Encourage students to use the other five reading strategies when appropriate as they finish reading the rest of the poem. (See page 10 of this Guide.)

ENGLISH LEARNERS

1. Make sure students understand these terms:

   rich with corn, page 248, line 1

   silver stars/crimson bars, page 248, lines 13–14

   stood fast, page 250, line 27

   a royal will, page 252, line 34

   A shade of sadness, a blush of shame, page 252, line 37

   nobler nature within him stirred, page 252, line 39

2. Students might benefit from reading along with the recording of the poem provided in *The Language of Literature* Audio Library. ◌

After Reading

Recommended Follow-Up

- Thinking Through the Literature, page 740, *The Language of Literature*
- Choices & Challenges, pages 741, *The Language of Literature*
- SkillBuilders, pages 256–257, *The InterActive Reader*™

Informal Assessment Options

Retell Have students retell the events in this poem as a story from the point of view of one of the following people: Barbara Frietchie, one of her neighbors, Stonewall Jackson, or a Confederate soldier.

Spot Check Look at the notes students made in the margins. Make sure their answers show an understanding of what they read. Ask volunteers to share the three adjectives they wrote on page 255 to describe Frietchie.

Formal Assessment Options in *The Language of Literature*

Selection Test, pages 121–122, Formal Assessment Book

For more teaching options, see pages 737–741 in *The Language of Literature* Teacher's Edition.

Additional Challenge

1. **Write a News Article**
   Have students write a paragraph that might have appeared in a Civil War–era newspaper about the events described in the poem. Remind students to report the *who, what, where, when, why,* and *how* of the events. Encourage them to "quote" Frietchie, Jackson, soldiers, or townspeople by writing comments that these people might have said. You may wish to have some newspapers on hand for students to use as writing models.

2. **MARK IT UP** **Identify Contrasts**
   Ask: *How would you describe the important contrasts in this poem?* Have students mark details in the poem to support their ideas.

End Unit Lesson Plans

Reading a Magazine Article

Introducing the Concept

Most students have read magazine articles. However, they may find that sorting out the blend of headings, text, and visuals can be difficult. Tell students that using these strategies will help.

Teaching Tips for the Magazine Article

A **Title and headings:** Note that the title of this article is "What a Kick!" Point out to students that the title is a play on the word *kick* (soccer players kick the ball, but "a kick" is also used to describe something that's fun or enjoyable).

B **Visuals and captions:** Suggest that students preview the visuals in a magazine article to get an idea of the topic before they begin reading. Previewing the visuals on this magazine article should tell students that the article's topic is soccer.

C **Bulleted list:** Point out that the bulleted items in this article are clues to the topic. A bulleted list can also summarize important points or detail a process.

D **Terms in different typeface:** Remind students that boldface type is heavier than regular type and italic type is slightly slanted.

E **Special features:** Tell students that the special feature in this article is a chart that explains why readers should play soccer. Point out that a magazine article's special feature is always tied to the topic but often provides information on a related subtopic.

Additional Questions

1. According to one of the captions, when did team U.S.A. win the Women's World Cup title? (July 10, 1999)
2. What is the world's most popular team sport? (soccer)
3. How many reasons to play soccer does the chart provide? (five)

Additional Tips for Reading a Magazine Article

- **Reading items in any order:** Tell students that they don't have to read the items in a magazine article in any particular order. After previewing the article, readers can read the features or the captions first—whatever catches their interest.

- **Ignore advertising:** Students may be distracted by the glossy ads that appear in some articles. Encourage students to mentally screen out these ads.

- **Understand slang terms:** Point out that magazines aimed at teenagers often use informal language and popular slang. Students whose first language isn't English may have trouble understanding such slang as *'rents* (meaning "parents") and *crush* (meaning "a boyfriend or girlfriend"). You might suggest that students jot down any words and terms they don't understand and ask a friend to translate.

Reading a Textbook

Introducing the Concept

Many students have trouble reading textbooks. The titles, headings, and features on a textbook page can confuse students and hinder learning. Tell students that these skills and strategies will help them learn to read textbooks.

Teaching Tips for the Textbook Page

A **Graphics:** Point out that the time line on this page shows years in the period *Before Christ,* or B.C. The years appear in descending order. In a time line showing years in the period *Anno Domini* ("Year of Our Lord"), or A.D., the years would appear in ascending order. You might tell students that they may also encounter the time abbreviation B.C.E., or *Before the Common Era.* This is another term for the period "Before Christ": Years in this period also appear in descending order on a time line.

B **Title and headings:** Have students note that the title of the lesson is "Athens: A City-State." Based on this title, students may predict that the lesson will be on the government of ancient Athens.

C **Main idea or objectives:** Make sure students understand that the question under "Thinking Focus" introduces the lesson's main idea. As students read the lesson, they should keep the question in mind and try to answer it.

D **Vocabulary words:** Encourage students to highlight or note definitions as they read.

E **Visuals and captions:** Tell students that the visuals on this page provide a glimpse of the government of ancient Athens in action. Point out that the pictures of the tokens are directly tied to information found in the primary source paragraph.

F **Words in special type:** You might demonstrate how to use the respelling to pronounce *Xenophon.* Tell students that the capitals in the first syllable indicate that this syllable is stressed. The lowercase letters in the other two syllables indicate that these syllables are not stressed.

G **Set-off text:** Tell students that the text set off on this page is a primary source. Explain that a primary source gives firsthand, or eyewitness, information. The two lines following the paragraph indicate the author and name of the piece and the approximate date it was written.

Additional Questions

1. What did the ancient Greeks use to cast their votes? **(tokens)**

2. Who is the author of the primary source paragraph? **(Xenophon)**

Additional Tips for Reading a Textbook

- **Take notes before reading:** Before students begin reading, have them write down or discuss all they know about the topic.

- **Use the PACER method:** When students read a lesson in a textbook, encourage them to follow the PACER method: **p**review the entire lesson, use section subheadings to **a**nalyze the purpose of a passage, **c**arefully read the text, **e**valuate the material, and, finally, **r**eview their notes.

- **Use a graphic organizer:** As students read, suggest that they use a graphic organizer to help make sense of the material. For example, they might create a spider map to keep track of a lesson's main ideas and supporting details.

Reading a Chart

Introducing the Concept

Charts are among the most familiar ways to present information visually. You might explain to students that although charts may seem simple to read, there are some strategies for reading a chart accurately.

Teaching Tips for the Chart

A **Title:** Make sure that students know what "nutritional value" means. In this chart, the insects are compared according to how much nourishment each has when used as food.

B **Headings:** Show students that, in this chart, the insects are the row headings. The nutrients are the column headings. To find the insect with the most iron, for example, read the iron column from top to bottom. To find the protein in a cricket, read the cricket row from left to right. To find out the iron content of a cricket, look for the place where the iron column and the cricket column intersect (9.5).

C **Symbols or abbreviations:** In this chart, *NA* means "not available." *(g)* means "gram," and *(mg)* means "milligram."

D **Credit:** Although students will encounter many charts without credit information, they should always look for a credit. It is one way to tell if the information they are reading is reliable.

Additional Questions

1. Which food has the greatest amount of protein? **(lean ground beef)**

2. How much calcium is in lean ground beef? **(information is not available)**

3. Which insect has the greatest amount of calcium? **(cricket)**

4. Where is the book *Bugs in the System* mentioned? **(in the credit)**

Other Types of Charts and Graphs

In their reading, students will encounter several types of charts and graphs, such as the four shown below. When reading a pie chart, students must simply remember to read the labels. When they encounter a bar or line graph, remind them to read the labels on the horizontal and vertical axes before trying to understand the graph's content. In a flow chart, remind them to follow the arrows.

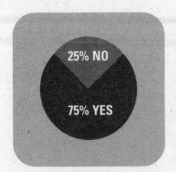

Pie Chart shows percentages

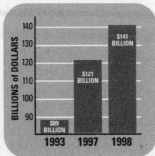

Bar Graph compares numbers

Line Graph shows change over time

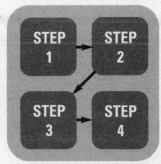

Flow Chart explains the steps of a process

Reading a Map

Introducing the Concept

There are as many different types of maps showing a variety of features as there are charts and graphs representing information. You might want to show students examples of different types of maps (see list below).

Teaching Tips for the Map

A **Title:** Map titles carry the most important information in the map. Many titles have dates reflecting a time period; others have names of specific regions or areas; and some have names of battles or economic activity.

B **Key or legend:** Tell students that keys or legends can include arrows, symbols, colors, letters, numbers, and lines that represent an item or activity on the map.

In addition to the key, this map provides an inset map of the United States that indicates where Umpqua National Forest is located. Remind students that inset maps may show the relation of a specific geographic location to a wider area.

C **Geographic labels:** Tell students to watch for different type styles used in geographic labels. On complicated political maps, for example, recognizing the type style (italics, all caps, different sizes, boldface) will help students distinguish rivers, capital cities, state and country names, mountain ranges, etc.

D **Scale:** Note that on this map the scale measures distance in miles. Maps used in textbooks and other reference materials will often use a scale that represents distance in miles and kilometers.

E **Compass rose:** A compass rose shows which way the directions—north (N), south (S), east (E), and west (W)—point on the map. Examples include

Additional Questions

1. What is the elevation of Pyramid Rock? (4793)

2. How many road numbers are shown on this map? (six)

3. Name two creeks on the map. (Bulldog Creek and Big Bend Creek)

4. What road would you take to get to Fuller Lake? (1543)

Basic Types of Maps

- **Physical maps** show mountains, hills, plains, rivers, lakes, oceans, and other physical features of an area.

- **Political maps** show political units, such as countries, states, counties, districts, and towns. Each unit is typically shaded a different color, represented by a symbol, or shown with a different typeface.

- **Historical maps** illustrate such things as economic activity, migrations, battles, and changing national boundaries.

Reading a Diagram

Introducing the Concept

While diagrams can be an important aid in illustrating and understanding written texts, they pose their own set of challenges for readers. After the first glance, many diagrams require close study and interpretation. Explain to students that although diagrams may look easy because of the pictures, they sometimes contain complex information. These strategies should help them sort through many different kinds of diagrams.

Teaching Tips for the Diagram

A **Title:** Remind students that a diagram's title is not necessarily at the top. It might very well be at the bottom or on the side. Some diagrams don't even have titles.

B **Images:** Generally, the images will give readers the fastest idea of what a diagram is about. However, only by looking at the images together with the surrounding captions and labels can they completely understand a diagram. Suggest to students that when reading a diagram, they make a quick assessment of the diagram based on the images and the title, and then check their assessment after studying the diagram's other elements.

C **Caption and labels:** In many diagrams, the captions and labels contain critical information about the images. Remind students not to skip over this text; if they do, they might miss the point of the diagram.

D **Arrows and other markers:** Point out to students that these markers often illustrate the diagram's most important concept. For example, in the ecosystem diagram, the arrows show the movement of energy among organisms—this is the most important thing about an ecosystem.

Additional Questions

1. What would happen to the primary consumers if all the producers disappeared? (**The primary consumers would have nothing to eat.**)

2. What would happen to the primary consumers if all the secondary consumers disappeared? (**They would have no predators, and their population would increase. As they increased in number, the primary consumers would require more food. This might diminish the numbers of the producers, who are the food source for the primary consumers.**)

3. Why are bacteria and fungi important? (**In decomposing plant and animal remains, they "clean up" plant and animal waste and also provide nutrients for growing plants.**)

4. What would happen to an ecosystem if dead plants and animals did not decay? (**They would pile up, taking up extra room. Also, they would not fertilize the soil, which would reduce nutrients in the soil and make it harder for plants to grow.**)

Main Idea and Supporting Details

Introducing the Concept

Many students have trouble identifying a paragraph's main idea. Acknowledge that distinguishing a paragraph's main idea from its supporting sentences is not always easy. Tell students that there are some strategies that can help.

Teaching Tips for Main Idea and Supporting Details

• **Main idea:** A paragraph's main idea is presented in a general statement. The other sentences in the paragraph support this general statement with more specific details.

• **Summarize:** Students might try to summarize and restate a main idea as a headline or title.

• **Supporting details:** Types of supporting details include sensory details, facts, examples, reasons, and anecdotes.

Additional Questions

1. How might you restate the main idea in the second paragraph as a headline? (Communities Cut Back on Trash)

2. What types of details are used to support the paragraph's main idea? (examples)

Additional Tips

Tell students that not all main ideas are stated in the first sentence. Some main ideas appear in the middle of a paragraph; some are stated in the last sentence. Sometimes, especially in narrative or descriptive writing, a main idea is implied rather than stated. When the main idea is implied, students must figure out the major point that ties all the sentences together. In the following paragraph, for example, all of the sentences are tied together by the following implied main idea: It's a beautiful day.

> The sun sparkled on the lake. Everywhere birds sang in the leafy trees. The soft, warm grass spread across the meadow like an inviting green carpet. A cloudless, blue sky promised a long, lazy afternoon. The air smelled as fresh and clean as the laundry blowing in the gentle breeze.

Problem and Solution

Introducing the Concept

Familiarity with common text structures, such as problem and solution, can help students mentally organize what they read and improve their comprehension. Explain to students that a text describing a problem and solution can often be broken down into recognizable parts.

Teaching Tips for the Problem and Solution Text

- **Statement of problem:** Point out to students that in some cases, as on the pupil page, the problem is clearly stated at the beginning of a text and identified as a problem ("the problem is . . . "). In other cases, the statement of the problem might not be so obvious.

- **Explanation of problem:** Show students that in this text, the writer explains the effects of the problem (broken arms and legs, etc.) as well as giving the reasons for the problem (it is difficult for riders and skaters to share a path). In explaining a problem, a writer might also list examples or write persuasively about the problem's importance.

- **Proposed solution:** Note that the solution, like the statement of a problem, may be stated clearly ("the solution is . . . ") or it may be less direct.

- **Support for proposal:** This is another place where a writer will often try to write persuasively, in order to convince the audience that the proposed solution is a good one.

- **Evaluating the solution:** Urge students to develop opinions about every proposed solution they read, whether in their school work or independent reading.

Additional Example

The following paragraph contains another problem and proposed solution. Share it with students and ask them to identify its different elements and evaluate the proposed solution.

Beach Bummer

As soon as the weather gets warm, hundreds of city dwellers show up at the city's eight beaches with their blankets, volleyballs, and picnic baskets. Families, teenagers, dog owners, and even kite fliers play together peacefully and all is well until the loud buzz of the jet skis begins. Suddenly, swimmers have to watch where they're going and the people sitting on the beach have to start shouting just to hear each other. The cries of the sea gulls and the rush of the waves are completely drowned out by this horrible noise.

Jet skis are a lot of fun to ride, and they have their place, but they should not be allowed to take over every beach in the city. The city should choose one or two beaches and limit the jet skiers to those beaches only. Then the jet skiers can have their fun without ruining the beach for everyone else.

Answers

Statement of problem: "all is well until the loud buzz of the jet skis begins"

Explanation of problem: "Suddenly, swimmers have to watch . . . this horrible noise."

Proposed solution: "The city should choose one or two beaches and limit the jet skiers to those beaches only."

Support for proposal: first and last sentences of final paragraph.

Sequence

Introducing the Concept

Whenever writers give introductions, describe a process, or simply tell a story, they are using a sequential text structure. You might explain to students that recognizing this text structure will make it easier for them to follow the steps in a sequence, and it will also help them organize their thoughts when taking notes. Share these strategies with students.

Teaching Tips for Sequence

- When reading a text that they can mark up, students might find it helpful to number the steps in a sequence (1, 2, 3, etc.).

- Have students also look out for sequence clues such as dates, which are particularly helpful in reading history texts, and times of day.

- Warn students that a sequence of events is sometimes given out of order for reasons of emphasis or suspense. This possibility makes it especially important for them to keep track of sequence clues and signal words. When reading such a text, numbering the steps in their true chronological order can be especially helpful.

More Practice in Recognizing a Sequence

Reproduce the text below for your students. Have them read the text and answer the questions that follow.

> After the Revolutionary War, Andrew Jackson moved to the Tennessee frontier. In 1784, he began to study law. He built a successful legal practice and also bought and sold land. Jackson then bought a plantation near Nashville and ran for Congress. He was elected. After the War of 1812 broke out, he was appointed a general in the army. At the Battle of New Orleans in 1815, Jackson defeated the British even though his troops were greatly outnumbered. He became a national war hero. He earned the nickname "Old Hickory," after a soldier claimed that he was "tough as hickory."

1. Circle all of the words or phrases that signal sequence in this paragraph. (**After the Revolutionary War; in 1784; After the War of 1812 broke out; in 1815; after a soldier claimed . . .**)

2. Which happened first: Jackson's election to Congress or his move to Tennessee? (**His move to Tennessee**)

3. Was Jackson appointed a general in the Revolutionary War or the War of 1812? (**The War of 1812**)

4. After what event did Jackson become a national war hero? (**After he defeated the British in the Battle of New Orleans in 1815**)

Cause and Effect

Introducing the Concept

Writing organized by causes and effects shows that one event took place as a result of another event. Tell students, however, that events that follow one another do not necessarily have a cause-and-effect relationship. The events may be sequential. Students can use these strategies to determine whether events have a causal relationship.

Teaching Tips for Cause and Effect

- **Effect:** Tell students to look for effects in a piece of writing by asking a question based on the title of the piece, such as "What happens when a volcano erupts?"
- **Cause:** Tell students that they can look for causes by asking a question, such as "Why does a volcano erupt?"
- **Signal words:** Point out that not all cause-and-effect writing contains signal words. In such a case, students can use the "because test" to determine whether two events have a cause-and-effect relationship. Tell students to link the events with the word *because*. If the sentence still makes sense, the relationship is causal.

Additional Questions

1. Why might exploding lava cause death and destruction? **(because ash, gases, and hot lava blast from a volcano)**
2. What happened as a result of the thick ash that was carried to a campsite? **(two men suffocated and died)**

Additional Tips

Tell students that not all events are linked by a series of causes and effects. Sometimes a single cause can have more than one effect. Also, several causes can result in a single effect. You might use the following chart to demonstrate a single cause with multiple effects.

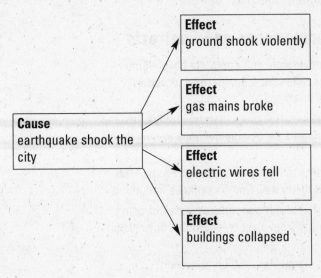

Comparison and Contrast

Introducing the Concept

Tell students that comparison and contrast can appear in any kind of writing, but that they are especially common in science and social studies materials. For instance, social studies textbooks often compare and contrast different eras in history, such as the Greek and Roman empires. A science textbook might compare and contrast ways of generating energy, such as nuclear and solar power.

Teaching Tips for Comparison and Contrast

- **Direct statements:** Show students direct statements of comparison and contrast in the sample article: "The biggest difference in today's space suits is that astronauts can wear them on space walks outside of the spacecraft"; "The new space suits give the same kind of protection as the old ones."

- **Comparison signal words:** Mention other comparison signal words and phrases, such as *both, neither, as well as, additionally*, and *likewise*.

- **Contrast signal words:** Other words and phrases that signal a contrast are *yet, still, in contrast*, and *instead*.

Additional Questions

1. What contrast does the article make between conditions on Earth and conditions in space? **(oxygen exists on Earth but not in space)**

2. To what other type of suit does the author compare 1960s space suits? **(flight suits worn by some pilots)**

3. According to the article, what is the most important difference between modern space suits and space suits of the 1960s? **(astronauts can wear modern space suits on space walks outside the spacecraft)**

4. What comparison does the author make between today's space suits and those of the future? **(future space suits will be more comfortable than those of today)**

Additional Tips for Recognizing Comparisons and Contrasts

- **Comparisons without signal words:** Not all comparisons and contrasts have signal words. Have students watch for statements that still make a comparison or contrast clear, such as "I like soccer. My brother prefers basketball."

- **Multiple comparisons:** Some texts compare and contrast more than two things. Instead of a Venn diagram, have students make a chart with side-by-side columns to help them clarify the multiple elements.

- **Comparisons in everyday life:** Encourage students to notice all the ways comparison-and-contrast structure is used in texts they read every day. Some examples include:
  - dictionary definitions, especially definitions of abstract concepts or states of being (for instance, the definition of *freedom* is "liberty from slavery, detention, oppression." In other words, *freedom* is not those things).
  - charts and graphs in textbooks, newspapers, magazines, and on television
  - reviews of TV shows, movies, video games, albums, and restaurants

Argument

Introducing the Concept

As students begin to read nonfiction on a regular basis, they will come across many arguments. You might want to tell students that they do not have to agree with every argument they read, but they should be aware that some arguments are well-supported while others lack support and factual evidence.

Teaching Tips for the Argument

- **Signal words:** Looking for signal words can help students determine the writer's position or opinion. Some additional examples include *agree, disagree, feel, oppose,* and *accept.*
- **Support:** Writers may use statistics, the opinions of experts, case histories, or narratives to support an argument. Tell students that not all arguments use expert opinions, but referring to experts can certainly help validate the writer's argument. In the example, the writer chose to include an expert opinion in order to strengthen a counterargument.
- **Evaluate the evidence:** Have students evaluate the argument by asking them to look closely at the evidence the author provides to back up the conclusions. Does the evidence make sense? Does it seem accurate?
- **Errors in reasoning:** Overgeneralizations and other errors in reasoning are common instances of unsupported inferences and fallacious reasoning.
- **Accuracy:** Students should question the accuracy of facts and statistics. Just because a statement is in print doesn't make it true.

Additional Questions

1. What is the expert opinion in the argument? (**Trainers believe that sea parks and aquariums support the well-being of dolphins.**)
2. What action or change is the writer calling for? (**making it illegal to take dolphins from the sea and display them for our entertainment.**)

Avoiding Errors in Reasoning

Some writers use fallacious reasoning to persuade the reader to feel a certain way or to do something. Some examples of faulty reasoning include the following:

- **Overgeneralizations** are statements that are so broad that they can't possibly be true. (*Everybody loves dogs. Everyone should own a dog.*) Using words such as *some, many, few, almost,* and *sometimes* can help you avoid an overgeneralization.
- **Circular reasoning** repeats an idea in different words rather than giving reasons to support it. (*Running is exhausting because it makes you tired.*)
- **Either/or statements** suggest that there are only two choices available in a situation. (*I'll either love the new song, or I'll hate it.*) Remind students that there might be other possibilities to consider in either/or statements.

Social Studies

Introducing the Concept

Acknowledge that social studies books can be frustrating because there are so many details to remember. Explain that the books are designed to make the most important information easy to find.

Teaching Tips for the Social Studies Page

A **Title:** Encourage students to read the title of each social studies lesson. Knowing the general topic of the lesson is an effective prereading strategy.

B **Goals or objectives:** Encourage students to go back to the goal or objective after reading and make sure that they can answer what it asks of them.

C **Vocabulary terms:** Tell students that boldfaced, italicized, or underlined terms often appear on tests. After reading, students should define those terms in their own words.

D **Display text:** Explain that items such as the Aristotle quotation are made prominent because they contain key concepts or vivid descriptions.

E **Pictures and captions:** Captions often include additional information. Looking at pictures and captions can make it easier to remember facts and details.

F **Other visuals:** Remind students to read the titles of any time lines, charts, tables, or other graphics in the lesson, so they will know what the graphic represents.

G **Time frame:** Understanding the order of historical events is a key part of doing well in a social studies class. Be sure that students understand that for B.C. dates, the numbers decrease as they move toward the present. For example, 1200 B.C. came before 700 B.C.

Additional Tips for Reading in Social Studies

One problem many students have with social studies is that the material seems like a series of disconnected facts. Students have trouble connecting the facts into meaningful patterns and remembering what they read. Suggest these tips to help them.

- **Make predictions:** Have students write down one or two predictions based on the title of the lesson and on what they have read in preceding lessons. After reading, encourage them to look at their predictions to see if they were right.

- **Find relationships to prior reading:** Ask how the material relates to subjects they have covered before. For example, how was the period after the Trojan War different from the period before the war?

- **Overcome lack of prior knowledge:** Most students will not have prior knowledge of the historical events they read about. To help overcome this difficulty, encourage them to create word webs, Venn diagrams, and other graphic organizers as they read. Knowing how facts relate to one another makes them easier to remember.

- **Use textbook aids:** Encourage students to use the aids provided in their social studies textbook, such as

  - special sections on how to read maps and charts
  - tips on how to interpret political cartoons
  - explanations on how to recognize text structures such as cause and effect

Science

Introducing the Concept

Textbooks pose special reading challenges for students. Science textbooks, for example, contain highly specialized vocabulary and complicated, sometimes unfamiliar concepts. They also rely heavily on visuals, such as diagrams and illustrations. Point out to students that reading a science page requires some special skills. Offer them these additional strategies.

Teaching Tips for the Science Page

A **Title and headings:** Remind students that the heading "Fact or Fiction?" is specific to the sidebar, and less important than the main heading, "Water Table."

B **Vocabulary words:** Encourage students to note or mark definitions as they read. Point out that on this page, the definitions precede the boldface vocabulary words.

C **Text structures:** Point out to students that recognizing the structure of a text will help them take effective notes. For example, if the text gives a process description, the students can take notes as numbered steps. If it breaks information down into categories, they can take notes in the form of a heading and description for each category.

D **Figure references:** Explain to students that in some cases, figure references point them to diagrams or illustrations that are critical to their understanding of the text. For this reason, they should be sure to look at the figure in the margin as soon as they are told to.

E **Diagrams, photos, and illustrations:** Point out to students that the lesson's vocabulary terms are also labels on the diagram. You might also explain to them that the circle at the left of the diagram is a magnification of the rock or soil in the diagram.

F **Special features:** Let students know that sidebars and other special features are often extraneous to the lesson. Remind them not to get bogged down in such features when first reading the lesson; it's more important to stick to the main text.

Additional Tips for Reading in Science

- **Watch for cues in the text about connecting the science concept to everyday experiences.** Students may have little or no prior knowledge of the subject matter in a science lesson. However, many science lessons begin with a paragraph or two relating some everyday experience to the science concept. (For example, it might compare the spray from a soda can to the eruption of a volcano.) As they read about new concepts, students should carefully consider the relationship between these and other everyday experiences and the concept.

- **Don't assume knowledge of familiar vocabulary terms; be sure to read definitions carefully.** Some science terms are familiar, everyday words that have a more specific meaning in science. (For example, the word *heat* is generally used to describe a feeling of warmth or hotness. In science, however, *heat* refers to a form of energy associated with the motion of atoms or molecules.) When they encounter familiar words among science vocabulary terms, readers should take care to read each term's definition and not assume that they already know it.

- **Be alert to surprising information, or information that contradicts prior knowledge.** Readers may find that a science lesson contradicts what they think they know about the concept. (For example, the fact that falling objects accelerate at the same rate, no matter what their weight, is often surprising to people.) Readers should be alert to such contradiction, and be ready to consciously revise their understanding of the material.

Mathematics

Introducing the Concept

Many student textbooks, especially those in math and science, pose special challenges for readers. In addition to scanning the titles and headings, students must deal with very specific vocabulary and symbols. Let students know that reading a math page takes some special skills. Share these helpful strategies with students.

Teaching Tips for the Math Page

A **Title and subheads:** Point out that on this page, the first heading is labeled "Goal 1: Multiplying Fractions." Explain to students that because the entire lesson is called "Multiplying Fractions and Mixed Numbers," they can reasonably predict that Goal 2 will be "Multiplying Mixed Numbers."

B **Objectives:** Suggest that students rewrite the lesson objectives in the form of questions. For example, "How do you solve problems involving multiplication of positive fractions?" Seeing these goals as questions will help them understand the point of the lesson.

C **Explanations:** Point out that while this explanation gives directions for a procedure, some explanations give general instruction about a concept, which may be more abstract and require extra concentration.

D **Special features:** Boxed or highlighted text, special notes, and other devices often contain special tips, strategies, or short summaries of important concepts. They are designed to make the material easier to understand and remember.

E **Worked-out solutions to problems:** Remind students to walk through each step of these sample problems, making sure that they understand how the problems work and how the answer has been arrived at. Sample problems are their key to solving the other problems in the set.

Additional Tips for Reading in Mathematics

- **Reread previous material:** If the text refers to material you studied earlier, be sure to reread the previous material.

- **Check directions carefully:** Carefully read directions for each exercise or problem set. In some cases, the directions may not ask you to solve a problem, but to answer questions about it.

- **Watch for boldfaced words:** Look out for boldface vocabulary words; be sure that you understand their definitions.

- **Check special vocabulary:** Remember that words we use every day have different meanings in mathematics. For example, the words *product, base,* and *power* have special meanings in math.

- **Read math in special ways:** One does not always read left to right in math. For example, fractions are to be read from top to bottom.

- **Watch for special words and symbols:** Read every word and symbol very carefully to avoid mistaking words such as *hundred* for *hundredth* or *1.0* for *.10*.

Reading an Application

Introducing the Concept

An application must be read carefully in order to be filled out correctly. Remind students that a few strategies can help them read applications accurately.

Teaching Tips for the Application

A **Sections:** Encourage students to always scan something before reading it. This will help them put the different sections in context once they begin to read carefully.

B **For office use only:** Many applications have a section like this for the people administering the application. Students should look out for this label and avoid writing in these sections.

C **Special markings:** Remind students to notice how the dividing lines, boxes, or special tips group information in a logical order.

D **Signature:** Caution students to read carefully any agreement that requires their signature. Be sure they understand that a signature is legally binding in many cases.

More Practice with Applications

Reproduce the form below for your students and ask them the questions that follow.

BICYCLE REGISTRATION	**CITY OF SANTA RITA**	**NO.** _____

RIDER	ADDRESS	PHONE
BOY'S **GIRL'S** **SIZE**	**FRAME COLOR**	**MAKE**
SERIAL NUMBER	**OTHER IDENTIFICATION**	

AFFIDAVIT: I hereby certify that the above described bicycle is the property of the undersigned for use by the person named above.

DATE: _____   Signature: _____

KEEP THIS REGISTRATION RECEIPT IN A SAFE PLACE

TRANSFER OF REGISTRATION: The above described bicycle has been disposed by the above owner

New Owner: _____   Signature: _____

Address: _____   Date: _____

Return Transfer to: **RECORD SECTION**
Police Department
1454 Overlook Drive
Santa Rita, CA 90300

STAMP THE REGISTRATION NUMBER INTO THE FRAME

1. What is the purpose of this form? **(To register a bicycle with the city)**

2. What features are used to identify the bicycle? **(Whether it's a boy's or a girl's bike, the size of the bike, its frame color, its make, its serial number, and any other identification)**

3. What should you do with the registration receipt when you have finished registering your bicycle? **(Keep it in a safe place)**

Reading a Public Notice

Introducing the Concept

Public notices can provide students and their families with valuable information. Explain that although public notices are usually designed to be as easy to read as possible, they can still present some challenges.

Teaching Tips for the Public Notice

A **Audience:** Explain that knowing whom the notice is designed to reach can help students filter out irrelevant notices and get more information out of relevant ones. The census notice shown is for the person or people at 11120 Elmwood Avenue.

B **Instructions:** Tell students that whenever they read a notice, they should look for instructions or requests. The census notice asks the recipient to fill out and mail the census form. Point out that in this case, instructions are scattered through the text.

C **Author:** Every notice was created by someone, and knowing who created a notice can help students judge its reliability. The census letter is signed by Kenneth Prewitt, the director of the Bureau of the Census. The census bureau is part of the federal Department of Commerce.

D **Sources for more information:** Mention that, since space on a notice is usually limited, many notices give sources where readers can find out more. This notice suggests calling the local census office and visiting a Web site. Other notices may give addresses or contact names.

E **Special features:** The census notice includes brief instructions in Spanish, Chinese, Korean, Vietnamese, and Tagalog. More extensive instructions in those languages are on the back of the notice (not shown). Other notices may have different special features, such as maps, timetables, or checklists.

Additional Questions

1. Is this notice from the government or from a private organization? (the government)

2. Is it from the federal, state, or local government? (federal)

3. What persuasive reason does the letter give for filling out the census form? (so that the recipient's community can get the government funds it is entitled to)

4. Why do you think the letter provides information in six languages? (to make it easier for non–English speakers to fill out the form; to make it more likely that everyone will be counted)

Other Types of Public Notices

Students will encounter other public notices, such as

• **posted rules** for use of parks, swimming pools, beaches, libraries, community centers, and other public areas;

• **announcements** of community events, meetings, and elections; and

• **information on public health and safety,** such as road signs.

Mention that even though many of these notices will not use complete sentences, students can use the same techniques to understand them that they used on the census letter.

Reading Web Pages

Introducing the Concept

Ask students to describe their experiences searching for information on the World Wide Web. Explain that the Web contains a massive amount of information, so users must be Web-savvy to find what they need.

Teaching Tips for the Web Page

A **Web address:** Tell students to bookmark or write down the Web addresses (URLs) of sites they may need to return to. If they write down the address incorrectly or return to the page later to find the link broken, they can try entering the first part of the address (such as http://www.pbs.org) and then look for links to the page they want.

B **Title:** A well thought-out Web page will include a title that summarizes the page's content. With so many Web pages to choose from, it is important for students to read titles and skim content of pages instead of printing out everything they find.

C **Menu bars:** Explain that most Web pages let users access pages in any order. Remind students to look at menu bars carefully to see what categories the site offers. Students may need to use the "back" button to find the menu bar again after accessing a page, or the menu bar may appear on every page of the site.

D **Links:** Explain that a link may lead to another page on that site or to a different site altogether. Just because a site links to a page does not mean that the person who did the linking has checked that the page is accurate or up to date.

E **Interactive areas:** For safety reasons, caution students to avoid giving their home address or phone number or sending pictures of themselves to interactive sites unless they check with a parent or teacher first.

Glossary of Web-Related Terms

bookmark: a saved link to a Web page. If you bookmark a site on your computer, you can call it up again from your bookmark list on that same computer without having to type in the Web address. A bookmark list is sometimes called a hot list or a favorites list.

Boolean search: a search for two or more terms linked by *and* or *or,* such as "students AND discipline" or "vacations OR holidays." The term *Boolean* refers to British mathematician George Boole (1815–1864).

browser: a computer program that lets you look at and interact with material on the World Wide Web. Some commonly used browsers are Netscape Navigator and Internet Explorer.

.com: when used as part of a Web address, usually indicates a commercial (private) site. Other such designations include *.net* (commercial), *.edu* (college or university), *.org* (nonprofit), *.gov* (governmental), and *.mil* (military). For example, www.mcdougallittell.com is a commercial site, and www.pbs.org is a nonprofit site.

http: Hypertext Transfer Protocol, the computer rules for exchanging information on the Web. Web addresses include the http coding, a colon, and two backslashes (http://).

netiquette: etiquette on the Internet. Typing a message in all capital letters is poor netiquette because it is the online equivalent of shouting.

URL: a Uniform Resource Locator, or Web address, such as http://www.mcdougallittell.com.

Reading Technical Directions

Introducing the Concept

Reading technical directions can be challenging because of difficult vocabulary and complex instructions. Tell students that the following strategies will help them make sense of technical directions.

Teaching Tips for Technical Directions

A Reading directions from beginning to end at least once gives readers an overall picture of what they must do. Tell students that this is one of the most important steps in reading technical directions.

B Directions will usually provide letters or numbers to show the order in which the steps occur. If no numbers or letters are given, tell students they may find it helpful to insert the numbers themselves.

C Tell students to underline or circle specific words that call for an action. Underlining an action verb can help a reader become more aware of the directions in each step.

D Remind students to read the text and visuals together to make each step clear.

E Warnings or notes are very important because they often refer the reader to another page for more information, or they may tell the reader to take certain precautions before attempting a step.

Additional Practice Using Technical Directions

If students require additional practice, make copies of this short version of technical directions for using a camera's focus range.

Using the Focus Range

1. The focus range of the camera is 0.6 m (2 ft) to infinity.

Close-Up Correction

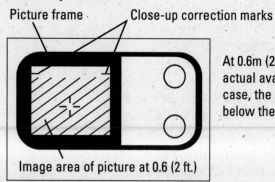

Picture frame · Close-up correction marks

At 0.6m (2 ft.), the shaded area is the actual available image area. In this case, the subject should be positioned below the close-up correction marks.

Image area of picture at 0.6 (2 ft.)

Warning The shutter will not release if the subject is closer than 0.6 (2 ft). When the subject is extremely close to the camera, the subject will be out of focus. For more on how to avoid taking out-of-focus pictures see page 25.

▌▌▌ MARK IT UP ⟩

1. Circle the available image area when a subject is 2 ft. from the camera. **(Shaded area)**

2. Where are you supposed to position the subject? **(below the close-up correction marks)**

3. Where do you look for more information on out-of-focus pictures? **(page 25)**

Reading Product Information: Food Label

Introducing the Concept

Nutrition labels appear on most packaged food products. You might tell students that learning how to read these labels will help them avoid foods that have little nutritional value.

Teaching Tips for the Food Label

A **Serving Size:** Make sure students understand that "serving size" refers to the recommended portion of the food to be eaten at one time. All of the numbers and percentages on the label are based on this portion.

B **Percent Daily Value:** Remind students that a percentage is a fraction of 100. Eating the recommended portion of this food accounts for 13% of the daily value of total fat. One must eat other foods to make up the remaining 87%.

C **Fat and Sodium Nutrients:** Tell students that if a portion has 20% or more of total fat, it's considered a high-fat food. If it has no more than 5%, it's considered low-fat.

D **Sugars and Protein:** Even though a percent daily value for sugars has not been established, point out that the FDA recommends no more than 50 grams a day for the added sugars in such processed foods as cakes and cookies. There is no such limit for the naturally occurring sugars found in fruit, milk, or yogurt.

E **Vitamins and Minerals:** Encourage students to compare the percent daily value of these nutrients with those for fat and sodium. Since the values of fat and sodium are much higher than those for vitamins and minerals, the food represented by this label may be one to avoid.

F **Small Print:** Point out that some groups, including growing teenagers and nursing mothers, may need more than a 2,000-calorie diet. Tell students that if they need a higher-calorie diet, their intake of the nutrients listed on a nutrition label should be higher.

Additional Questions

1. How many calories are in one serving of this food? (**160 calories**)
2. What percent daily value of cholesterol does a serving of cookies provide? (**0%**)
3. A serving contains 0% of which vitamins and minerals? (**vitamin A, vitamin C, calcium**)

Other Types of Product Information

Students encounter many different types of product information in their daily life. For example:

• **Labels on over-the-counter medicines** tell how to take these preparations safely and effectively.

• **Warranties** on appliances and electronic goods explain the consumer's rights and responsibilities if something goes wrong with the product.

• **Clothing labels** provide cleaning instructions for the item. Failure to read this information carefully can result in ruined, shrunken clothing.

Reading a Schedule

Introducing the Concept

Schedules come in many forms and are sometimes difficult to read. Discuss with students the various practical uses of schedules, and point out to them that the ability to read a schedule properly is an important real-world skill.

Teaching Tips for the Schedule

A **Title:** Remind students that when reading a schedule, they should be sure that they are looking at the right one. Mixing up schedules is an easy mistake that can cause a lot of confusion.

B **Date or Day Labels:** Again, it's also important to make sure you're looking at the right day or date. Remind students to check these labels very carefully.

C **Event Names:** Mention to students that the names of classes or other events are really the heart of this particular schedule.

D **Time Markers:** Point out to students that time is indicated in two places on this schedule. Explain to them that this makes the schedule easier for people to look up a class either by the time of day ("What can I do at 6:00?") or by the class name ("What time is Tae Kwon Do offered?").

Other Kinds of Schedules

Students will encounter all kinds of schedules while in or out of school. Reproduce the bus schedule for your students and ask them the questions that follow.

Bus Route 333: Grand Avenue			Weekday Mornings—EASTBOUND		
Lawrence Station	Chestnut St. Mall	Grand & Lincoln	Memorial Hospital	Grand & Delaware	Three Rivers Station
4:57 A.M.	5:03 A.M.	5:06 A.M.	5:10 A.M.	5:16 A.M.	5:19 A.M.
5:38	5:44	5:48	5:53	5:59	6:02
5:55	6:02	6:06	6:11	6:18	6:22
6:15	6:22	6:26	6:31	6:38	6:42
6:35	6:42	6:46	6:51	6:58	7:02
7:00	7:08	7:13	7:19	7:28	7:33
7:15	7:23	7:28	7:34	7:43	7:48
7:30	7:38	7:43	7:49	7:58	8:03
7:55	8:03	8:08	8:14	8:23	8:28
8:25	8:33	8:38	8:44	8:52	8:57
8:50	8:58	9:03	9:09	9:17	9:22
9:20	9:28	9:33	9:39	9:47	9:52
9:50	9:58	10:03	10:09	10:17	10:22
10:20	10:28	10:33	10:39	10:47	10:52
10:50	10:58	11:03	11:09	11:17	11:22
11:20	11:28	11:33	11:39	11:47	11:52
11:50	11:58	12:03 P.M.	12:09 P.M.	12:17 P.M.	12:22 P.M.

1. Along what street does this bus drive? (Grand Avenue)

2. If you want to travel from Lawrence Station to Grand & Lincoln and arrive by 7:30 A.M., what time should you leave? (7:15 A.M.)

Vocabulary
Mini-Lessons
with Graphic Organizers

1 Explain to students that sometimes they can figure out the meaning of an unfamiliar word or term by thinking about the context, or the surrounding words of the sentence or passage.

2 Write the following paragraph on the board and read it aloud:

> The *disarray* in her room made it impossible to move. Clothes and papers covered the floor, and books and magazines threatened to spill from every shelf.

3 Then model how to use context to figure out the meaning of *disarray*:

> *You might say:* I'm not sure what disarray *means. I can look for context clues in the sentence this word is in and in the surrounding sentences. The phrases "made it impossible to move," "clothes and papers covered the floor," and "books and magazines threatened to spill" help me figure out that* disarray *means "a state of great disorder, or a mess."*

4 Now write the following paragraph on the board and read it aloud. Have a volunteer underline the context clues that could be used to help determine the meaning of the word *inaudible*.

> Children ran screaming up and down the aisles, and the man beside me snored loudly. I tried to block out the noise, but I'm afraid I couldn't hear you. Your speech was *inaudible*.

Point out to students that in the example above, a type of clue known as **details from general context** helped them figure out the meaning of *inaudible*. Encourage students to use this strategy throughout the year, along with other common types of context clues:

Definition and Restatement

The cats that live behind our garage are **feral**, or wild.

(The phrase following *feral* helps define the word as meaning "wild or untamed.")

Example

He studies **pachyderms**, including the elephant, rhinoceros, and hippopotamus.

(The *elephant*, *rhinoceros*, and *hippopotamus* are examples of pachyderms.)

Comparison and Contrast

He wasn't **apologetic**; on the contrary, he didn't seem at all sorry that he was two hours late.

(The words *on the contrary* help you understand that "not at all sorry" is the opposite of *apologetic*. Therefore, *apologetic* must mean "being very sorry.")

Here's How

See the next three pages for useful lessons on context clues that you can duplicate for students.

Context Clues (Example)

A good way to make sense of an unfamiliar word is to look at the **context**: the other words in the sentence and other sentences in the paragraph that might give clues to the meaning of the word. There are a number of ways you can use context clues to help you determine a word's meaning.

Sometimes a sentence will provide an **example** that will help you understand the meaning of the word. Examples are often signaled by words or phrases such as

like	for instance	this	such as	especially
these	for example	other	includes	

Here's How **Using Examples in Context to Figure Out an Unfamiliar Word**

To get rid of that sore throat, try an old-fashioned *remedy* such as gargling with saltwater or sipping peppermint tea.

1. Identify the unfamiliar word.
   (I'm not sure what the word *remedy* means.)

2. Read to see if there is a word that signals that an example may follow.
   (I see the phrase *such as*. Those words could lead to an example.)

3. Find the example or examples.
   (The phrases *gargling with saltwater* and *sipping peppermint tea* follow the phrase *such as*. These are examples of remedies.)

4. Ask yourself how the example or examples relate to the unfamiliar word.
   (Both examples are things you can do to make you feel better.)

5. Use this information to figure out what the word means.
   (Since both examples are things that can make you feel better, *remedy* must mean "something that makes you feel better.")

6. Now, look up the unfamiliar word in the dictionary and jot the word and definition down in your personal word list.
   remedy: something that relieves pain or cures disease

Copyright © McDougal Littell Inc.

Context Clues (Comparison or Contrast)

A good way to make sense of an unfamiliar word is to look at the **context:** the other words in the sentence and other sentences in the paragraph that might give clues to the meaning of the word. There are a number of ways you can use context clues to help you determine a word's meaning.

Sometimes a sentence will provide a **comparison** or a **contrast** that will help you understand the meaning of the word. Certain words or phrases signal comparison or contrast.

Some Comparison Signals		Some Contrast Signals	
like	similar to	but	although
as	also	unlike	however
related	resembling	rather than	on the other hand

Here's How Using Comparison or Contrast to Figure Out an Unfamiliar Word

The set for the play looked as *flimsy* as a house of cards, but it was as sturdy as the brick walls of the theater.

1. Identify the unfamiliar word.

(I'm not sure what the word *flimsy* means.)

2. Read to see if there is a word or phrase that signals that a comparison or a contrast may follow.

(I see the words *as* and *but. As* could signal a comparison, and *but* could signal a contrast.)

3. Identify the comparison or contrast.

(The first part of the sentence compares the flimsy set with a house of cards, while the second part of the sentence contrasts the set with a sturdy wall.)

4. Use this information to figure out what the unfamiliar word means.

(The comparison is with something that is weak and the contrast is with something strong and sturdy, so I think that *flimsy* means "weak, not sturdy.")

5. Find the word in the dictionary and record it in your personal word list.

flimsy: light, thin; lacking solidity or strength

6. A sentence may contain only comparison or only contrast as a context clue. You can still use the strategy above to find the meaning.

Copyright © McDougal Littell Inc.

Context Clues (Restatement)

A good way to make sense of an unfamiliar word is to look at the **context**: the other words in the sentence and other sentences in the paragraph that might give clues to the meaning of the word. There are a number of ways you can use context clues to help you determine a word's meaning.

Sometimes a writer will **restate** the meaning of a difficult word within a sentence, defining it for you. Restatements or definitions are often signaled by words or phrases such as

or	which is	that is
also called	also known as	in other words

Here's How **Using Restatement in Context to Figure Out an Unfamiliar Word**

Although I have a bike, I prefer to be a *pedestrian.* In other words, I'd rather walk.

1. Identify the unfamiliar word.

(I'm not sure what the word *pedestrian* means.)

2. Read to see if there is a word that signals that a restatement may follow.

(I see the phrase *in other words.* What follows may include a restatement or definition.)

3. Find the restated information.

(The phrase *in other words* is followed by *I'd rather walk.*)

4. Use this information to figure out what the unfamiliar word means.

(Because the second sentence says that *I'd rather walk* is another way of saying "I prefer to be a pedestrian," I think that *pedestrian* must mean "someone who walks.")

5. Now, look up the unfamiliar word in the dictionary and jot the word and definition down in your personal word list.

pedestrian: a person traveling on foot; a walker

Copyright © McDougal Littell Inc.

Word Parts: Prefixes, Suffixes, and Compound Words

1 Explain to students that sometimes they can figure out the meaning of an unfamiliar word by thinking about the meaning of the word parts it contains.

2 Write the word *unsuccessful* on the board and read it aloud. Model how to use the base word and affixes to figure out the meaning of the word.

You could say: *I'm not sure what* unsuccessful *means. I can try breaking the word into parts. I see the prefix* un-, *which means "not." I see the base word* success, *which means "the achievement of something desired, planned, or attempted." I also see the suffix* -ful, *which means "full of." By combining the meanings of these word parts, I can figure out that* unsuccessful *must mean "not achieving something desired, planned, or attempted."*

3 Explain to students that they can also break down compound words, which are made up of two words put together. Tell students that they can sometimes tell the meaning of a compound word by looking at the meaning of each word part. This strategy may be particularly useful for students learning English.

4 Write the word *sickbed* on the board and read it aloud. Model how to break it into parts and figure out the meaning.

You could say: *I'm not sure what* sickbed *means. I can try breaking it into two words. I see that it's made up of the words* sick *and* bed. *Is it a bed that's sick? That doesn't make much sense. I think it must be a bed for a sick person.*

As the year progresses, you may wish to review this strategy. The following list provides additional words for you and your students to model. Have volunteers draw vertical lines between the word parts, and ask them to explain how to use those parts to figure out the meaning of each word.

hemisphere	bicycle	bookstore	unicorn	magnify	breadstick
microscope	doormat	translate	reaction	breakfast	director
active	mysteriously	natural	glamorous	knockout	

Here's How

See the next three pages for useful lessons on working with suffixes, prefixes, and compound words. You can duplicate these lessons for students.

5 Share with students the following lists of commonly used prefixes, suffixes, and compound words.

Prefixes	Suffixes	Compound Words
hemi- (half)	-tion (action or process)	doghouse
bi- (two)	-or (one who performs a specified action)	toehold
uni- (one)	-ive (inclined to)	jackhammer
magni- (large)	-ate (to make)	hammerhead
micro- (small)	-ly (in what way)	cottonwood
trans- (across)	-al (relating to)	fingernail
pre- (before)	-ous (full of)	sunset
post- (after)	-dom (state or quality of)	daybreak
un- (not)	-hood (state or quality of)	playpen

Copyright © McDougal Littell Inc.

Prefixes

A **prefix** is a word part attached to the beginning of a base word or root. The meaning of a prefix combines with the meaning of the base word or root. For example, the prefix *in-* often means "not," as in *indirect,* which means "not direct."

Here's How **Using Prefixes to Determine Word Meaning**

1. When you first encounter an unfamiliar word, try to determine whether the word has a prefix.

antisocial

(The base word seems to be *social,* since it can stand on its own, so the prefix must be *anti-.* I also recognize the prefix from seeing it in other words.)

....

2. If you recognize the prefix from a word you do know, make an educated guess about its meaning.

(I know that *antislavery* means "opposed to slavery," so maybe *anti-* means "opposed to.")

Based on what you know about the prefix and the base word, make a guess about the meaning of the entire word.

(*Antisocial* must mean "opposed to society.")

....

3. Look up the word's definition in the dictionary and compare it with your guess.

antisocial *adj.* Rejecting the society of others; not sociable

(*Antisocial* does have to do with being opposed to society; my guess was correct.)

....

4. Look at other words in the dictionary with the same prefix. Look to see what they have in common.

antitheft *adj.* Designed to prevent theft

antibody *n.* A protein in the blood or tissue that destroys or weakens bacteria

(Basically, the prefix *anti-* means "against" or "opposing.")

....

5. Look in the dictionary for more words with the same prefix. Make yourself familiar with their definitions.

antidepressant, antihistamine, anti-Semitic, antismog, antithesis

---

Copyright © McDougal Littell Inc.

Suffixes

A **suffix** is a word part attached to the end of a base word or root. Most suffixes determine a word's part of speech. Familiarity with common suffixes can help you determine the meaning of some unfamiliar words.

Here's How Using Suffixes to Determine Meaning

1. When you first encounter an unfamiliar word, try to determine whether the word has a suffix.

> **accelerator**

(The base word seems to be *accelerate,* since it can stand on its own, so the suffix must be *-or.* I also recognize the suffix from seeing it in other words.)

2. If you do recognize the suffix from a word you know, make an educated guess about its meaning.

(I know that *narrator* means "one who narrates," so *-or* probably means "one that performs a specific action.")

Based on what you know about the prefix and the base word or root, make a guess about the meaning of the entire word.

(I know that *accelerate* means "to increase the speed of," so *accelerator* must mean "one who increases the speed of something.")

3. Look up the word's definition in the dictionary and compare it with your guess. If the word isn't listed on its own, you may need to look for it within the entry for the base word.

> **accelerator** *n.* A device or substance that increases speed, often the gas pedal of a car

(*Accelerator* means "something that increases speed"; my guess was close.)

4. Try to think of other words with the same suffix. What do they have in common?

> **acceptor, actor, collector, duplicator**

(Basically, all these words mean "someone who" or "something that" does whatever the base word suggests—*accepts, acts, collects, duplicates*—so *-or* must mean "someone who" or "something that.")

Copyright © McDougal Littell Inc.

Compound Words

A **compound word** is a word made up of two words put together. The meanings of the two word parts combine to form a new meaning. Sometimes the meaning of a compound word is obvious when you look at the meaning of each word part. For example, the word *homework* is made up of the words *home* and *work.* It simply means work (usually from school) that you do at home. Other times, the meaning is not as clear, but it is usually still related to the meaning of the two word parts.

Here's How   Understanding Compound Words

1. When you see an unfamiliar compound word, look first for its two word parts.

   windshield

   (The word parts of *windshield* are *wind* and *shield.*)

2. Look at the meanings of the two parts and think of how they are related to *windshield.*

   (*Windshield* has something to do with both *wind* and *shield.* Since the word is *windshield* and not *shieldwind,* it sounds more like a kind of *shield* than a kind of *wind.* I think it must be something that shields the wind.)

3. Look up the word's definition in the dictionary and compare it with your guess.

   windshield *n.* a framed pane of glass in front of the passengers of a car to protect them from the wind

   (My guess was correct.)

4. Some compound words have a meaning that doesn't make obvious sense. When you encounter such a word, break it into its word parts, and see what sense you can make of it.

   breakneck

   (The word parts of *breakneck* are *break* and *neck.* It sounds like it has something to do with a broken neck.)

5. Look up the word's definition in the dictionary and compare it with your thoughts.

   breakneck *adj.* dangerously fast: *a breakneck pace*

   (Although *breakneck* doesn't literally mean "a broken neck," it does mean "dangerously fast." Someone driving dangerously fast might risk having a broken neck. So there is at least a loose connection between *breakneck* and broken necks.)

Copyright © McDougal Littell Inc.

1 Explain to students that sometimes they can figure out the meaning of an unfamiliar word if they recognize its root from other, familiar words. You may want to explain that a **root** is a word part that contains the most important element of that word's meaning. A root must be combined with other word parts, such as prefixes or suffixes, in order to form a word.

2 Write the word *originate* on the board and read it aloud. Model how to use the root to help determine the word's meaning.

You could say: *I've never seen the word* originate *before. The root is probably* orig-; *I've seen* orig- *in other words, such as* original. *I know that* original *refers to the first of something, or something newly created. I think* originate *sounds like a verb, so perhaps it means "to create or make something new."*

3 Now write the following table on the board:

Root	Meaning
agri-	field
alter-	other
anim-	life, spirit
cap-	head
grad-	step
hab-	hold
hosp-	host
mar-	sea
sem-	half

4 Have volunteers use the information in the table as they try to define the words below. Make sure they explain the process they used to figure out the meaning of each word.

gradual	captain	capitol	agriculture	alternative
habitat	hospital	animate	semicircle	submarine

5 As the year progresses, you may wish to review this strategy. The following table provides you with additional words, roots, and meanings.

Root	Meaning	Examples
ann-	year	annual, anniversary
cam-	field	camp, campus
-claim, -clam	shout, call	exclamation, proclaim
clar-	clear	clarity, declare
flex-, flec-	bend	flexible, reflect
liber-	free	liberty, liberate
ment-	mind	mental, demented
min-	small, lesser	minute, mini, minus
oct-	eight	octopus, octagon
sim-	same, like	similar, simile
stell-	star	stellar, constellation

Here's How

See the next page for useful lessons on using word roots to determine meaning. You can duplicate these lessons for students.

Copyright © McDougal Littell Inc.

Roots

Many English words, especially long ones, can be broken into smaller parts. A **root** is the core of a word, or the part that contains the most important element of the word's meaning.

Many words in English have their roots in other languages, particularly Greek and Latin. Knowing the meaning of Greek and Latin roots can help you understand unfamiliar words.

Here's How Using Word Roots to Determine Meaning

1. When you first encounter an unfamiliar word, try to determine the word's root.

   antiquity

   (The root might be *antiqu-* or *-ity*. Since *-ity* appears at the end of so many words, it is probably not the root. The root must be *antiqu-*.)

2. If you recognize the root from a word you do know, make an educated guess about the word's meaning.

   (I know that *antiques* are old pieces of furniture, so maybe *antiquity* also has something to do with old things and age or with furniture.)

3. Look up the word's definition in the dictionary and compare it with your guess.

   antiquity *n.* Ancient times

   (*Antiquity* does have to do with old things and age; one of my guesses was correct.)

4. Read the word's etymology at the end of the dictionary entry.

   [French, from Latin *antiquus,* old.]

   (Basically, *antiqu-* means old.)

5. Try to think of other words with the same root. (Hint: for words without prefixes, try looking at nearby words in the dictionary.)

   antiquarian, antiquated, antique

Copyright © McDougal Littell Inc.

1 Tell students that an **idiom** is a set phrase that means something different from the literal meaning of its individual words. Explain to students that they can sometimes figure out the meaning of an unfamiliar idiom by thinking about its context, or the surrounding words of the sentence or passage.

2 Write the following sentence on the board and read it aloud:

> **The conductor *flies off the handle* and knocks over her music stand every time the violinist makes a mistake.**

3 Then model how to use context to figure out the meaning of *fly off the handle.*

> **You could say:** fly off the handle. *I can look for context clues in the rest of the sentence. The conductor is reacting to the violinist's mistake, which probably makes her unhappy. In addition to* flying off the handle, *the conductor also knocks over her music stand, which seems to show that she's angry. I think that to* fly off the handle *means "to lose one's temper."*

4 The following boldface sentences contain commonly used idioms. Write these sentences on the chalkboard (without the translations given in parentheses). Ask students to read the sentences and use context clues to figure out the meaning of the idioms.

> **I'm sorry I'm late; I got *tied up* at work.** (I got busy at work.)
>
> **After playing soccer all day, Jacqui was so *wiped out,* she could hardly move.** (Jacqui was so tired, she could hardly move.)
>
> **Oh no! I've been so busy this week that Eric's birthday completely *slipped my mind.* I hope he's not too upset with me.** (I completely forgot about Eric's birthday.)
>
> **There are so many dishes to wash—would you mind *giving me a hand* with them?** (Would you mind helping me wash them?)
>
> **There's a tiger in the back yard? You must be *pulling my leg.*** (There's a tiger in the back yard? You must be joking with me.)
>
> **After being ten points behind for almost the entire game, the Grasshoppers finally won *by the skin of their teeth.*** (After being ten points behind for almost the entire game, the Grasshoppers finally won, but they only barely won.)

5 As the year progresses, you may wish to review this strategy. The following list provides you with more idioms to share with your students.

Idiom	Meaning
I never thought I'd *end up* in a big city.	arrive at, result in, finish
That's it! You've *hit the nail on the head.*	to be completely right
My mother quit smoking *cold turkey.*	immediate, complete withdrawal
He gave her a *dirty look.*	to scowl at someone
Jerry knew the answer *right off the bat.*	instantly, immediately
Nikki will *have a fit* if she sees you here.	become extremely upset
Why are you so *down in the dumps?*	discouraged or depressed
Miguel's *come down with* the flu.	become ill with
The baby is *out cold.*	fast asleep or unconscious
I think Madeleine is *playing possum.*	pretending to be asleep
I can never *keep a straight face* when he sings.	hold back from laughing

Here's How

See the next page for a useful lesson on understanding idioms. You can duplicate this lesson for students.

Copyright © McDougal Littell Inc.

Understanding Idioms

An **idiom** is a set phrase whose meaning is different from the literal meaning of its individual words. For example, the idiom *raining cats and dogs* has nothing to do with cats or dogs; it simply means "raining very hard."

Most idioms are so commonly used in everyday speech that people use them without thinking about them. However, unfamiliar idioms can be very confusing. If you didn't know that *he put his foot in his mouth* really means "he said something clumsy or embarrassing," you might wonder what someone is doing with his foot inside of his mouth!

When you see an unfamiliar idiom, you can sometimes find clues in the idiom's context, or surrounding words and paragraphs.

Here's How Understanding Idioms

"Come on, it's three o'clock already, and we haven't even started our homework," said Andre. "We have to *get cracking*."

1. Identify the unfamiliar idiom.

   (I'm not sure what *get cracking* means. Does it mean "to crack something"?)

2. Look for context clues, such as a restatement or explanation.

   (I see that Andre's first sentence is "Come on, it's three o'clock already, and we haven't even started our homework." It seems that Andre is explaining why he and the others have to *get cracking*.)

3. Use this information to figure out what the idiom means.

   (When Andre says "Come on, it's three o'clock already, and we haven't even started our homework," it seems that he's in a hurry to have the homework done. I think *get cracking* means "start working.")

4. Some idioms appear in regular dictionaries under the definition of the phrase's main word. Look up this idiom in a regular dictionary or in a dictionary of idioms, under *cracking* or *get*.

   (**get** *v. -idioms.* **Get cracking.** To begin work; get started.)

5. If you can't find an idiom in a dictionary, ask a teacher, a fellow student, or another adult what it means.

Copyright © McDougal Littell Inc.

Using Words with Multiple Meanings

1 Explain to students that many words have more than one meaning. They can figure out which meaning of a word is being used in a sentence or passage by looking for clues in the surrounding context.

2 Write the following sentence on the board and read it aloud:

Under this *ruler,* fair laws that granted equal rights to everyone were passed.

3 Then model how to use context to figure out which meaning of the word is being used:

MODEL

I'm not sure which meaning of ruler *is being used in this sentence.* Ruler *can mean "a measuring stick," and it can also mean "one who governs." I can look for context clues in the sentence. The phrases "fair laws" and "were passed" help me figure out that, in this sentence,* ruler *means "one who governs."*

4 Now write the following sentence on the board and read it aloud. Have a volunteer underline the context clues that could be used to help determine which meaning of the word *gravity* is intended.

I could tell by their serious expressions that my friends understood the *gravity* of the situation.

5 If students are not familiar with a word or its multiple meanings, encourage them to look up the word in a dictionary. Sometimes dictionaries provide sample contexts to show the different meanings of a word. Tell students to compare the sample contexts and figure out the one that best fits the sentence. As the year progresses, you may wish to review these strategies.

The following chart provides you with additional words and some of their multiple meanings. Have students create sentences that demonstrate their understanding of the words' multiple meanings.

Word	Meanings	Word	Meanings
record	1. report set down in writing 2. disk played on a phonograph 3. unequaled achievement	scale	1. instrument used for weighing 2. series of musical notes 3. outer covering of fish
change	1. to alter something 2. small amount of money 3. variety	article	1. individual item 2. essay 3. words used to signal nouns
letter	1. character of the alphabet 2. written message 3. award for athletic skill	critical	1. very important 2. dangerous condition 3. faultfinding
star	1. heavenly body 2. famous actor 3. design with five or more points	counter	1. opposed to something 2. surface upon which food is prepared 3. one who counts
goal	1. purpose 2. zone into which players aim a ball 3. score awarded in a game	model	1. person who displays clothing 2. small object that represents a larger one 3. construction that serves as a plan

Here's How

See the next page for a useful lesson on words with multiple meanings that you can duplicate for students.

Copyright © McDougal Littell Inc.

Words with Multiple Meanings

Because language constantly changes to meet the needs of those who use it, many words in English have more than one meaning. These multiple meanings may lead to confusion, causing readers to misinterpret a writer's message.

Here's How Selecting the Appropriate Meaning of a Word

1. When you are not sure which definition of a word applies in a particular sentence, look for clues in the surrounding context.

> **When my father makes his famous spaghetti sauce, he uses more than a *dash* of garlic.**

(I know that *dash* is a verb that is used to describe someone running very fast, but in this sentence the word seems to be used as a noun. Maybe *dash* can be a different part of speech and have another meaning.)

2. If the meaning you know does not make sense in the context of the sentence and you don't have enough clues to help you figure out the meaning, look up the word in a dictionary. Look for the definition that makes sense in the sentence.

(I see that there are several meanings for the word *dash,* including "to run quickly," "a small amount of something," and "a line used as punctuation.")

3. Decide which dictionary definition works best in the sentence you are examining.

(In this sentence, *dash* refers to the amount of garlic the father adds to his dish, so in this case, *dash* probably is a noun meaning "a small amount of something added to other things.")

Copyright © McDougal Littell Inc.

Teaching Decoding Strategies

Teaching Decoding Strategies

By middle school, your students have had years of instruction in decoding strategies, primarily in phonics, structural analysis, and context clues. Readers are taught these strategies to help them determine the meaning of words unfamiliar in print but known as part of their receptive vocabulary or to determine the meaning of totally unfamiliar words.

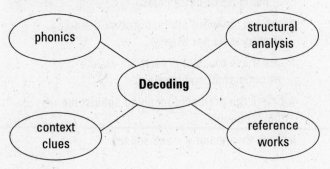

Phonics

Phonics is a system of teaching the basic sound-letter relationships in the English language. Many early grade educators believe phonics lays the foundation for young readers understanding the relationship between spoken and written words. Instruction is usually coupled with decodable text so students can apply skills to predictable reading and develop automaticity—the ability to recognize words in text automatically and effortlessly. Good readers use phonics skills automatically in conjunction with other decoding strategies.

In the primary grades, phonics receives the main emphasis as a decoding strategy. The chart below shows when phonics instruction usually occurs.

Phonics	Grade where taught
consonants (initial, medial, final)	through first half grade 2
consonant digraphs (/th/ *th*, etc.)	through first half grade 2
consonant clusters (*st, bl, br,* etc.)	through grade 2
short vowels	through grade 1
long vowels	through grade 2
r-controlled vowels (*er, ir, ar,* etc.)	through grade 2
diphthongs (*oi, oy,* etc.)	through grade 2
variant vowels (*ough, au, aw,* etc.)	through grade 2

As a result of phonics instruction, many young students can decode the vast majority of phonetically regular words they read. In the intermediate grades and beyond, the problem becomes how to decode irregular and multisyllabic words which appear increasingly in reading materials.

Structural Analysis

Structural analysis is a strategy used to figure out the meaning of multisyllabic words. Students are taught to "chunk" words; that is, break words into recognizable parts based on syllabication rules or meaningful word parts.

Syllabication rules Instruction and practice in syllabication rules helps students break words into smaller parts and then use phonics skills to pronounce the word. The following pages contain lessons devoted to teaching students these high-utility syllabication skills.

Rule 1: When there are two consonants between two vowels, divide between the two consonants, unless they are a blend or a digraph.

Rule 2: When there are three consonants between two vowels, divide between the blend or the digraph and the other consonant.

Rule 3: When there are two consonants between two vowels, divide between the two consonants between vowels unless they are a blend or a digraph. The first syllable is a closed syllable, and the vowel sound is short.

Rule 4: Do not split common vowel clusters, such as vowel digraphs, r-controlled vowels, and vowel diphthongs.

Rule 5: When you see a VCV pattern in the middle of a word, divide the word before or after the consonant. If you divide after the consonant, the first vowel sound is short. If you divide before the consonant, the vowel sound is long.

Rule 6: Always divide compound words between the individual words.

Rule 7: When a word includes an affix, divide between the base word and the affix (prefix or suffix).

When students use these syllabication rules to pronounce the word, they can match the word with a word already in their speaking vocabulary.

Meaningful word parts Another instructional strategy teaches students to look for meaningful word parts, beginning with the root or base word and moving on to prefixes and suffixes. Using knowledge of these parts, the reader assembles a meaning and attempts to match clues with words already in the speaking or receptive vocabulary. You can help your students use structural analysis by teaching the procedure outlined below.

Example Sentence and Procedure

His heart beat <u>thunderously</u>. There had been so many hope-filled moments before, all of them ending in bitter disappointment. (from *Zebra*)

1. Find the root or base word and recall its meaning. (thunder)

2. Find the prefix and/or suffix and recall its meaning(s). (ous, ly)

3. Use the knowledge clues to predict the word's meaning. (a sound like thunder)

4. Check predicted meaning against the rest of the sentence. (His heart beat sounded like thunder.)

5. Does the meaning make sense? (yes)

For additional suggestions on teaching structural analysis skills, see *The Language of Literature*.

Context Clues

Using context clues means using the knowledge provided by surrounding words and phrases to figure the meaning of words. Students are taught to look for clues such as restatements, examples, comparisons, contrasts, definitions, and general description. In addition to context clues, readers often use other decoding strategies.

You can help your students use context clues by teaching the procedure beneath the sample sentence.

Example Sentence and Procedure

In 1917 the United States entered World War I as an active <u>combatant</u>. Like many socially prominent women, Eleanor (Roosevelt) threw herself into the war effort.

1. Look at the surrounding context for a description of the word or other clues.

2. Look at the word and apply other decoding strategies as necessary.

3. Use these clues to predict the word's pronunciation and meaning.

4. Check the predicted meaning against the rest of the sentence.

5. Does the meaning make sense?

For additional suggestions on teaching context clues, see *The Language of Literature*.

Quick Diagnostic Test

Use the list below to determine how well your students read multisyllabic words. The lists are organized by syllabication rule. If your students are unable to read some or all of these words, teaching them high-utility syllabication rules may help improve their decoding skills. Use the lessons on the following pages to assist you.

(Rules 1, 3)	(Rule 5)
Picture	model
happen	robot
feather	crazy
follow	never
usher	final

(Rule 2)	(Rule 6)
angler	whirlwind
merchant	grasshopper
tumbler	grapevine
children	wastebasket
purchase	earring

(Rule 4)	(Rule 7)
party	readjustment
poison	rebound
feature	childish
royal	unavoidable
chowder	unselfish

Syllabication

LESSON 1: Consonant Blends and Digraphs in Multisyllabic Words

This lesson will help students chunk, or syllabicate, multisyllabic words that contain consonant blends and digraphs. Your students most likely recognize blends and digraphs when they see them in print; however, they may have problems decoding multisyllabic words if they attempt to syllabicate between the two letters in the blend or digraph. If you think your students would benefit from a review of blends and digraphs, begin with Parts 1 and 2. If not, you may go directly to Parts 3 and 4.

Part 1: Quick Review of Consonant Blends

Following are common consonant blends with examples of each. The two letters in each blend represent two sounds.

br	break, brand	sl	slick, slam
cr	crane, crack	-ld	field, hold
dr	drive, drip	-lk	milk
fr	free	-lp	help
gr	green	-lt	melt
pr	press	sc	scare
tr	true	sk	ski, risk
bl	blue	sm	smart
cl	clue, close	sn	snare, snack
fl	flame, flute	sp	spell, clasp
gl	glue, glide	st	state, twist
pl	please, plan	sw	switch, sway

DIRECT INSTRUCTION

To help your students focus on consonant blends, write the following sentences on the board.

1. <u>Brown</u> bears <u>slide</u> on the <u>frost</u>.
2. The <u>grand</u> <u>prize</u> was a <u>silk</u> <u>scarf</u>.
3. <u>Flutes</u> <u>fly</u> in <u>blue</u> <u>skies</u>.
4. <u>Sly</u> <u>smelt</u> <u>swim</u> in <u>swift</u> surf.

Ask a student to read aloud the first sentence. Call attention to the words *brown, slide,* and *frost.*

You could say: What two letters do you see at the beginning of *brown (br),* at the beginning of *slide (sl),* at the beginning and end of *frost (fr, st)*? These are called consonant blends. The consonant blends are made up of two consonant letters and stand for two sounds. You will always say both sounds when you sound out a word.

Follow the same procedure with the remaining sentences.

Answers: #2: grand (*gr*), prize (*pr*), silk (*lk*), scarf (*sc*); #3: Flutes (*fl*), fly (*fl*), blue (*bl*), skies (*sk*); #4: Sly (*sl*), smelt (*sm, -lt*), swim (*sw*), swift (*sw*)

Part 2: Quick Review of Consonant Digraphs

Following are consonant digraphs and examples of each. The two letters in each digraph represent one sound.

ch cheat, check, touch
sh shine, fish, push
th (voiced) that, the, this
th (voiceless) think, teeth, thumb, thank
wh (hw blend) where, whoops, when, white, wheel

DIRECT INSTRUCTION

Write these sentences on the chalkboard.

1. How <u>much</u> <u>fish</u> does a <u>whale</u> eat?
2. <u>She</u> will <u>think</u> <u>the</u> <u>thing</u> is <u>cheap</u>.
3. <u>When</u> will you <u>change</u> and <u>wash</u> <u>the</u> <u>sheets</u>?
4. Do <u>white</u> hens have <u>teeth</u>?

Ask a student to read aloud the first sentence.

You could say: What two letters do you see at the end of *much (ch),* at the end of *fish (sh),* at the beginning of *whale (wh)*? The consonant digraphs are made up of two consonant letters but represent only one sound. You will say only one sound when you sound out a word.

Follow the same procedure with the remaining sentences.

Answers: #2: She (*sh*), think (*th*), the (*th*), thing (*th*), cheap (*ch*); #3: When (*wh*), change (*ch*), wash (*-sh*), the (*the*), sheets (*sh*); #4: white (*wh*), teeth (*th*)

Part 3: Syllabication Strategy: Consonant Blends and Digraphs

In the following lesson, students will use their knowledge of consonant blends and digraphs to syllabicate words. You may find it helpful to review the most basic syllabication rule: *Each syllable has one and only one vowel sound.*

DIRECT INSTRUCTION

Write Rule 1 and the example words on the chalkboard. Remind students that V stands for vowel and C stands for consonant. Ask a student to give examples of vowel and consonant letters.

> **Rule 1: VCCV**
> **When there are two consonants between two vowels, divide between the two consonants, unless they are a blend or a digraph.**
>
> **picture   happen   abrupt   feather**

Have a student read Rule 1. Ask a student to explain the rule in his or her own words and then to read the first word.

You could say: Find the VCCV pattern in the word *picture* (*ictu*). Do you see a blend or digraph? (no) Where would you divide this word according to Rule 1? (between the *c* and the *t*) Look at each syllable. Pronounce the word. Do you recognize the word?

Repeat the process with the remaining words.

Answers: hap/pen; a/brupt, feath/er

Write Rule 2 and the example words on the chalkboard.

> **Rule 2: VCCCV**
> **When there are three consonants between two vowels, divide between the blend or the digraph and the other consonant.**
>
> **angler   merchant   tumbler   children**

Have a student read Rule 2. Ask a student to explain the rule in his or her own words and then to read the first word.

You could say: Find the VCCCV pattern in the word *angler.* (*angle*) Do you see a blend or digraph? (yes) Where would you divide this word according to Rule 2? (between the *n* and the *gl*) Look at each syllable. Pronounce the word. Do you recognize the word?

Repeat the process with the remaining words.

Answers: (mer/chant), (tum/bler), (chil/dren)

Part 4: Strategy Practice

Write the following words on the board. Have students divide the words according to the two rules, identify the rule, and pronounce the word.

Practice applying Rule 1

	Answers		Answers
scatter	scat/ter	whether	wheth/er
garden	gar/den	zipper	zip/per
crafty	craft/y	fashion	fash/ion
scarlet	scar/let	forget	for/get
traffic	traf/fic	respect	re/spect

Practice applying Rule 2

	Answers		Answers
hungry	hun/gry	toddler	tod/dler
concrete	con/crete	purchase	pur/chase
hundred	hun/dred	address	ad/dress
worship	wor/ship	supply	sup/ply
handsome	hand/some	employ	em/ploy

Cumulative practice

	Answers		Answers
written	writ/ten	nothing	noth/ing
constant	con/stant	lather	lath/er
secret	se/cret	sandal	san/dal
surplus	sur/plus	merchant	mer/chant
kindling	kin/dling	silver	sil/ver

LESSON 2: Short Vowels in Multisyllabic Words

When your students have trouble figuring out words unfamiliar in print, they are most likely having problems decoding the letters that stand for the vowel sound(s) in the word. Usually this is because the relationship between vowel sounds and letters that represent them isn't as predictable as the relationship between consonant sounds and the letters that represent them.

This lesson will help your students syllabicate words that contain short vowels. If you think your students would benefit from a review of short vowels, you may begin with Part 1. If not, you may skip directly to Parts 2 and 3.

Part 1: Quick Review of Short Vowels

Of the vowel sounds in English, the short vowels have the most predictable relationship between the sounds and the letters that represent them.

DIRECT INSTRUCTION

To help students focus on short vowels, write the list below on the board.

at	end	in	on	up
bat	bend	fin	odd	cup
and	vest	lick	mop	duck
fad	tell	drip	trot	lump

Have a student read the first column of words.

You could say: **What vowel sound do you hear in each of these words? (/a/ or short a) What letter represents that sound in each of these words? (the letter *a*)**

Follow the same procedure with the remaining lists.

Answers: column 2: /e/ or short e; column 3: /i/ or short i; column 4: /o/ or short o; column 5: /u/ or short u

Part 2: Syllabication Strategy: Short Vowels

Use the following syllabication strategy to help your students figure out some of the vowel sounds in multisyllabic words. You will note that Rule 3 expands upon Rule 1 introduced in Lesson 1.

DIRECT INSTRUCTION

Write Rule 3 and the example words on the board. Remind students that V stands for vowel and C stands for consonant.

> **Rule 3: VCCV**
> **When there are two consonants between two vowels, divide between the consonants, unless they are a blend or a digraph. The first syllable is a closed syllable, and the vowel sound is short.**
>
> **butter   lather   follow   usher**
> **summer   traffic   tender   invent**

Have a student read Rule 3 and explain the rule in his or her own words.

Have a student read the first word.

You could say: **Find the VCCV pattern in the first word. (*utte*) Do you see a blend or a digraph? (no) Where would you divide this word according to Rule 3? (between the two *t*'s) What vowel sound do you hear in the first syllable? (short) Look at each syllable and pronounce the word. Do you recognize the word?** Repeat this process with the remaining words.

Answers: but/ter, lath/er, fol/low, ush/er, sum/mer, traf/fic, ten/der, in/vent

Part 3: Strategy Practice

Write the following on the board. Have students divide the words according to the rule and pronounce the word.

	Answers		Answers
under	un/der	billow	bil/low
bother	both/er	enter	en/ter
bottom	bot/tom	number	num/ber
rather	rath/er	object	ob/ject
practice	prac/tice	dipper	dip/per
snapper	snap/per	silver	sil/ver
after	af/ter	grammar	gram/mar
cashew	cash/ew	sudden	sud/den
pulpit	pul/pit	vintage	vin/tage
pencil	pen/cil	member	mem/ber

LESSON 3: Vowel Clusters in Multisyllabic Words

This lesson will show students how to chunk, or syllabicate, multisyllabic words that contain vowel clusters: long vowel digraphs, r-controlled vowels, and vowel diphthongs. If your students aren't aware of vowel clusters, they might syllabicate between the two vowels in the cluster. In that case, they will syllabicate incorrectly and mispronounce the word when they attempt to sound it out. If you think your students would benefit from a review of vowel clusters, begin with Parts 1–3. If not, skip to Parts 4 and 5.

Part 1: Quick Review of Long Vowel Digraphs

In words with vowel digraphs, two vowel letters are represented by one vowel sound.

DIRECT INSTRUCTION

Write the list below on the board.

cream	play	boat
beast	gray	coal
bean	paint	goat
green	aim	row
peel	stain	slow

Have a student read the first column of words.

You could say: **What vowel sound do you hear in each of these words? (long e) What letters stand for the long e sound in *beast*? (*ea*) What letters stand for the long e sound in *green*? (*ee*) These are called vowel digraphs. Vowel digraphs are made up of two vowel letters that stand for one sound.**

Follow the same procedure with the remaining lists.

Answers: column 2: long a, *ay* in *gray*, *ai* in *paint*; column 3: long o, *oa* in *boat*, *ow* in *slow*

Part 2: Quick Review of R-controlled Vowels

In words with r-controlled vowels, the vowel sound is influenced by the *r* that follows it.

DIRECT INSTRUCTION

Write the list below on the board.

fern	car	born
dirt	star	cord
fur	arm	sort
her	yarn	more
birth	farm	horn

Have a student read the first column of words.

You could say: **These words all have the "er" sound. What letters stand for the "er" sound in *fur*? (ur) in *her*? (er) in *birth*? (ir) These are called r-controlled vowels. The r-controlled vowels are made up of a vowel and the letter r. In words with r-controlled vowels, the vowel sound is influenced by the *r* that follows it.**

Follow the same procedure with the remaining columns.

Answers: column 2: all words have the ar sound, letters are *ar;* column 3: all words have the or sound, letters are *or.*

Part 3: Quick Review of Vowel Diphthongs

DIRECT INSTRUCTION

To help students focus on vowel diphthongs write this list on the board.

oil	ouch
boil	cloud
boy	how
spoil	scout
toy	towel

Have a student read the first column of words.

You could say: **These words all have the oi sound. What letters stand for the oi sound in *boil*? (oi) in *boy*? (oy) These are called vowel diphthongs. Vowel diphthongs are made up of two vowel letters that stand for two vowel sounds.**

Follow the same procedure with the remaining column.

Answers: column 2: all words have the ow sound, letters are *ou* or *ow.*

Part 4: Syllabication Strategy: Vowel Clusters

Use the following syllabication strategy to help your students syllabicate words that contain vowel clusters.

DIRECT INSTRUCTION
Write Rule 4 and the example words on the board.

> **Rule 4:**
> **Do not split common vowel clusters, such as long vowel digraphs, r-controlled vowels, and vowel diphthongs.**
>
> **party   poison   feature   royal   chowder   garden**

Have a student read Rule 4. Have a student explain the rule in his or her own words.

Have a student read the first word.

You could say: Do you see a vowel cluster in this word? (yes) If you do, what is the cluster? (*ar*) Where would you avoid dividing this word according to Rule 4? (between the *a* and *r*) Where do you think you should divide the word? (after the cluster, between the *r* and *t*) Look at each syllable and pronounce the word. Do you recognize the word?

Repeat this process with the remaining words. In the case of *poison, feature,* and *royal,* students will be asked to syllabicate words for which they haven't learned all of the syllabication rules. Encourage them to try out what they know and attempt a pronunciation based on what they've learned so far.

Answers:

poison: (*oi*) avoid dividing between cluster; divide after the cluster

royal: (*oy*) avoid dividing between cluster; divide after the cluster

feature: (*ea*) avoid dividing between cluster; divide after the cluster

chowder: (*ow*) avoid dividing between cluster; divide after the cluster

garden: (*ar*) avoid dividing between cluster; divide after the cluster

Part 5: Strategy Practice

Write the following on the board. Have students divide the words according to the rules they know, and pronounce the word.

	Answers		Answers
carton	car/ton	peanut	pea/nut
powder	pow/der	council	coun/cil
circus	cir/cus	purpose	pur/pose
mountain	moun/tain	moisture	mois/ture
maintain	main/tain	voyage	voy/age
fertile	fer/tile	mayor	may/or
darling	dar/ling	freedom	free/dom
coward	cow/ard	tailor	tai/lor
hornet	hor/net	eager	ea/ger
barter	bar/ter	order	or/der

LESSON 4: Short and Long Vowels in Multisyllabic Words

This lesson will help your students develop flexibility in applying syllabication strategies as they attempt to decode multisyllabic words.

Part 1: Quick Review

If you have skipped over Lessons 1–3, you may want to preview this lesson to be sure your students are prepared for a more complicated syllabication strategy.

Part 2: Syllabication Strategy: Is the vowel sound long or short?

Use the following syllabication strategy to help your students decide whether a vowel letter stands for a long or short vowel sound.

DIRECT INSTRUCTION

Write Rule 5 and the example words on the board. Remind students that V stands for vowel and C stands for consonant.

Rule 5: VCV

When you see a VCV pattern in the middle of a word, divide the word either before or after the consonant. If you divide the word after the consonant, the first vowel sound will be short. If you divide the word before the consonant, the first vowel sound will be long.

   model   robot   crazy   never

Have a student read Rule 5 and explain the rule in his or her own words.

Ask a student to read the first word.

You could say: Find the VCV pattern in the first word. (*ode*) Where should you first divide the word? (after the *d,* the first consonant) What happens to the vowel sound in the first syllable? (The vowel sound is short) Say the word. Do you recognize it? (yes) When the consonant is part of the first syllable, the first syllable is called "closed."

Ask a student to read the second word.

You could say: Find the VCV pattern in the second word. (*obo*) Where should you first divide the word? (after the *b,* the first consonant) What happens to the vowel sound in the first syllable? (The vowel sound is short) Say the word. Do you recognize it? (no)

Try the second part of the rule. Where should you divide the word? (before the consonant) What happens to the vowel sound in the first syllable? (The vowel sound is long) Say the word. Do you recognize it? (yes) When the consonant is part of the second syllable, the first syllable is called "open."

Repeat this process with the remaining words.

Answers: crazy: (*azy*) Divide after the *z,* the first consonant; vowel is short; no, do not recognize the word. Divide before the *z;* the vowel is long; yes, recognize the word.

never: (*eve*) Divide after the *v;* vowel sound is short; yes, recognize the word.

Part 3: Strategy Practice

Write the following words on the board. Have students divide the words and pronounce the words.

	Answers		Answers
legal	le/gal	final	fi/nal
gravel	grav/el	prefix	pre/fix
basic	ba/sic	level	lev/el
driven	driv/en	moment	mo/ment
minus	mi/nus	paper	pa/per
panic	pan/ic	soda	so/da
spider	spi/der	devil	dev/il
honor	hon/or	tiny	ti/ny
seven	sev/en		

LESSON 5: Compound Words

When students encounter multisyllabic words, they often don't try the obvious; i.e., to look for words or word parts they already know within the longer word. Lessons 5 and 6 will help students develop these skills.

Part 1: Syllabication Strategy: Compound Words

Use the following syllabication strategy to help your students determine where to divide a compound word.

DIRECT INSTRUCTION

Write Rule 6 and the example words on the board.

> **Rule 6:**
>
> **Divide compound words between the individual words.**
>
> **grapevine   lifeguard   whirlwind
> butterfly   grasshopper**

Have a student read Rule 6. Ask a student to explain the rule in his or her own words.

You could say: **When you see a multisyllabic word, stop and see if it is made up of one or more words that you already know.**

Have a student read the first word.

You could say: **How many words do you see in the first word? (two) Where should you divide the word? (between *grape* and *vine*)**

Repeat the process with the remaining words in the first row.

Answers: (life/guard), (whirl/wind)

Have a student read the first word in the second row.

You could say: **How many words do you see in the word? (two) Where should you divide the word? (between *butter* and *fly*) Where else should you divide the word? (between the two *t*s) How do you know? (Rule 1 says to divide two consonants between vowels.)**

Repeat the process with the remaining words. (grass/hop/per)

Part 2: Strategy Practice

Write the following words on the board. Have students divide the words, identify the rule(s) they use, and pronounce the word.

	Answers		Answers
shipwreck	ship/wreck	buttermilk	but/ter/milk
postcard	post/card	notebook	note/book
screwdriver	screw/dri/ver	volleyball	vol/ley/ball
oatmeal	oat/meal	washcloth	wash/cloth
windmill	wind/mill	wastebasket	waste/bas/ket
dragonfly	dra/gon/fly	peppermint	pep/per/mint
pancake	pan/cake	hardware	hard/ware
earthquake	earth/quake	handlebar	han/dle/bar
pigtail	pig/tail	earring	ear/ring
wristwatch	wrist/watch	weekend	week/end

LESSON 6: Affixes

This lesson will give students help in dividing multisyllabic words that contain one or more affixes. These are the kinds of words that give students the most problems because they tend to be long and can look overwhelming. If you think your students would benefit from practice with identifying prefixes and suffixes, start with Parts 1 and 2. If not, go directly to Parts 3 and 4.

Part 1: Quick Review of Prefixes

Recognizing prefixes in multisyllabic words can help your students chunk words into manageable parts. You may use the following list of common prefixes and their meanings to expand upon the lesson described below.

auto-	self	by-	near, aside
mis-	bad	under-	below
pre-	before	un-	not
re-	again	de-	from, down
with-	back, away	dis-	opposite
bi-	two	uni-	one
on-	on	be-	make
tri-	three		

DIRECT INSTRUCTION

Write the following prefixes and their meanings on the board.

auto-	self	bi-	two	un-	not

You could say: **The word part on the left side of each pair is called a prefix. Prefixes can be added to root words or base words to change the meaning of the word. Think of a word that begins with this prefix.**

Write the word on the board.

Follow the same procedure with the remaining prefixes. If you wish, include additional prefixes. Save the words and use them for syllabication practice later.

Possible answers: *auto-* (autobiography); *bi-* (bicycle, bifold); *un-* (unhappy, unlikely)

Part 2: Quick Review of Suffixes

Recognizing suffixes in multisyllabic words can help your students chunk words into manageable parts. You may use the following list of common suffixes and their meanings to expand upon the lesson described below.

-ness	state or quality of	-less	without
-like	resembling	-ship	state or quality of
-ish	relating to	-ful	full of
-ways	manner	-er	one who
-ly	like, or resembling	-ous	full of
-ion	state or quality of	-ment	action or process

DIRECT INSTRUCTION

Write the following suffixes and their meanings on the board.

-ness	state or quality of	-ly	resembling
-ful	full of		

You could say: **The word part on the left side of each pair is called a suffix. When suffixes are added to root words or base words, they often change the part of speech of the root or base word. Think of a word that ends with this suffix.**

Write the word on the board.

Follow the same procedure with the remaining suffixes. If you wish, include additional suffixes. Save the words and use them for syllabication practice later.

Possible answers: *-ness* (happiness, sadness); *-ly* (quickly, lively); *-ful* (thankful, eventful)

Part 3: Syllabication Strategy: Affixes

Use the following syllabication strategy to help your students determine where to divide words that contain affixes.

DIRECT INSTRUCTION

Write Rule 7 and the examples on the board.

Rule 7:

When a word includes an affix, divide between the base word and the affix (prefix or suffix).

rebound	restless	unavoidable
preschool	childish	readjustment
disprove	joyous	unselfish

Ask a student to read Rule 7 and to explain the rule in his or her own words.

Have a student read the first word in column 1.

You could say: **What prefix do you see in *rebound*?** *(re)* **Where should you divide *rebound* according to Rule 7?** *(re/bound)* Continue with the remaining words in column 1. In each case, have students apply the rule, divide the word, pronounce the word, and then see if they recognize it.

Answers: pre/school; dis/prove

Have a student read the first word in column 2.

What suffix do you see in *restless*? *(less)* **Where should you divide *restless*?** *(rest/less)* Continue with the remaining words in column 2. In each case, have students apply the rule, divide the word, pronounce the word, and then see if they recognize it.

Answers: child/ish; joy/ous

Have a student read the first word in column 3.

What affixes do you see in this word? *(un, able)* **Where should you divide the word?** *(un/avoid/able)* Continue with the remaining words in column 3. In each case, have students apply the rule, divide the word, pronounce it, and then see if they recognize it. Note: In *avoid, a* is also considered a prefix, and *able* is considered a suffix. You can further divide the word as follows: un/a/void/a/ble.

Answers: re/adjust/ment and re/ad/just/ment; un/self/ish

If you wish to extend this lesson, have students analyze each word to see if they should apply additional syllabication rules.

Part 4: Strategy Practice

Write the following words on the board. Have students divide the words, identify the rule(s) they use, and pronounce the words.

	Answers
uniform	uni/form (or u/ni/form)
fairly	fair/ly
beautiful	beau/ti/ful
unlikely	un/like/ly
recall	re/call
misfit	mis/fit
rigorous	rigor/ous (or rig/or/ous)
hopelessness	hope/less/ness
childlike	child/like
unwind	un/wind
selfish	self/ish
opinion	opin/ion (and o/pin/ion)
hardship	hard/ship
sticker	stick/er
sideways	side/ways
department	de/part/ment
disbelieve	dis/believe (and dis/be/lieve)
withstand	with/stand
become	be/come
refreshment	re/fresh/ment

Comprehension
Mini-Lessons
with Graphic Organizers

1 For students who have trouble grasping the main idea of a paragraph or passage, discuss these points.

- The main idea is the most important idea a writer makes in a paragraph or passage.
- The writer may state the main idea in a sentence. This sentence can appear at the beginning, middle, or end of a paragraph or passage.
- The writer may not always state the main idea. Sometimes it is implied. The reader must then figure it out by thinking about the details and putting the main idea in his or her own words.

2 Duplicate the following paragraph. A master is provided on page 121. Have students follow along as you read it aloud, using it to model the stated main idea.

> **Astronauts once believed the moon was completely dry and barren, but recent discoveries have changed this view. Lunar probes have found frozen water in a deep crater near the moon's south pole. Scientists now believe the frozen water may have come from comets that struck the moon's surface.**

You could say: *Writers often put the main idea in the first sentence. "Astronauts once believed the moon was completely dry and barren, but recent discoveries have changed this view" seems like the main idea. The second sentence tells how lunar probes have found frozen water. The third sentence tells how scientists believe the frozen water came into the moon's surface. Both sentences are details that support the first sentence. It is, therefore, logical to conclude that the first sentence is the main idea.*

3 Duplicate the following paragraph. A master is provided on page 121. Have students follow along as you read it aloud, using it to model implied main idea.

> **Tomatoes originated in South America. Some time during the mid-1500s Spanish priests brought them to Europe. Today there are more than 4,000 varieties. China and the United States produce almost thirty percent of the world's supply of tomatoes.**

You could say: *Let's look at the first sentence. It tells me where tomatoes originated. The second sentence gives me another detail about tomatoes. The third and fourth sentences also give additional details about tomatoes. In this case, the writer chose not to state the main idea. I'll have to figure it out by looking at all the details and seeing how they relate to tomatoes. Each sentence gives a detail about tomatoes over time. Therefore, the implied main idea is a brief history of tomatoes.*

4 Duplicate the following paragraphs and read them aloud. A master is provided on page 122.

> **People did not always have the convenience of walking into a movie theater or renting a video to watch at home. In the late 1800s, traveling projectionists would bring films to country towns and small cities. They would set up their movie projectors in old, dusty halls and show silent films. By 1905, stores in major cities were converted into theaters by adding folding chairs and screens. These theaters became known as nickelodeon theaters because they charged 5 cents for a short, silent film.**
>
> **Exhibitors in these new locations looked for creative ways to make up for the lack of sound in film. For example, movie theaters often provided a pianist who would vary the music according to the action of the film. Lecturers would give their own commentary or describe the action. Sometimes off-screen actors would be hired to provide the dialogue.**

5 Duplicate and distribute the Main Idea Web on the next page. Have students work in pairs to fill in the webs with main ideas and details from both paragraphs. Correct responses are shown in the Answer Key on page 182.

Make additional copies of the Main Idea Web and have them available for students to use when necessary throughout the year.

Copyright © McDougal Littell Inc.

Name

Date

Detail:

Detail:

Main Idea:

Detail:

Detail:

Copyright © McDougal Littell Inc.

Main Idea

Astronauts once believed the moon was completely dry and barren, but recent discoveries have changed this view. Lunar probes have found frozen water in a deep crater near the moon's south pole. Scientists now believe the frozen water may have come from comets that struck the moon's surface.

Tomatoes originated in South America. Some time during the mid-1500s Spanish priests brought them to Europe. Today there are more than 4,000 varieties. China and the United States produce almost thirty percent of the world's supply of tomatoes.

Copyright © McDougal Littell Inc.

Main Idea

People did not always have the convenience of walking into a movie theater or renting a video to watch at home. In the late 1800s, traveling projectionists would bring films to country towns and small cities. They would set up their movie projectors in old, dusty halls and show silent films. By 1905, stores in major cities were converted into theaters by adding folding chairs and screens. These theaters became known as nickelodeon theaters because they charged 5 cents for a short, silent film.

Exhibitors in these new locations looked for creative ways to make up for the lack of sound in film. For example, movie theaters often provided a pianist who would vary the music according to the action of the film. Lecturers would give their own commentary or describe the action. Sometimes off-screen actors would be hired to provide the dialogue.

Copyright © McDougal Littell Inc.

1 Ask students if they have ever told a friend a story with events that weren't in the exact order in which they occurred. If details were out of order, the friend could ask questions to clarify the sequence. Explain that it is important to keep track of the sequence of events in order to understand the meaning of the story or how the plot moves forward, especially since the writer isn't available to answer questions. The following points will be useful to students who need more help.

- Sequence is the order in which events happen. Sequence refers to the chronological order in a story or piece of nonfiction. It may also refer to steps in a process or in following directions.

- Writers sometimes use words such as *first, next, after, before, then,* and *later* to connect ideas and indicate the order in which events occur.

- Words, phrases, or dates that tell when something is happening can also help readers figure out the sequence of events.

- The order of the events may not be the same as the order of the sentences in a paragraph or story. A paragraph or story may begin telling about an event that happens in the present. Other sentences may tell about events that happened in the past leading up to the present.

- When events are not clearly laid out, it may help the reader to visualize in his or her mind how the events happened.

2 Duplicate the following paragraph. A master is provided on page 125. Have students follow along as you read it aloud, using it to model **sequence.**

> **Once the screening process was complete, Michelle was ready to be a movie extra. On her first day of the filming, she reported to an abandoned school building at 6:30 A.M. After she registered and checked in at the wardrobe line, Michelle waited with her friends for several hours. Some chocolate donuts helped to pass the time. Finally, at 9:30 A.M. it was time to shoot the scene. By 1:30 P.M. Michelle was standing in line waiting to get paid after a long day's work.**

You could say: *The first sentence tells me that Michelle passed a screening process. The second and third sentences tell me what happened at the shooting. Sentences four and five provide additional details that are not part of the sequence. The last two sentences give me details about the rest of her day as an extra. So if I were to list the order of events, I would say that Michelle went to an abandoned school building to be an extra; then she registered and waited until it was time for her scene; next she shot her scene; and, finally, she got paid.*

3 Duplicate the following paragraph. A master copy is provided on page 125. Have students follow along as you read it aloud.

> **The night before her first day of school, Sarah had a nightmare. She got up late and was running behind schedule. Then, as she dashed out the door, she almost forgot her lunch. Sarah ran to catch the bus, but by the time she was within a few feet from it, the driver began to drive away. Suddenly, the bus stopped, so she ran towards it once again. As Sarah was approaching the bus, she tripped over her feet and fell to the ground. Finally, she boarded the bus—her face flushed red with embarrassment.**

4 Duplicate and distribute the Sequence/Flow Chart on the next page. Work with students to fill in the first event. Then have them complete the chart. Tell students to highlight any words or phrases that helped them determine the order of events. Ask volunteers to share how they mapped out the events of the paragraph. Possible responses are shown in the Answer Key on page 182.

5 Make additional copies of the chart on page 124 for use throughout the year.

Copyright © McDougal Littell Inc.

Name   **Date**

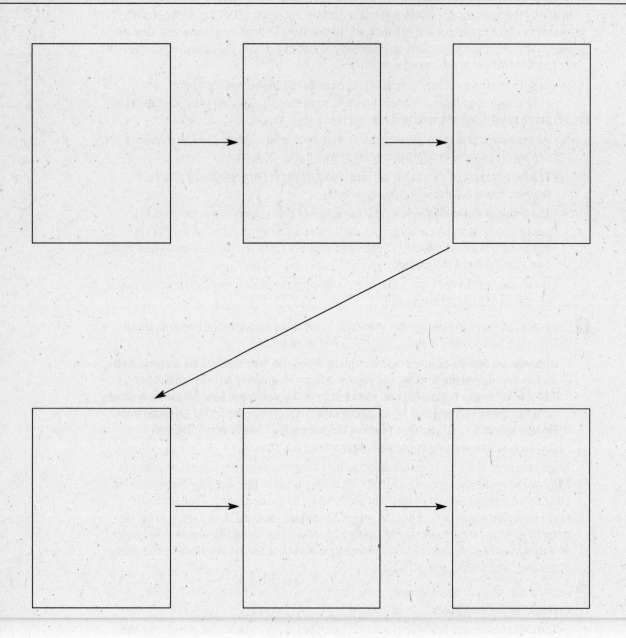

Copyright © McDougal Littell Inc.

Sequence

Once the screening process was complete, Michelle was ready to be a movie extra. On her first day of the filming, she reported to an abandoned school building at 6:30 A.M. After she registered and checked in at the wardrobe line, Michelle waited with her friends for several hours. Some chocolate donuts helped to pass the time. Finally, at 9:30 A.M. it was time to shoot the scene. By 1:30 P.M. Michelle was standing in line waiting to get paid after a long day's work.

The night before her first day of school, Sarah had a nightmare. She got up late and was running behind schedule. Then, as she dashed out the door, she almost forgot her lunch. Sarah ran to catch the bus, but by the time she was within a few feet from it, the driver began to drive away. Suddenly, the bus stopped, so she ran towards it once again. As Sarah was approaching the bus, she tripped over her feet and fell to the ground. Finally, she boarded the bus—her face flushed red with embarrassment.

Copyright © McDougal Littell Inc.

1 Write the following sentence on the board, and read it aloud.

> **The room was filled with smoke because Cristian burned the popcorn.**

Ask students which event caused the other event to happen *(burning the popcorn caused the room to fill with smoke)*. Introduce the concept of cause and effect by discussing the following points.

- A **cause** is an action or event that makes something else happen.
- An **effect** is what happens because of a certain action or event.

Explain that cause-and-effect relationships may contain one or more of these characteristics.

- Writers use clue words or phrases *(because, since,* and *as a result)* to indicate causes and effects. However, clue words alone do not automatically indicate a cause-effect relationship. One event must make another event happen.

- A single cause can result in more than one effect *(burning the popcorn caused the room to fill with smoke and the fire alarm to go off)*. Also, several causes can lead to a single effect *(Because we woke up late this morning and had car problems, we missed our flight.)*.

- Sometimes a series of events are linked in a cause-and-effect chain in which one event causes another, which in turn causes another, and so on. *(Because Pat didn't study, she failed the test. Because she failed the test, she was punished.)*

Watch out for events that happen in sequence. Just because one event follows another doesn't mean the first event caused the second one. *After they went shopping for groceries, it began to rain.* (It didn't start raining because they went grocery shopping.)

2 Duplicate the following paragraph or use the master on page 130. Ask students to follow along as you read it aloud, using it to model **cause-effect.**

> **Last December there was a blizzard. Because of the strong winds and heavy snow, many people got into car accidents. Others were forced to stay home. The airport canceled all its flights, and many people could not travel to their destinations.**

You could say: The second sentence has a signal word that may indicate a cause-effect relationship. *(Because* of the strong winds and heavy snow, many people got into car accidents.) *If you look at sentences three and four, it is logical to say that the blizzard also caused people to stay home and caused the airport to cancel all flights. These sentences show how one cause can result in more than one effect.*

Now look at the last sentence. It is an example of a cause-and-effect chain in which the first event (the blizzard) *caused the second event* (the cancellation of flights), *which in turn caused a third* (people could not travel to their destinations).

3 Write on the board these signal words: *because, so, since.* Duplicate the following paragraph or use the master on page 130. Have students follow as you read it aloud.

> **Last year, Anna's dad changed jobs and moved his family to another state. As a result, Anna left behind her old friends and began sixth grade at a new school. On the first day of classes, she nervously looked for a place to sit. She found an empty seat next to a girl with glasses. The girl smiled at Anna and began talking to her. Since then, the two girls have been best friends.**

4 Duplicate and distribute the Cause-and-Effect Chart on the next page. Work with students to fill in the first cause-and-effect relationship. Possible responses are shown in the Answer Key on page 183.

5 Make copies of the additional cause-and-effect charts on pages 128–129 and have them available for students to use at appropriate times throughout the year.

Copyright © McDougal Littell Inc.

Cause	→	Effect(s)

Copyright © McDougal Littell Inc.

Single Cause with Multiple Effects

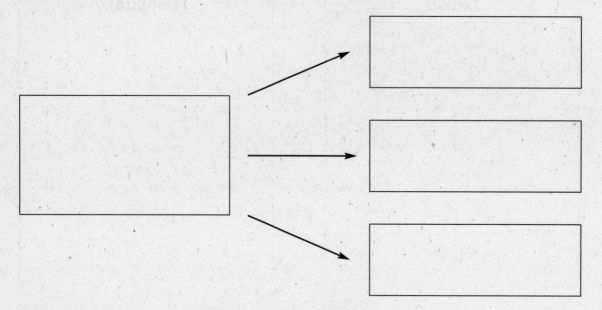

Multiple Causes with Single Effect

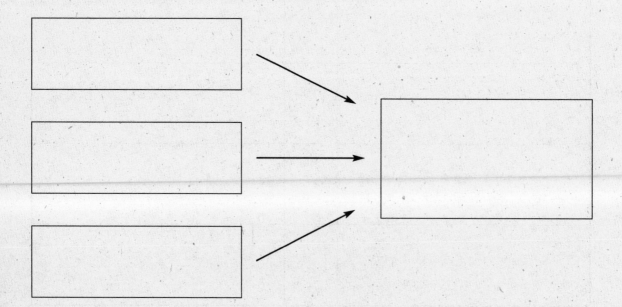

Copyright © McDougal Littell Inc.

Cause-and-Effect Chain

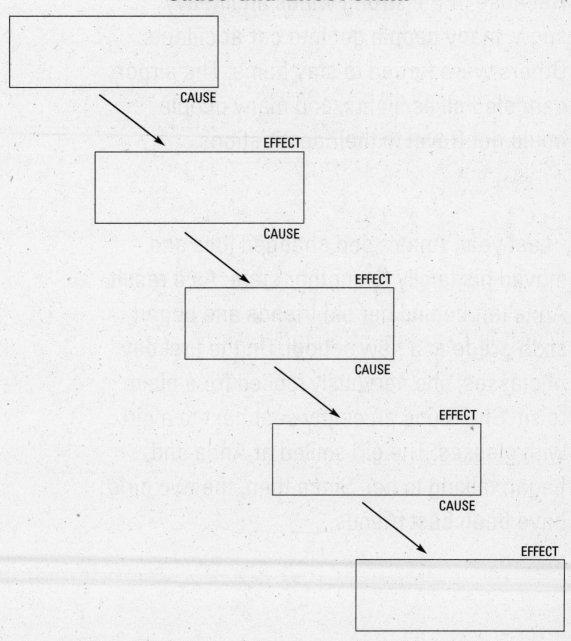

Copyright © McDougal Littell Inc.

Cause-and-Effect

Last December there was a blizzard. Because of the strong winds and heavy snow, many people got into car accidents. Others were forced to stay home. The airport canceled all its flights, and many people could not travel to their destinations.

Last year, Anna's dad changed jobs and moved his family to another state. As a result, Anna left behind her old friends and began sixth grade at a new school. On the first day of classes, she nervously looked for a place to sit. She found an empty seat next to a girl with glasses. The girl smiled at Anna and began talking to her. Since then, the two girls have been best friends.

Copyright © McDougal Littell Inc.

1 The following points will be helpful to students who have trouble understanding the terms *comparison* and *contrast.*

- **Comparing** means to think about the ways in which two or more people or two or more things are alike. *(Jen and Peter play soccer.)* Writers sometimes use words such as *both, same, alike, like, also, similarly,* and *too* to make comparisons. *(Jen and Peter both play soccer.)*

- **Contrasting** means to think about ways in which two or more people or two or more things are different. *(Penguins live only in cold climates. Pelicans can be found worldwide.)* Writers sometimes use words or phrases such as *unlike, but, although, instead, yet, even though, however,* and *on the other hand* to contrast two or more things. *(Penguins live only in cold climates unlike pelicans which can be found worldwide.)*

- Sometimes there are no signal words. Readers must figure out what the writer is comparing and contrasting from the details given.

2 Duplicate the following paragraph. A master is provided on page 133. Have students follow along as you read it aloud, using it to model **comparison and contrast.**

> **Sandra and Gaby are twins, though they are not identical twins. Both wear glasses and both are right-handed, but the similarities stop there. Gaby wears braces and has shoulder-length hair. Sandra, on the other hand, does not use braces and her hair is long.**

You could say: *The first sentence tells me that two people, Sandra and Gaby, are being compared. The second sentence contains the word* both, *which signals a way in which Sandra and Gaby are alike. The third sentence gives me more information about Gaby. The fact that the sentence is only about Gaby is a clue that the information presented about her may be different from information later presented about Sandra.*

The last sentence contains the phrase on the other hand, *which signals a difference between Sandra and Gaby. Therefore, Sandra and Gaby are alike in that they both wear glasses and are right-handed. The difference is that Gaby wears braces and has shoulder-length hair while Sandra does not wear braces and has long hair.*

3 For reference, write on the board the signal words and phrases listed in the second bulleted item. Then duplicate the following paragraph and read it aloud. A master is provided on page 133.

> **Baseball and softball are two popular sports. Baseball teams have nine players while softball teams, or what is known as slow-pitch softball, have ten players. Both games share similar equipment although there are a few differences in the size and make-up of the equipment. Many slow-pitch games use a 12-inch ball, while baseball players use a ball that measures from 9 to 9 1/4 inches. Softball bats may be made of wood, metal, plastic, or fiberglass. Baseball bats are usually made of ash wood. Batters may bunt and runners may steal bases in baseball, but slow-pitch rules prohibit bunting and base stealing.**

4 Duplicate and distribute the Venn diagram on the next page. Have students fill in the diagram, using information in the paragraph along with what they already know about softball and baseball to compare and contrast the two sports. Possible responses are shown in the Answer Key on page 183.

5 Have volunteers share the information in their diagrams by first describing the similarities between the two sports and then describing their differences.

6 Make additional copies of the diagram on page 132 and have it available for students to use at appropriate times during the year.

Copyright © McDougal Littell Inc.

Name _____ **Date** _____

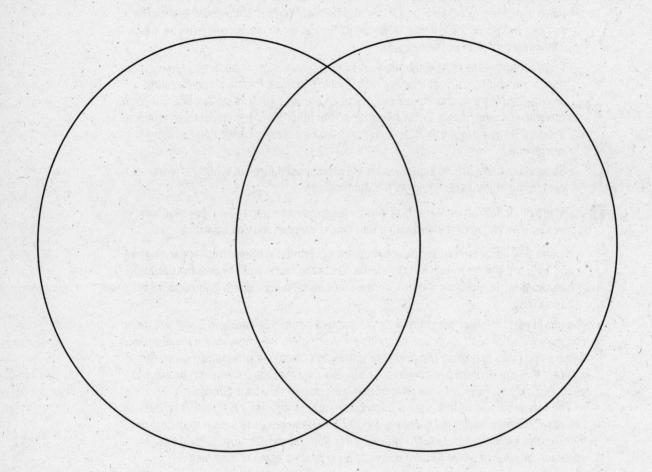

Copyright © McDougal Littell Inc.

Compare

Sandra and Gaby are twins, though they are not identical twins. Both wear glasses and both are right-handed, but the similarities stop there. Gaby wears braces and has shoulder-length hair. Sandra, on the other hand, does not use braces and her hair is long.

Contrast

Baseball and softball are two popular sports. Baseball teams have nine players while softball teams, or what is known as slow-pitch softball, have ten players. Both games share similar equipment although there are a few differences in the size and make-up of the equipment. Many slow-pitch games use a 12-inch ball, while baseball players use a ball that measures from 9 to 9 1/4 inches. Softball bats may be made of wood, metal, plastic, or fiberglass. Baseball bats are usually made of ash wood. Batters may bunt and runners may steal bases in baseball, but slow-pitch rules prohibit bunting and base stealing.

Copyright © McDougal Littell Inc.

1 Present students with the following situation:

The park where you play basketball after school is usually clean and tidy. Today, however, bits of paper and trash are everywhere and the garbage cans are overflowing. What inference can you make? (Students will most likely say that the park's sanitation workers did not clean the park.) For students who need more help making inferences, discuss the following points.

- It is not possible for writers to include every detail about what is happening in a work of literature.
- Often writers purposely choose to hint at details rather than state them; this can add meaning and suspense for the reader.
- Inferences are logical guesses based on clues in the text and on the reader's own knowledge and common sense.
- To make inferences, readers must: look for details that the writer provides about character, setting, and events; think about what they already know about a topic; and connect the story to their own personal experiences.

2 Duplicate the following paragraph. A master is provided on page 136. Ask students to follow along as you read it aloud, using it to model the skill **making inferences.**

> **Josh stood behind the curtain, twisting his hands. He tried to go over his lines but found he couldn't remember them. Peering from around the curtain, he watched with a sinking, uncomfortable feeling in his stomach as the audience filled the theater.**

You could say: In the first sentence, Josh is twisting his hands. Twisting the hands is a nervous gesture, so Josh is probably nervous about something. The second sentence tells me that he must be preparing to perform in a play. Actors in a play must memorize their lines. Josh is backstage but is having trouble remembering his lines. He seems to be getting more and more anxious. The third sentence tells me that the play is about to begin. People are filling the theater. Unfortunately, Josh's stage fright is beginning to affect him physically.

3 Duplicate the following passage. A master is provided on page 136. Have students follow along as you read it aloud.

> **While Josh waited in the wings, he saw Principal Sanchez on the other side of the stage. The principal was straightening his tie and getting ready to welcome the audience. Josh studied the crowd one last time before the curtain rose. The front row was filled with five smiling people, all with his same red hair and freckles. They applauded when the principal finished his remarks. Then, suddenly, Josh found himself moving onto the stage. He heard his lines spoken clearly and confidently. With a shock he realized that he was doing the speaking. The play had begun.**

4 Duplicate and distribute the Inference Chart on the next page. Work with students to fill in the first row. Then have them add to the chart any other inferences they make about the passage. Sample responses are shown in the Answer Key on page 183.

Copyright © McDougal Littell Inc.

Selection Information	+	My Opinion/ What I Know	=	My Inference/ My Judgment
	+		=	
	+		=	
	+		=	
	+		=	

Copyright © McDougal Littell Inc.

Josh stood behind the curtain, twisting his hands. He tried to go over his lines but found he couldn't remember them. Peering from around the curtain, he watched with a sinking, uncomfortable feeling in his stomach as the audience filled the theater.

While Josh waited in the wings, he saw Principal Sanchez on the other side of the stage. The principal was straightening his tie and getting ready to welcome the audience. Josh studied the crowd one last time before the curtain rose. The front row was filled with five smiling people, all with his same red hair and freckles. They applauded when the principal finished his remarks. Then, suddenly, Josh found himself moving onto the stage. He heard his lines spoken clearly and confidently. With a shock he realized that he was doing the speaking. The play had begun.

Copyright © McDougal Littell Inc.

1 To introduce the concept of predicting, ask students to make a guess about what the weather will be like in a few hours based on what they already know. Use the following points to explain how the strategy applies to reading a story.

- When you **predict,** you try to figure out what will happen next based upon what has already happened.

- To make a **prediction,** you must combine clues in a story plus your own knowledge and experience to make a reasonable guess.

- Good readers make and revise predictions about characters, setting, and plot as they read. Sometimes, they don't even realize they're doing it.

- Sometimes you must first make a guess or inference about what is happening before you can predict what will happen next. *(When the clouds parted, the sun began to beat down. Roberto started to sweat in his heavy coat.)* You might infer that Roberto didn't know that the weather would warm up so much. You could then use the inference to predict that he is about to take off his coat.

2 Duplicate the following paragraph. A master is provided on page 139. Have students follow along as you read it aloud, using it to model the skill of **predicting.**

> **Mr. Wong looked at his kitchen floor with satisfaction and then went to clean his bucket and mop.**

You could say: *The first sentence tells me that Mr. Wong is carrying a bucket and mop away from the kitchen. Since those items are usually used in cleaning, I think that Mr. Wong has just washed the floor. I'll read further to see if my prediction is right.*

> **Just then, Jane threw open the kitchen door, holding a large glass trophy.**

You could say: *The second sentence tells me that Jane has won a prize for something. Since I think the floor is wet, the floor is probably slippery. Jane should be careful when she steps inside. I'll read further to see if I'm on target.*

> **Shouting, "Dad, look what I won!" Jane ran into the house. Before she had taken two steps, however, she slipped and fell down hard on the wet kitchen floor.**

You could say: *My predictions were right. Based on what just happened to Jane, I can also predict that her trophy will break in the fall.*

3 Duplicate the following passage. A master is provided on page 139. Instruct students to follow along as you read it aloud. Afterwards, students should be ready to infer what has happened and to predict what will happen next.

> **"It's got to be here somewhere." Anna flung clothes and magazines in the air. After several minutes of intense effort, she found the key just where she left it—in the lock of her diary.**
>
> **Sighing with relief, Anna flung herself on her bed. Grabbing a pencil from the bedside table, she began to write excitedly in the diary. "I've got to write down what happened before I forget," she said to herself.**
>
> **Just then the phone in the kitchen rang. "It must be Jen!" exclaimed Anna. "I've got to tell her." Quickly locking the diary and placing it under her pillow, she ran downstairs to talk to her friend.**
>
> **As soon as she had disappeared, Anna's little brother came out of his hiding place in the hall. He had been watching his sister through the partly opened door. Now, on silent feet, the boy tiptoed silently toward the door to Anna's room.**

4 Duplicate and distribute the Predicting Chart on the next page. Have students work in pairs to complete the chart. Possible responses are shown in the Answer Key on page 184.

Copyright © McDougal Littell Inc.

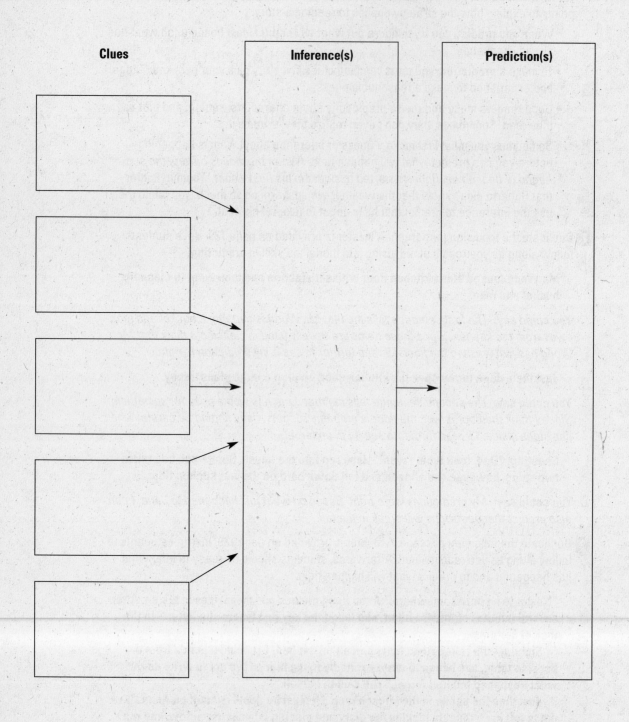

Clues

Inference(s)

Prediction(s)

Copyright © McDougal Littell Inc.

Mr. Wong looked at his kitchen floor with satisfaction and then went to clean his bucket and mop.

Just then, Jane threw open the kitchen door, holding a large glass trophy.

Shouting, "Dad, look what I won!" Jane ran into the house. Before she had taken two steps, however, she slipped and fell down hard on the wet kitchen floor.

"It's got to be here somewhere." Anna flung clothes and magazines in the air. After several minutes of intense effort, she found the key just where she left it—in the lock of her diary.

Sighing with relief, Anna flung herself on her bed. Grabbing a pencil from the bedside table, she began to write excitedly in the diary. "I've got to write down what happened before I forget," she said to herself.

Just then the phone in the kitchen rang. "It must be Jen!" exclaimed Anna. "I've got to tell her." Quickly locking the diary and placing it under her pillow, she ran downstairs to talk to her friend.

As soon as she had disappeared, Anna's little brother came out of his hiding place in the hall. He had been watching his sister through the partly opened door. Now, on silent feet, the boy tiptoed silently toward the door to Anna's room.

Copyright © McDougal Littell Inc.

1 Use examples from textbooks, newspapers, magazines, and pamphlets as you discuss the following points about distinguishing fact and opinion:

- A **fact** is a statement that can be proven through observation, experience, and research. A fact may include supporting evidence such as statistics or quotations from a recognized expert.

- An **opinion** is a statement that tells what a writer thinks, believes, or feels about a subject. It cannot be proven true or false.

- A writer may use words and phrases such as the following to signal an opinion: *according to, I think, in my opinion, perhaps, seem, ought to, should, bad, good, better, worse, excellent, terrible.* A writer may also use words that appeal to the reader's emotions.

- Sometimes a writer will use one or more facts to support an opinion.

- A single statement can contain both a fact and an opinion.

- A statement that you agree with is not necessarily a fact.

2 Duplicate the following paragraph. A master is provided on page 142. Have students follow along as you read it aloud, using it to model the skill of **distinguishing between fact and opinion.**

> **Living in a big city is the best experience a person can have. Big cities are fun. There is always something to do in a big city. Most big cities offer museums, art galleries, theater, comedy, sports, and/or concerts year-round.**

You could say: Actually, I agree with the point the writer is making, but I know that these statements may not be facts. First I look for numbers, statistics, or quotations from experts. If I don't find any, there's a good chance that the statements are the writer's opinion.

Next I look for words that might signal opinions. The first sentence contains the signal word best. The word best immediately signals an opinion. This statement can't be proven. The second sentence does not contain any signal words, and I don't think it can be proven. Some people may think that big cities are not fun. The third sentence is a bit tricky. It contains the signal word always, so immediately you have to ask if it can be proven. If not, then it is an opinion. The last sentence uses the signal word most. It states the fact that most, not all, big cities offer something year-round.

3 For reference, write on the board the signal words and phrases listed in the third bulleted item. Then duplicate the following paragraph and read it aloud. A master is provided on page 142.

> **In my opinion, dogs make better companions than cats. Besides being cute and playful animals, dogs can be trained to protect their owners. Cats, on the other hand, are lazy animals that run when strangers approach them. Dogs can be trained to provide special services. There are guide dogs specially trained to guide a blind person and hearing dogs trained to alert a person who can't hear.**

4 Duplicate and distribute the Two-Column Chart on the next page and ask students to use it to list the facts and opinions in the paragraph. Suggest that they highlight any signal words that helped them distinguish between the two types of statements.

5 Have volunteers share their completed charts, explaining why they listed each statement where they did. Correct responses are shown in the Answer Key on page 184.

6 Make additional copies of the chart on page 141 and have them available for students to use at appropriate times during the year.

Copyright © McDougal Littell Inc.

Name _____ **Date** _____

Copyright © McDougal Littell Inc.

Fact and Opinion

Living in a big city is the best experience a person can have. Big cities are fun. There is always something to do in a big city. Most big cities offer museums, art galleries, theater, comedy, sports, and/or concerts year-round.

In my opinion, dogs make better companions than cats. Besides being cute and playful animals, dogs can be trained to protect their owners. Cats, on the other hand, are lazy animals that run when strangers approach them. Dogs can be trained to provide special services. There are guide dogs specially trained to guide a blind person and hearing dogs trained to alert a person who can't hear.

Copyright © McDougal Littell Inc.

1 Duplicate the following passage and have students follow along as you read it aloud. A master is provided on page 145.

> The hot, dusty park was packed with thousands of people. They were all waiting for the sun to go down so the fireworks could start. Almost every patch of grass was covered with blankets, and the blankets were piled high with lawn chairs, coolers, radios, and people. Mai sat in the dirt, alone. Her ankle was swollen with pain.
>
> She had been chasing her little brother Peter through the park when she fell and twisted her ankle. By the time she looked up, Peter had run off into the crowd. She looked around for her parents, but she saw only strangers.
>
> "Mom? Dad?" she called out, but no one answered. The sky drew darker.

Ask students when and where this story takes place *(in a park in the evening, just before a fireworks display)*. Have them tell who the story is about *(Mai and her brother Peter)*. Ask them what the story problem is *(Mai is lost in a crowd with a hurt ankle. She can't find her family anywhere)*.

2 Discuss with students the following elements of a narrative:

- The **setting** is when and where a story takes place. It is important for two reasons. First, it helps the reader visualize the story where it occurs. Also, a setting creates a context for the events that take place.

- **Characters** are the people in a story. The main character is the person whom the story is mostly about. Characters in a story can also be animals or imaginary creatures.

- The **plot** is the series of events that happen in a story. Most stories have a problem, or **conflict,** that the main character must try to resolve. The **resolution** is the solution to the problem.

3 Continue the story at left by duplicating the following passage. A master is provided on page 146. Have students follow along as you read it aloud.

> Mai started to panic. Once it got dark, she'd never be able to find her family. She stood up and tried to walk a few steps.
>
> "Ah-ouch!" she muttered. She felt like crying, but not in front of all these people. Instead, she took a deep breath, hobbled a few more steps and looked around again. As it grew darker, she could see people waving around bright sparklers. Many children were wearing glowing rope necklaces. There were a few fireflies out, as well. Where on earth did Peter go?
>
> She knew that her parents' blanket wasn't too far from the lakefront, so she started to limp toward the lake. A single cannonball firecracker shot up into the sky. It was the warning! The fireworks were about to begin.
>
> Mai walked a little faster. It was getting pretty hard to see. A red flashlight bobbed in the distance. She remembered that Peter had brought a red flashlight with him. Could that be Peter? The red flashlight came toward her.
>
> "Mai! Mai, is that you?" Her little brother came running out of the darkness. "Mom and Dad are really worried."
>
> "Peter!" she cried. "I'm so glad it's you."
>
> "What happened to you, anyway?" he asked. "You disappeared."
>
> She noticed that her ankle didn't hurt quite so much any more. She could walk without limping. "Oh, nothing," she said. "I just lost track of you, that's all."

4 Duplicate and distribute the Story Map on page 144. Work with students to fill in the setting and characters. Then have them complete the plot portion of the map. Possible responses are shown in the Answer Key on page 184.

5 Make additional copies of the Story Map for use at appropriate times during the year.

Copyright © McDougal Littell Inc.

Setting	Characters

Plot

Problem:

Events:

1

2

3

4

Resolution:

Copyright © McDougal Littell Inc.

Narrative Elements

The hot, dusty park was packed with thousands of people. They were all waiting for the sun to go down so the fireworks could start. Almost every patch of grass was covered with blankets, and the blankets were piled high with lawn chairs, coolers, radios, and people. Mai sat in the dirt, alone. Her ankle was swollen with pain.

She had been chasing her little brother Peter through the park when she fell and twisted her ankle. By the time she looked up, Peter had run off into the crowd. She looked around for her parents, but she saw only strangers.

"Mom? Dad?" she called out, but no one answered. The sky grew darker.

Copyright © McDougal Littell Inc.

Narrative Elements

Mai started to panic. Once it got dark, she'd never be able to find her family. She stood up and tried to walk a few steps.

"Ah-ouch!" she muttered. She felt like crying, but not in front of all these people. Instead, she took a deep breath, hobbled a few more steps and looked around again. As it grew darker, she could see people waving around bright sparklers. Many children were wearing glowing rope necklaces. There were a few fireflies out, as well. Where on earth did Peter go?

She knew that her parents' blanket wasn't too far from the lakefront, so she started to limp toward the lake. A single cannonball firecracker shot up into the sky. It was the warning! The fireworks were about to begin.

Mai walked a little faster. It was getting pretty hard to see. A red flashlight bobbed in the distance. She remembered that Peter had brought a red flashlight with him. Could that be Peter? The red flashlight came toward her.

"Mai! Mai, is that you?" Her little brother came running out of the darkness. "Mom and Dad are really worried."

"Peter!" she cried. "I'm so glad it's you."

"What happened to you, anyway?" he asked. "You disappeared."

She noticed that her ankle didn't hurt quite so much any more. She could walk without limping. "Oh, nothing," she said. "I just lost track of you, that's all."

Copyright © McDougal Littell Inc.

Additional Graphic Organizers

On the following pages you will find additional graphic organizers that can be used in a number of different situations to help students comprehend and monitor what they read. Consult the chart below to decide how and when to use each graphic organizer.

Graphic Organizer	Purpose	When and How to Use
K-W-L Chart (page 88)	To help students comprehend a nonfiction selection	*Before Reading:* 1. Identify the topic for students. 2. Have students write what they already **know** about it in the *K* column. 3. Have them write what they **want** to find out in the *W* column. *During Reading:* 4. Have students record what they **learn** in the *L* column.
Q & A Notetaking Chart (page 89)	To help student memorize key facts in a nonfiction selection	*During Reading:* 1. Tell students that as they read they should turn each heading or main idea into a question and write it in column 1. *After Reading:* 2. Have students answer the questions they wrote without opening their books. 3. Have students reread the selection to find answers to any questions they could not answer.
Concept Web (page 90)	To guide students to think of related words or concepts	*Before Reading:* Have students form small groups. List key concepts or vocabulary words on the board. Ask students to discuss meanings, fill out a web for each concept or word by writing it in the center of the web, and then writing related terms in the ovals around the center.
Reflection Chart (page 91)	To help students stop and think about key points or events	*During Reading:* 1. Ask students to note important or interesting passages in the left column. 2. Have them record in the right column their thoughts about each passage noted.
Event Log (page 92)	To help students keep track of story events	*During Reading:* 1. Have students list each event as they read about it. *After Reading:* 2. Students should use the list to give an oral retelling or summary of the selection.

Graphic Organizer	Purpose	When and How to Use
Story Frames (page 93)	To help students summarize story events	*After Reading:* 1. Ask students to draw sketches of key events in the selection. 2. Have them use the sketches to retell the selection orally.
Plot Diagram (page 94)	To help students classify events as being part of the exposition, rising action, climax, or falling action	*After Reading:* 1. Review the terms *exposition, rising action, climax,* and *falling action* with students. 2. Encourage students to use the diagram to list the events that form each of these plot phases.
Character Profile Chart (page 95)	To help students identify character attributes	*During or After Reading:* Have students write the character's name at the center and then list qualities and behaviors that exemplify these qualities in the surrounding boxes.
New Word Diagram (page 96)	To help students understand new vocabulary they encounter	*During or After Reading:* 1. Have students write a new word in the box at the top of the diagram. 2. Encourage them to think of—or look in the dictionary for—synonyms and antonyms of the word and record them in the appropriate boxes. 3. Ask students to think of real people or characters they've read about who they associate with the concept of the word. They can then add the names to the diagram.
Reading Log (page 97)	To encourage students to keep track of what they read	*After Reading:* Have students record on this form each selection they read during the year. Review the form periodically with students.

Topic: _____

K What I Know	W What I Want to Find Out	L What I Learn

Copyright © McDougal Littell Inc.

Turn the Heading or Main Idea of Each Passage into a Question	Write a Detailed Answer Here
1.	
2.	
3.	
4.	
5.	
6.	
7.	

Copyright © McDougal Littell Inc.

Copyright © McDougal Littell Inc.

Quotation or Paraphrase from Text (include page number)	Thoughts About It

Copyright © McDougal Littell Inc.

Event 1
Event 2
Event 3
Event 4
Event 5
Event 6
Event 7
Event 8
Event 9
Event 10

Copyright © McDougal Littell Inc.

Copyright © McDougal Littell Inc.

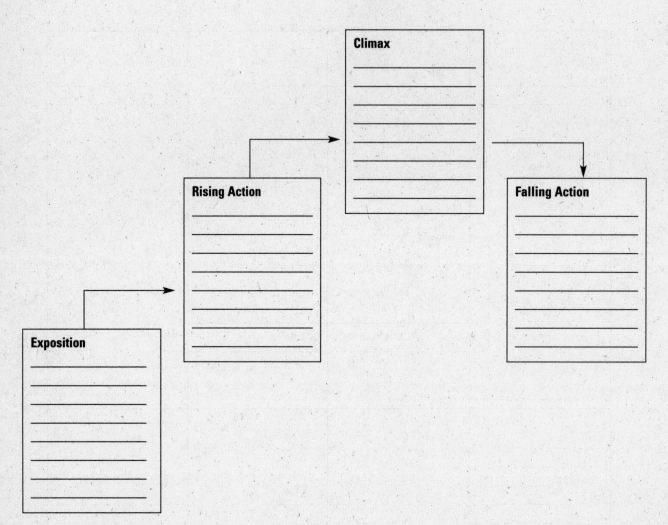

Copyright © McDougal Littell Inc.

Quality: _____
Example: _____
_____
_____
_____

Quality: _____
Example: _____
_____
_____
_____

Quality: _____
Example: _____
_____
_____
_____

_____
Character's Name

Quality: _____
Example: _____
_____
_____
_____

Quality: _____
Example: _____
_____
_____
_____

Quality: _____
Example: _____
_____
_____
_____

Copyright © McDougal Littell Inc.

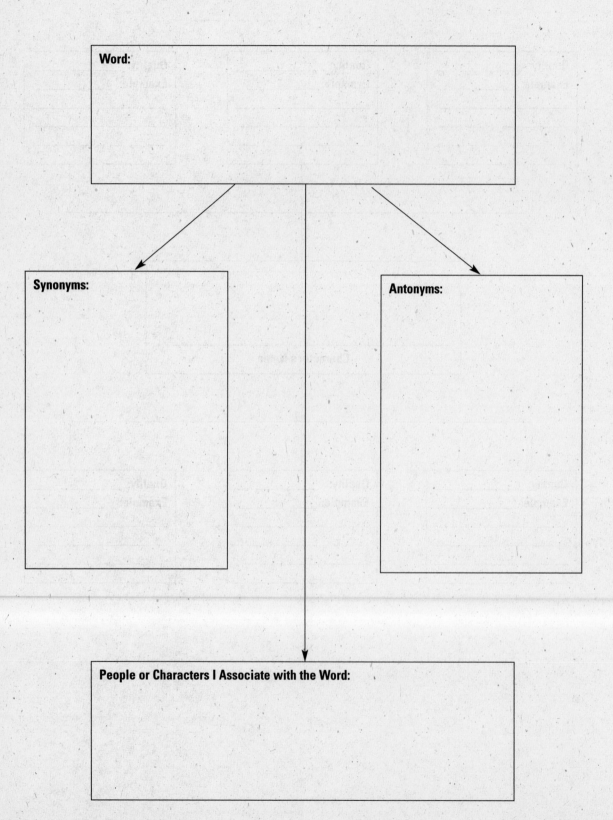

Word:

Synonyms:

Antonyms:

People or Characters I Associate with the Word:

Copyright © McDougal Littell Inc.

Name   **Date**

Selection Title	Type of Literature	Date Finished	Reactions

Copyright © McDougal Littell Inc.

Answer Key

This key answers all questions asked in *The InterActive Reader Plus, The InterActive Reader Plus with Additional Support,* and *The InterActive Reader Plus for English Learners.* Pause & Reflect answers have parenthetical notes (Plus, AS, or EL) as necessary to indicate the books to which they apply.

Eleven, page 2
Connect to Your Life, page 2
Typical answers will include presents, birthday party, starting middle school, feeling more grown-up.
Key to the Story, page 2
Possible response: Don't be sad. Sometimes it takes time before you feel like your new age.
Pause & Reflect, page 4 (Plus)
1. On your birthday you are still all the ages that you were before.
2. Possible response: Yes, because you don't instantly feel older on your birthday; it takes time.
Pause & Reflect, page 4 (AS and EL)
Possible response: Yes, because you don't instantly feel older on your birthday; it takes time.
Pause & Reflect, page 5
1. Students should circle "if I was one hundred and two I'd have known what to say when Mrs. Price put the red sweater on my desk" (lines 37–39).
2. plastic buttons, ugly, stretched out
Reading Check, page 6
Possible response: Rachel's teacher becomes angry because Rachel has shoved the red sweater to the corner of her desk.
Mark It Up, page 7
Students might circle the following details: "crying"; "bury my face in my stupid clown-sweater arms"; "face all hot and spit coming out of my mouth"; "little animal noises"; "body shaking."
Reading Check, page 7
Possible response: She means that her birthday, which should have been a happy, special day, has been ruined by her upsetting day at school.
Pause & Reflect, page 8
1. Possible response: Rachel is embarrassed because she thinks she is acting like a baby. On her eleventh birthday she should be acting more maturely.
2. Possible response: Yes, because it is very upsetting not to be able to stop yourself from crying in front of people.
Challenge, page 8
Students may star the following similes: "the way you grow old is kind of like an onion or like the rings inside a tree trunk" (lines 22–23); "or like my little wooden dolls" (lines 23–24); "eleven years rattling inside me like pennies in a tin Band-Aid box" (lines 33–35); "sitting there like a big red mountain" (lines 80–81); "it's hanging all over the edge like a waterfall" (line 93); "far away like a runaway balloon" (lines 134–135). Possible response: The similes help you understand Rachel's feelings by comparing them to things in the real world of an eleven-year-old that you can picture in your mind.

Active Reading SkillBuilder, page 9
Possible responses:
Rachel's Birthday: realizes that even though she is a new age, she still has the old ages inside her; wishes she was older when the teacher puts the sweater on her desk; feels young in front of the teacher; forces herself to think of the birthday celebration she will have at home; cries in front of the class, which makes her feel like a three-year-old and not her new age; instead of having a happy, special day in school, she was upset
My Memories: hoping for a special day when I would feel different; wanting to feel older, more mature; realizing that one day doesn't make you different from the day before; getting excited about my birthday party later that day
1. Rachel thought she would feel different when she woke up on the morning of her eleventh birthday, but she learns that one day doesn't change her. She realizes that even though she is a new age, she still has the old ages inside her.
2. Yes, because I remember waking up on my birthday thinking that I could suddenly change, now that I was older.
3. I always wanted to be older on my birthday because I have always been the youngest person in my class. I wanted to be the first person to turn a new age.

Literary Analysis SkillBuilder, page 10
(Possible responses are provided.)
Rachel
Trait: sensitive
Evidence: acts embarrassed at being singled out; cries after she is forced to put the sweater on
Trait: inarticulate
Evidence: can't find the words to explain convincingly to Mrs. Price that the sweater is not hers
Trait: respectful
Evidence: doesn't feel that it is her place to argue with a teacher
Mrs. Price
Trait: insensitive
Evidence: doesn't notice or care that Rachel is upset; doesn't apologize for her mistake
Trait: authoritarian
Evidence: demands that Rachel put on the sweater, not just keep it on her desk
Trait: persistent
Evidence: refuses to let the issue go

Words to Know SkillBuilder, page 11
A.		B.	
1. invisible		1. synonym	
2. except		2. antonym	
3. expect		3. antonym	
4. sudden		4. synonym	

C. Accept responses that accurately use all the Words to Know.

Matthew Henson at the Top of the World, page 12

Connect to Your Life, page 12

Possible responses: (Important Items) sleds, blankets, insulated boots, food; (Extras) candy, family photos

Pause & Reflect, page 15 (Plus)

1. to take a job with the government
2. brave, popular, respected, hardy

Pause & Reflect, page 15 (AS and EL)

to take a job with the government

Reader's Success Strategy, page 16

Students may list the following events: born on August 8, 1866; moved to Washington D.C.; his mother died; his father could no longer care for him; sent to live with his uncle; alone, homeless, and penniless at age thirteen because his uncle could no longer support him and his father had recently died; worked as a dishwasher in a small restaurant and slept in a cot in the kitchen; became a cabin boy on the *Katie Hines*; Captain Childs took a fatherly interest in Mathew; Captain Childs died; Mathew left the *Katie Hines* at Baltimore and found a place aboard a fishing schooner bound for Newfoundland; left the ship as soon as he was able and made his way back to Washington D.C.; found a job as a stock clerk at B. H. Steinmetz and Sons; Steinmetz recommended him for a job with Lieutenant Peary; Peary offered him a job as his personal servant; traveled to Nicaragua with Peary; went on five expeditions to Arctic regions with Peary; reached the North Pole on the final expedition; worked as a parking-garage attendant in Brooklyn; became a clerk in the U.S. customshouse in lower Manhattan; invited to join the Explorers Club in New York; Congress authorized a medal for all the men on the North Pole expedition.

Reading Check, page 16

Possible responses: Captain Childs took a fatherly interest in him; the captain saw to Matthew's education; he read widely in geography, history, mathematics, and literature.

Pause & Reflect, page 17 (Plus)

1. Possible responses: poverty, the deaths of his mother and father, loneliness, or hard work
2. He wanted adventure and enjoyed listening to sailors' stories.
3. He found work on another ship but was treated very badly by the crew.

Pause & Reflect, page 17 (AS and EL)

1. He wanted adventure and enjoyed listening to sailors' stories.
2. He found work on another ship but was treated very badly by the crew.

Reread, page 18

Possible response: They are both adventurous, brave, and hardworking.

Pause & Reflect, page 19 (Plus and AS)

1. (opportunity 1) a survey trip to Nicaragua; (opportunity 2) joining an expedition to the Arctic regions
2. Possible responses: (Henson) adventurous, persistent, hardworking; (Peary) ambitious, educated, respected

Pause & Reflect, page 19 (EL)

(opportunity 1) a survey trip to Nicaragua; (opportunity 2) joining an expedition to the Arctic regions

Reading Check, page 21

exhaustion and frostbite

Pause & Reflect, page 21

1. repairing the sleds, hunting with the Eskimos, handling the dogs
2. Some students may say yes, because Peary was resourceful and would probably have reached his goal somehow. Others may say no, because Henson's strength and skills made him the best explorer on the team.

Read Aloud, page 22

Possible response: I would feel exhausted. I would want the journey to end so I could have a long, long rest.

Pause & Reflect, page 24 (Plus and AS)

1. Peary had decided that he couldn't get along without Henson.
2. Possible response: After taking his readings and calculating that he was about three miles from the Pole, he traveled ten miles north and then realized he was traveling south. Students should circle details in lines 263–271.

Pause & Reflect, page 24 (EL)

Peary had decided that he couldn't get along without Henson.

Reader's Success Strategy, page 25

Possible response: (Before) Peary said that he couldn't get along without Henson; Peary had Henson plant the American flag at the North Pole; (After) Peary didn't speak to Henson on the return trip; Peary ordered Henson to get to work; Peary remained silent and withdrawn after arriving in New York

Reading Check, page 25

Possible response: because Peary became withdrawn and silent

Pause & Reflect, page 26 (Plus and AS)

1. worked different jobs, honored by the state of Maryland after his death
2. Possible responses: Henson's courage, determination, patriotism, dignity, skill

Pause & Reflect, page 26 (EL)

worked different jobs, honored by the state of Maryland after his death

Challenge, page 26

Most students will say no, Peary treated Henson unfairly. He could have paid tribute to Henson and should have acknowledged Henson's significant role in the expedition. Some may say yes, Peary gave Henson many opportunities and treated him more respectfully than he did the other crew members. Lack of recognition came from other authorities, not from Peary.

Active Reading SkillBuilder, page 27

(Possible responses are provided.)

Main Idea: Matthew Henson wanted adventure.

Details: Schoolbooks taught him to want more. So did the sailors who came to the restaurant and told stories. He left to go to Baltimore and find a ship.

Main Idea: Peary realized how valuable Henson was on the trip to Greenland.

Details: Henson established good relations with Eskimos. He handled dogs and equipment well. He hunted and cooked.

Main Idea: Henson was not recognized for his contribution for many years.

Details: He worked in a variety of unrelated jobs. His friends tried to get his work recognized. In 1937 he was invited to join the Explorers Club. In 1944 he received a medal from Congress.

Literary Analysis SkillBuilder, page 28

(Possible responses are provided.)

Period: working as a dishwasher; **Descriptive Words and Phrases:** "spun tales"; "strange and wonderful places"; "wide-eyed"; "adventures and dangers" (lines 65–69)

Period: headed for the Pole; **Descriptive Words and Phrases:** "mystical point" (line 186); ship "in a most perfect state of dirtiness" (lines 198–199); "trouble seemed to plague them" (lines 210–211); "killing work" (line 249); "grueling journey" (line 256)

Follow Up: Students' responses should range from short and dry to lengthy and colorful.

Words to Know SkillBuilder, page 29

A.
1. resentful
2. stamina
3. tyranny
4. surveyor
5. proposition
6. ardent
7. menial
8. deprivation
9. apt
10. validate

B. Students' letters should accurately use at least five Words to Know.

Summer of Fire, page 30

Connect to Your Life, page 30

(Possible responses are provided.)

Know: Wilderness fires can be started by people.

Want to Learn: How people fight wilderness fires

Learned: Wildfires do not necessarily damage the wilderness; sometimes they renew life there.

Pause & Reflect, page 33 (Plus)

1. dry farmland, lightning fires
2. Students should circle the following: "Park policy was to let wildfires burn unless they threatened lives or property" (lines 36–37); "The summer of 1988 was expected to be wet too" (lines 40–41).

Pause & Reflect, page 33 (AS and EL)

Students should circle the following: "Park policy was to let wildfires burn unless they threatened lives or property" (lines 36–37); "The summer of 1988 was expected to be wet too" (lines 40–41).

Reread, page 34 (Plus)

Possible response: Old Faithful was close to one of the major fires. It was surrounded by wooden buildings. The Old Faithful Inn is made of logs.

Reread, page 34 (AS and EL)

Students may say that the use of personification helps bring to mind images of a wild, raging fire.

Reading Check, page 34

information centers and buildings where people slept, ate, and shopped

Pause & Reflect, page 35 (Plus)

1. 5, 2*, 1, 3*, 4 (*These items may appear reversed as their order is difficult to note.)
2. Possible details include: "flames galloped" (line 62); "Roman candles" (line 64); "the sun was no brighter than a full moon" (line 68); "glowing embers" (line 70); "churning wall of dark smoke" (lines 98–99)

Pause & Reflect, page 35 (AS and EL)

5, 2*, 1, 3*, 4 (*These items may appear reversed as their order is difficult to note.)

Reading Check, page 35

Rain drenched the area around Old Faithful.

Pause & Reflect, page 36

1. Rain drenched the area around Old Faithful. Then snow arrived in West Yellowstone.
2. Possible responses: Although the fires were destructive to the wilderness, they also ushered in a new beginning for much of the region. Wildfire has always played its part in shaping the landscape of the wilderness.

Challenge, page 36

Possible responses: Educate people on the dangers of wildfires; douse discarded cigarettes; never underestimate the power and speed of wildfires.

Active Reading SkillBuilder, page 37

(Possible responses are provided.)

Box 1: May 24—fire season started when lightning struck a tree in northeastern part of the park

Box 2: later in the day—rain fell and extinguished fires

Box 3: June 23—fire near Shoshone started by lightning

Box 4: June 25—bolt of lightning kindled fire in northwest of park

Box 5: by mid-July—8,600 acres burned

Box 6: August 20—150,000 acres burned in park and neighboring forest

Box 7: by September 6—fire fighters defended Old Faithful

Box 8: by the afternoon of September 7—one of eight fires moved toward Old Faithful

Box 9: at the last moment—wind shifted fire to northeast and away from Old Faithful

Box 10: by early afternoon September 10—rain fell

Box 11: the next morning—snow fell

Box 12: until November—small fires burned

Literary Analysis SkillBuilder, page 38

(Possible responses are provided.)

1. mid-July—8,600 acres have burned and fire fighters are brought in
2. July 22—North Fork fire starts
3. August 15—North Fork fire reaches Madison
4. August 20—150,000 acres have burned in park and neighboring forests
5. September 6—fire fighters move in to defend Old Faithful
6. September 7—North Fork fire approaches Old Faithful

7. September 10—North Fork fire threatens park headquarters but rain falls

8. September 11—snow falls

9. November—snow and rain extinguish last of fires

Follow Up: Chronological order emphasizes the severity and duration of the fires and shows the powerlessness of humans in the face of this force of nature. The impression given is that without the snow and rain, the fires would still be raging. Spatial order is used effectively in some sections of the text to show the positions of various fires. Without the accompanying chronological order, however, spatial order would focus attention on individual areas of destruction, which would weaken the overall impression of the severity of the fires. The progress of the fire would be less clear to the reader. Cause and effect would place more emphasis on the reasons for the fires, which in most cases were caused by lightning.

Words to Know SkillBuilder, page 39

A. **1.** b   **B.** **1.** withering

2. a   **2.** tinder

3. a   **3.** geyser

4. c   **4.** oxygen

5. b

C. Students' reports should accurately use at least four Words to Know.

Ghost of the Lagoon, page 40

Connect to Your Life, page 40

Possible response:

Person: my grandmother; **Courageous Actions:** left her country to come to the United States; **Why:** She wanted her children to have a better life.

Key to the Story, page 40

Possible response: 2. scary; It was scary to feel the waves rock the ship. 3. warning; When the sky gets dark, sailors take it as a warning.

Pause & Reflect, page 42

1. Possible response: Mako is clever, resourceful, and loves the water.

2. Possible response: Yes, because it sounds pretty and warm, and it would be nice to be able to spend all day by the water. Students might underline the following: "like a castle" (lines 8–9), "Waterfalls trail down the faces of the cliffs" (lines 9–10), "waking hours were spent in the waters of the lagoon" (lines 13–14).

Reader's Success Strategy or **Reading Tip,** page 44

Possible responses: 1. Tupa destroys a canoe and three fishermen vanish; 2. Grandfather tells stories about Tupa; 3. Mako learns that his father was one of the three fishermen in the canoe destroyed by Tupa.

Reading Check, page 44 (AS)

Possible response: because Grandfather believes "there is evil in his very name"

Reading Check, page 44 (EL)

Mako learns that his father was one of the three fishermen in the canoe destroyed by Tupa.

Pause & Reflect, page 45 (Plus)

1. He attacks children.

2. Underline lines 87–88: "Your father," he explained gently, "was one of the three fishermen in the canoe that Tupa destroyed."

Pause & Reflect, page 45 (AS and EL)

He attacks children.

Pause & Reflect, page 47 (Plus)

1. Possible details to star: "coral gardens, forty feet below him" (line 138); "A school of fish swept by like silver arrows" (line 141); "ruby eyes" (line 142).

2. Possible response: Yes, because Mako seems brave and determined.

3. coral reef

Pause & Reflect, page 47 (AS and EL)

1. Possible response: Yes, because Mako seems brave and determined.

2. coral reef

Mark It Up, page 48

Possible details: "dense and green," "ferns," "green roof," "flock of parakeets," "a wild pig"

Reader's Success Strategy or **Reading Tip,** page 48

Possible responses: 4. Mako vows to kill Tupa; 5. Mako and Afa go on an expedition to the coral gardens; 6. Mako practices killing Tupa by spearing a coral reef.

Pause & Reflect, page 49

1. 1, 4, 3, 2

2. Possible response: Mako loves Afa. He believes no boy has ever had a finer companion.

Pause & Reflect, page 50 (Plus and AS)

1. Students' pictures should include a shark with eyes and gill slits.

2. Most students will predict: Yes, because Mako has practiced killing the shark and his love for Afa will give him courage.

Pause & Reflect, page 50 (EL)

Most students will predict: Yes, because Mako has practiced killing the shark and his love for Afa will give him courage.

Reader's Success Strategy or **Reading Tip,** page 51

Possible responses: 7. Mako and Afa hurry to get home in the dark; 8. Mako sees Tupa; 9. Afa falls into the water; 10. Mako saves Afa and kills Tupa.

Reading Check, page 52

It was the song to be sung at the feast given in Mako's honor for killing Tupa.

Pause & Reflect, page 52

1. Students should underline lines 280–281: "His dog, his companion, was in danger of instant death."

2. Possible response: It was exciting. You didn't know if Afa would reach the canoe in time or if Mako would be able to kill the shark.

Challenge, page 52

Students may star the following details: "How I should love to win that reward!" (line 74); "Your father . . . was one of the three fisherman in the canoe that Tupa destroyed" (lines 87–88);

"I shall slay Tupa and win the king's reward!" (lines 93–94); "He would paddle out to the reef and challenge Tupa!" (lines 155–156).

Active Reading SkillBuilder, page 53

(Possible responses are provided.)

1. Mako will encounter the ghost later in the story; Mako might find out that the ghost is just a myth.
2. Mako will find a way to kill the shark; Mako will be killed as his father was.
3. Mako will meet the ghost in the jungle on the reef; Mako and Afa will get lost in the jungle.
4. Mako will meet the ghost while he is on the water in his canoe; the canoe will overturn and Mako and Afa will have to swim to shore.
5. People will be angry because they think the community will be punished for the shark's death; people will be glad the shark is dead and honor Mako as a hero.

Literary Analysis SkillBuilder, page 54

(Possible responses are provided.)

Tupa attacks the fishermen—external conflict

Mako's mother forbids him to talk of killing Tupa—external conflict

Mako tries to grab Afa in the canoe—external conflict

Mako decides what to do when Afa falls overboard—internal conflict

Mako spears the shark—external conflict

Follow Up: Mako's fight to kill the shark is the main conflict. The other conflicts help to strengthen his determination.

Words to Know SkillBuilder, page 55

A.
1. harpoon
2. lagoon
3. reef
4. phosphorus
5. expedition

B.
1. reef
2. lagoon
3. harpoon
4. phosphorus
5. expedition

from Woodsong, page 56

Connect to Your Life, page 56

Students' signs should include a tip for dealing safely with wild animals.

Key to the Memoir, page 56

Possible response: Although the bear looks cute and cuddly, it is a wild animal. If you treat the bear like a pet, it might hurt you.

Pause & Reflect, page 59

1. snakes
2. Possible response: Bears eat meat, hibernate in the winter, bother dogs but not usually people, and are big and strong.

Reader's Success Strategy, page 59

Possible response: (Event) Scarhead comes to the trash-burning site and tears things apart. (Paulsen's Attitude) He becomes angry and throws a stick at Scarhead. (Event) Scarhead hovers over Paulsen but then withdraws. (Paulsen's Attitude) Paulsen is angry and goes to get his rifle. (Event) Paulsen aims his rifle at Scarhead but then decides against killing the bear. (Paulsen's Attitude) Paulsen is grateful to Scarhead for not hurting or killing

him and for teaching him the lesson that he shouldn't throw sticks at bears.

Read Aloud, page 59

He doesn't mind the bear and has become accustomed to him hanging around. He named him Scarhead and jokes about him like one of the other yard animals.

Pause & Reflect, page 60

1. The trash gives off a burnt-food smell.
2. Possible response: The bears might smell the burning trash and come to investigate.

Reader's Success Strategy, page 61

Possible responses: fearsome, powerful, fast, smart

Reading Check, page 62

The bear lowers his stance and turns back to the trash. Paulsen grabs his rifle and aims to shoot the bear, but decides not to.

Pause & Reflect, page 62

1. Possible response: Paulsen did not shoot the bear because he realized that the bear was just being a bear. He realized he should have known better than to throw something at the animal.
2. Paulsen learned that in the woods, he is no better than any other animal around him.

Challenge, page 62

Most students will say they think it was the right decision not to kill the bear. They may cite examples such as Paulsen's own conviction that "it is wrong to throw sticks at 400-pound bears" (lines 149–150). Some may say that Paulsen made a bad decision because now Scarhead will just continue to threaten the Paulsens' animals and destroy their property. Students might cite the following details: "my wife had a bear chase her from the garden to the house" (lines 27–28); "Twice we have had dogs killed by rough bear swats" (line 33); "they take a terrible toll of sheep" (lines 90–91); "ripped one side off the burn enclosure" (lines 105–106).

Active Reading SkillBuilder, page 63

(Possible responses are provided.)

Problem: Why was it a problem? Paulsen was having a bad day, and it made him angry.

Solution: What attempt was made to solve the problem? Paulsen threw a stick at the bear.

Results: Did this attempt succeed? No.

What happened? The bear threatened Paulsen and came close to attacking him, but didn't bother.

Then what happened? Paulsen got his gun to shoot the bear, but decided that it was wrong to do that.

Literary Analysis SkillBuilder, page 64

(Possible responses are provided.)

- ravens "pecked the puppies away from the food pans"
- seeing a bear for the first time is a novelty; then you begin to relax when they're around
- "having a bad day, and it made me mad"
- "hope never to throw a stick at a bear again"
- didn't think while being stared down by the bear
- thought crept in—why kill him?
- "hope he lives long"

- learned that I am just another animal in the woods

Follow Up: Details can be grouped into categories such as Sensory Details, Thoughts, Hopes, and Lessons Learned.

Words to Know SkillBuilder, page 65

A.
1. novelty
2. scavenging
3. rummaging
4. predator
5. menace

B.
1. predator
2. menace
3. novelty
4. scavenging
5. pets

All Summer in a Day, page 66
Connect to Your Life, page 66

Possible responses: When it is sunny, I feel happy. When it is snowing, I feel peaceful.

Key to the Story, page 66

Possible responses: They don't want to be seen with someone who is different. Some children are afraid to be around those who seem different. They're afraid others will think they're different too. They don't want to take the time to get to know someone who seems different.

Reading Check, page 68

The children are now nine years old and it has been raining for seven years; therefore they were two years old the last time the sun came out.

Read Aloud, page 69

Possible response: Margot feels very strongly that the sun is beautiful.

Pause & Reflect, page 69

1. Students might star the following details: "thousands upon thousands of days compounded and filled from one end to the other with rain" (lines 14–16); "sweet crystal fall of showers" (line 17); "storms so heavy they were tidal waves" (line 18).
2. the sun

Reader's Success Strategy, page 70

(Possible responses are provided.)

Description of Character or Action: Margot is described as "an old photograph dusted from an album, whitened away."
Character's Feelings: She feels lifeless and ghostlike.

English Learner Support, page 70

Possible response: An old photograph is faded and brittle. Margot looks pale and frail and feels lifeless.

Reading Check, page 71

Margot compares the sun to a penny and a fire. A penny is shiny, bright, and round. The sun is warm, bright, and round.

English Learner Support, page 71

Possible response: Both a penny and a fire are bright and round, like the sun.

Reread, page 71

Possible response: He wants to play a trick on her and he knows how badly she wants to see the sun.

Pause & Reflect, page 72

1. She gets the best grades.

2. Most students will say that she won't get out of the closet in time because no one can hear her, and the sun will be out only for a short time.

Reader's Success Strategy, page 73

(Possible responses are provided.)

Description of Character or Action: The children placed their hands on their ears and stood apart as they waited for the sun.
Characters' Feelings: great anticipation and excitement

Mark It Up, page 73

Students might underline the following: "jungle that covered Venus"; "nest of octopuses, clustering up great arms of fleshlike weed"; "color of rubber and ash"; "color of stones and white cheeses and ink."

Reading Check, page 73

a nest of octopuses

Reading Check, page 74

locked in the closet

Pause & Reflect, page 74

1. run, take off their jackets, play hide-and-seek, squint at the sun
2. The girl realizes that the rain is about to start again.

Reader's Success Strategy, page 75

(Possible responses are provided.)

Description of Character or Action: The children walk back with their hands at their sides and their smiles vanishing.
Characters' Feelings: They are very sad that it has begun to rain again.

Mark It Up, page 75

Students might underline the following: "as if someone had driven them, like so many stakes, into the floor"; "could not meet each other's glances"; "faces were solemn and pale"; "their faces down."

Pause & Reflect, page 76

1. Possible response: Cause—The children are distracted by the appearance of the sun.
2. Possible response: I would be mad that I missed the sun, but I would be hopeful of seeing it again soon once I returned to Earth.

Challenge, page 76

Possible response: Bradbury's abrupt ending forces the reader to think about Margot's reaction to the students and their reaction to Margot. It raises questions. Might things change between Margot and the others? Will the students feel bad about what they did?

Active Reading SkillBuilder, page 77

(Possible responses are provided.)

Setting: unbelievable but interesting; We don't have evidence that Venus can support life, but it provides a vivid background to the story.

Characters: believable and interesting; They act in ways we expect people to act—the classmates are disturbed by someone different from them and playful in the sun. Margot is withdrawn because she is in a place that is not comfortable for her.

Plot: believable and interesting; The idea of a group of children ganging up on another child is familiar and possible.

Literary Analysis SkillBuilder, page 78
(Possible responses are provided.)
Fantastic Details: rain for 7 years; jungle the color of rubber and ash; jungle mattress sighed and squeaked; huge raindrop; seven more years until the sun comes again
Realistic Details: rain; classroom; windows; songs and games; Ohio; homesickness; school shower rooms; closet; playing outside; thunder and lightning; the effects of sunlight on mood
Follow Up: The ways the children behave are similar to children today. Living on Venus where the sun comes out only for an hour every seven years is different.

Words to Know SkillBuilder, page 79

A. 1. tumultuously   B. 1. apparatus
    2. resilient   2. resilient
    3. concussion   3. concussion
    4. apparatus   4. tumultuously
    5. savor   5. savor

C. Students' notes should accurately use at least two Words to Know.

Chinatown *from* **The Lost Garden,** page 80
Connect to Your Life, page 80
Students' maps should be coherent and include a variety of symbols.
Mark It Up, page 82
Students should circle "the Chinese lived in Chinatown because they wanted to" (lines 18–19) and underline "before the fair housing laws they often had no choice" (line 20).
Pause & Reflect, page 83 (Plus)
  1. large in population
  2. Students should circle "the Chinese lived in Chinatown because they wanted to" (lines 18–19) and underline "before the fair housing laws they often had no choice" (line 20).
Pause & Reflect, page 83 (AS and EL)
large in population
Pause & Reflect, page 84
  1. Possible response: Chinatown is a small neighborhood with little greenery. People seem to live in small, rundown apartments. Outside Chinatown, people have more money, live in larger homes, and have plenty of parks and gardens.
  2. Possible response: I would feel sad and left-out, wondering why Chinese Americans couldn't live in nice neighborhoods.
Reader's Success Strategy, page 85
(Possible responses are provided.)
Paul: lives in the Chinatown projects, looks after his younger brothers and sisters, is tall and strong
Yep: lives outside Chinatown, explores Chinatown to learn about his heritage, is not tall and athletic
Pause & Reflect, page 86
  1. has good social skills
  2. Possible response: The author admires Paul's strength.
Mark It Up, page 87
Students may circle the following: "hopeless when it came to catching any ball in any shape or size" (lines 172–173); "Nor

could I dribble a basketball" (lines 173–174); "hopeless at catching a pass" (lines 181–182); "I was so bad that our opponents stopped covering me" (lines 183–184).
Reading Check, page 87
Possible response: Yep feels humiliated. The experience reinforces his belief that he is terrible at sports.
Pause & Reflect, page 88 (Plus)
  1. Students may say that after he broke the nun's glasses, he felt invisible because his classmates ignored him.
  2. Most students will say that Yep was unhappy and felt like a disappointment to his family because his entire family was athletic and he was not.
Pause & Reflect, page 88 (AS and EL)
Most students will say that Yep was unhappy and felt like a disappointment to his family because his entire family was athletic and he was not.
Reading Check, page 88
Possible response: Yep's inability to speak Chinese makes him feel like an outsider.
Reader's Success Strategy, page 89
(Possible responses are provided.)
Yep: is terrible at sports, does not speak Chinese, feels like an outsider
Harold: has a paper route, lives in the Chinatown projects, speaks Chinese, has exotic Chinese weapons made by his father
Pause & Reflect, page 90
  1. is not used to the games played in Chinatown; cannot understand Chinese; does poorly in the singing performance
  2. Yep was no longer comfortable acting like someone that wasn't really him.
Challenge, page 90
Possible response: Many different things contribute to a person's identity, including the culture you are from and the one in which you live. It can be confusing to figure out where you belong. Students should star passages that correspond with their answers.

Active Reading SkillBuilder, page 91
(Possible responses are provided.)
  1. **Supporting Facts:** Paul could almost always hit a home run when they played baseball.
  2. **Supporting Facts:** Yep couldn't catch the ball. He couldn't dribble a basketball.
  3. **Supporting Facts:** Yep didn't live in Chinatown like most of his classmates.
  4. **My opinion:** Agree, because Yep felt like an outsider with a different background. **Supporting facts:** He didn't live in Chinatown. His friends spoke Chinese that he didn't understand. The games he knew were different from the ones his friends in Chinatown played.

Literary Analysis SkillBuilder, page 92
(Possible responses are provided.)
Primary Source
  1. "If Uncle Francis and other members of our family left Chinatown to explore America, my experience was the reverse because I was always going into Chinatown to

explore the streets and perhaps find the key to the pieces of the puzzle."

Secondary Source
1. Unlike his family members, Laurence Yep found himself exploring the streets of Chinatown in search of his identity.
2. Accept all reasonable responses.

Words to Know SkillBuilder, page 93
A. 1. immensely (antonyms)   B. 1. entice
    2. palatial (synonyms)   2. vulgar
    3. shunned (antonyms)   3. stereotype
    4. gaudy (antonyms)   4. taboo
    5. tenement (antonyms)   5. remotely
Yep could not sing a single carol in Chinese.

The Circuit, page 94
Connect to Your Life, page 94
(Possible responses are provided.)
What Happens: leaving friends
Why This Is Hard: It's sad having to say goodbye to friends when you don't know when you will see them again.
What Happens: moving in
Why This Is Hard: It takes time to get used to new surroundings.
What Happens: starting at a new school
Why This Is Hard: You don't know anyone or where anything is.
Reread, page 96
Panchito is sad not to hear "Ya esora" anymore because then he knows that his family will have to move.
Pause & Reflect, page 97 (Plus)
1. Possible response: When the sharecropper stops saying "Ya esora," Panchito knows that his family will have to move.
2. upset
Pause & Reflect, page 97 (AS and EL)
upset
Reading Check, page 98
The family's two cherished possessions are Mama's galvanized pot and Papa's '38 Plymouth.
Reader's Success Strategy or **Reading Tip,** page 98
Possible responses: 2. The family packs their belongings; 3. They drive to a labor camp near Fresno.
Reading Check, page 99
The foreman suggested that they look for work from Mr. Sullivan.
Pause & Reflect, page 99 (Plus)
1. Possible response: I would be upset and anxious, wondering how we'll make it through a whole season living in such a rundown place.
2. Possible response: Panchito's parents don't own many things, but they take pride in the things they do own.
Pause & Reflect, page 99 (AS and EL)
1. Possible response: The family's new living quarters are dirty and desolate.
2. Possible response: I would feel depressed and worried.
Reader's Success Strategy or **Reading Tip,** page 100
Possible responses: 4. The family finds work with Mr. Sullivan; 5. They move into the garage at Mr. Sullivan's; 6. Panchito, his father, and his older brother begin work picking grapes.

Pause & Reflect, page 101 (Plus)
1. Possible response: Working in the fields is difficult because of the heat, the insects, and the dust.
2. Students should underline lines 150–151: "We did not want to get in trouble for not going to school."
3. Possible response: The two boys wear clean clothes, while Panchito and Roberto are dirty from working in the fields.
Pause & Reflect, page 101 (AS and EL)
1. Possible response: Working in the fields is difficult because of the heat, the insects, and the dust.
2. Students should underline lines 150–151: "We did not want to get in trouble for not going to school."
3. Possible response: No, because the work is very hard, the days are long, and I wouldn't get to go to school.
Reread, page 102
Possible response: Panchito is happy about starting school because he will not have to work in the fields all day.
Reader's Success Strategy or **Reading Tip,** page 102
Possible responses: 7. The grape season ends; 8. Panchito returns to school; 9. Panchito's father and brother pick cotton.
Pause & Reflect, page 103 (Plus)
1. Panchito is excited about starting school, but he feels bad that his brother won't be going with him.
2. Students might underline the following: "I felt dizzy . . . My mouth was dry . . . I could not begin" (lines 230–233); "I should have read" (line 236).
3. Possible responses: Will Panchito ever read out loud in class? Will he will make friends at his new school?
Pause & Reflect, page 103 (AS and EL)
1. Students might underline the following: "I felt dizzy . . . My mouth was dry . . . I could not begin" (lines 230–233); "I should have read" (line 236).
2. Possible responses: Will Panchito ever read out loud in class? Will he will make friends at his new school?
Pause & Reflect, page 104
1. "He then picked up a trumpet, blew on it and handed it to me." (lines 255–257)
2. understanding, gentle, kind
3. Possible response: The end of the story made me feel sad because just as things were going so well for Panchito, he came home to learn it was time to move once again.
Challenge, page 104
Students may mark the following: "As we drove away, I felt a lump in my throat" (line 88); "I knew he was sad" (line 191); "The sound gave me goose bumps" (line 257).

Active Reading SkillBuilder, page 105
(Possible responses are provided.)
Panchito
Detail: He feels a lump in his throat as they leave the strawberry fields; he doesn't want to see Roberto's sad face. **Inference:** Panchito is sensitive—he becomes attached to places and situations and shares in the emotions of others.
Detail: He feels nervous and empty as he enters the school building. **Inference:** He is uncertain about whether he will fit in or make friends or be able to do the work at his new school.

Detail: He seeks extra help from Mr. Lema during his lunch period. **Inference:** Panchito wants to succeed and is willing to work hard.

Papa

Detail: He does not say a word as they drive away from the strawberry fields on the last day. **Inference:** He is worried about finding another job so that he can provide for his family.

Detail: He looks at many cars and thoroughly checks out the one he buys. **Inference:** He is careful, thoughtful, and knowledgeable.

Mama

Detail: She is the one to talk with the farmer about the possibility of work. **Inference:** She speaks English well enough to communicate with others.

Detail: She cooks a special meal after the first day of grape harvesting. **Inference:** She is loving and caring toward her family; she provides them with the best that she possibly can.

Roberto

Detail: He warns Panchito about drinking the water. **Inference:** He looks out for his younger brother; he is experienced.

Detail: He is sad about not going to school but says nothing. **Inference:** He accepts the hardships of his life.

Mr. Lema

Detail: He gives up his lunch hour to help Panchito. **Inference:** He is a generous and kind man.

Detail: He offers to teach Panchito how to play the trumpet. **Inference:** He is concerned about Panchito as an individual and wants to add some beauty to his life.

Literary Analysis SkillBuilder, page 106

(Possible responses are provided.)

Detail: the yelling and screaming of my brothers and sisters; **Senses Used:** hearing; **Describes:** a person

Detail: tilting his head from side to side, like a parrot; **Senses Used:** sight; **Describes:** a person

Detail: Papa sighed, wiped the sweat off his forehead; **Senses Used:** touch, sight, hearing; **Describes:** a person

Detail: the walls, eaten by termites, strained to support the roof full of holes; **Senses Used:** sight; **Describes:** a place

Detail: I dropped to my knees and let the jug roll off my hands; **Senses Used:** sight, touch; **Describes:** an action

Detail: My body ached all over. I felt little control over my arms and legs; **Senses Used:** touch; **Describes:** a person

Detail: watched the dry, acid-stained skin fall to the floor in little rolls; **Senses Used:** sight, touch; **Describes:** a person

Detail: I felt my blood rush to my head; I felt dizzy; **Senses Used:** touch; **Describes:** a person

Words to Know SkillBuilder, page 107

A.
1. D
2. C
3. A
4. E
5. B

B.
1. hesitantly
2. surplus
3. vineyard
4. instinct
5. jalopy

Western Wagons/Night Journey, page 108

Connect to Your Life, page 108

Typical answers will describe where students would like to travel, why they would like to go there, how they would get there, and what they might see there.

Read Aloud, page 110

Possible responses: Yes, because I could make a fortune there. Or, no, because I don't know what sort of future a life out west would hold.

Reader's Success Strategy or **Reading Tip,** page 111

(Possible responses are provided.)

Stanza 1: Pioneers and their families traveled by wagon to California.

Stanza 2: They wanted a better life where there was gold or rich earth.

Stanza 3: Many people eagerly joined those going west.

Stanza 4: They'll face hardships, but life in the West holds promise.

Main idea: The pioneers were willing to risk what they had to explore the promise of life in the West.

Pause & Reflect, page 111

1. to escape overcrowded cities
2. Possible responses: brave, tough, determined, adventurous

Read Aloud, page 112

Possible response: I am bumped wide awake with the train's every move.

Reading Check, page 113

The speaker wants to see the land he loves.

Pause & Reflect, page 113

1. Students may star the following: "Bridges of iron lace" (line 6); "A lap of mountain mist" (line 8); "gullies washed with light" (line 19).
2. Most students will say yes, because it seems to be an interesting and beautiful ride.

Challenge, page 113

Possible response: The pioneers in "Western Wagons" are willing to risk what they have to explore the unknown. They share a spirit of adventurousness and daring. The speaker in "Night Journey" is similar in that while the other train passengers are sleeping, he is wide awake, aware of everything around him and enjoying his adventure.

Active Reading SkillBuilder, page 114

(Possible responses are provided.)

"Western Wagons"

Rhyming Lines: "The cowards never started, and the weak died on the road, / And all across the continent the endless campfires glowed."

"We're going West tomorrow, where promises can't fail. / O'er the hills in legions, boys, and crowd the dusty trail!"

"We shall starve and freeze and suffer. We shall die, and tame the lands. / But we're going West tomorrow, with our fortune in our hands."

Effect: The rhyme creates a cheerful and sentimental mood. This mood suggests that the hardships described are challenges to be faced and that the forging of new lands is an adventure.

"Night Journey"

Rhyming Lines: "Its rhythm rocks the earth, / And from my Pullman berth"

"Mist deepens on the pane, / We rush into a rain"

"The pistons jerk and shove, / . . . To see the land I love."

Effect: There are few couplets in the poem. Rhyming lines are mostly separated by other lines. The rhyme has the effect of unifying the poem but not dominating it. The poem sounds natural, like a person's thoughts spoken aloud.

Literary Analysis SkillBuilder, page 115

(A sample response for two lines of each poem is provided.)

Western Wagons

They went with axe and rifle, when the trail was still to blaze,

They went with wife and children, in the prairie-schooner days,

With banjo and with frying pan—Susanna, don't you cry!

For I'm off to California to get rich out there or die!

Night Journey

Beyond the mountain pass

Mist deepens on the pane,

We rush into a rain

That rattles double glass.

Follow Up: Students may say that the rhythm sets the mood and tone of the poems, making "Western Wagons" sound like a call or a cheer, and making "Night Journey" sound like a fast-moving, powerful locomotive.

Abd al-Rahman Ibrahima *from* Now Is Your Time! page 116

Connect to Your Life, page 116

Typical responses will include thoughts pertaining to personal identity.

Reader's Success Strategy, page 119

(Possible responses are provided.)

Event 2: Ibrahima was raised in the Muslim tradition.

Event 3: At the age of twelve, he was sent to Timbuktu to study.

Reading Check, page 119

Ibrahima was expected to assume a political leadership role, set a moral example, and be well versed in Islam.

Pause & Reflect, page 120 (Plus)

1. T, F, T, T
2. educated, long-haired, royal

Pause & Reflect, page 120 (AS and EL)

educated, long-haired, royal

Pause & Reflect, page 121 (Plus)

1. Ibrahima and Dr. Cox learned a lot from each other.
2. Possible response: The Fula helped Dr. Cox by healing his infected leg.

Pause & Reflect, page 121 (AS and EL)

Possible response: The Fula helped Dr. Cox by healing his infected leg.

Reading Check, page 121

The Fula won the first battles of the war.

Reading Check, page 122

Two causes of the Fula defeat: They were lured into a trap. The enemy had guns.

Two results of the defeat: Few Fula survived. Ibrahima was captured.

Pause & Reflect, page 122

1. 3, 4, 1, 2
2. Most students will say that Ibrahima was a good leader. They may support this by saying he was brave and pushed on, and his army followed him loyally.

Reading Check, page 123

The unlucky ones were left to die in agony.

Reading Check, page 124

Whoever held the gun had the power, whether he was evil or good.

Reader's Success Strategy, page 124

(Possible responses are provided.)

Event 4: Ibrahima was forced to march to the sea.

Event 5: He was inspected and put onto a large ship.

Event 6: Under harsh conditions, the journey began.

Pause & Reflect, page 125 (Plus)

1. Possible response: Ibrahima and the others were put on a boat and shipped out of Africa. They were mistreated, and many Africans died during the journey due to the terrible conditions.
2. Possible response: The conditions below deck were horrible. It was dark and hard to breathe below deck, and the whites kept shoving more and more people into the overcrowded space.

Pause & Reflect, page 125 (AS and EL)

Possible response: horrible, cramped, dark

Read Aloud, page 126

Possible response: Ibrahima felt that everything that had identified him as a Fula had been taken away.

Reading Check, page 127 (AS)

Ibrahima decided to return to Thomas Foster. His only other choice would have been to stay in the woods, where he would probably die.

Reading Check, page 127 (EL)

If had had stayed in the woods, he probably would have died.

Pause & Reflect, page 127 (Plus)

1. 2, 4, 1, 3
2. Possible response: Foster treated Ibrahima as a piece of property. He bought Ibrahima to be a worker, and that was Foster's main concern.

Pause & Reflect, page 127 (AS and EL)

2, 4, 1, 3

Pause & Reflect, page 128

1. kept his religious beliefs, married and raised a family, grew vegetables to sell in town
2. Most students will probably predict that Dr. Cox will help him, since Ibrahima's people helped Dr. Cox when he was in

need. Others might think it would not be possible for Ibrahima to get home because he belonged to Foster.

Reading Check, page 129

They suggested that he write a letter to his people, telling them where he was.

Reading Check, page 130

Marshalk erroneously sent the letter to Morocco, but the letter eventually reached Henry Clay, the American secretary of state, who wrote to Foster about Ibrahima's release.

Pause & Reflect, page 131 (Plus and AS)

1. 4, 3, 2, 1
2. No human being should be denied freedom.

Pause & Reflect, page 131 (EL)

4, 3, 2, 1

Challenge, page 131

Typical responses should show appropriate evidence from the text. Students may mark the following: "The white man made him turn around, and several other white men neared him, touched his limbs, examined his teeth, looked into his eyes, and made him move about" (lines 233–237); "He was told to work in the fields. He refused and he was tied and whipped" (lines 271–272); "The whippings forced him to work" (line 274).

Mark It Up, page 132

(Possible responses are provided.)

Fact: "Some of those who could no longer walk were speared and left to die in agony." (lines 169–171)

Opinion: "It was the lucky ones who were killed outright if they fell." (lines 171–172)

Fact: "Ibrahima was forty-five and had been in bondage for twenty years." (lines 316–317)

Opinion: "At forty-five Ibrahima was considered old." (lines 323–324)

Fact: "Finally, some time after the death of Dr. Cox in 1816, Ibrahima wrote the letter that Marshall suggested." (lines 371–373)

Opinion: "He had little faith in the procedure but felt he had nothing to lose." (lines 373–374)

Active Reading SkillBuilder, page 133

(Possible responses are provided. Those events without a date appear between two date lines.)

1774—beginning of Ibrahima's studies in Timbuktu
1781—Dr. Cox's arrival in a Fula village
—Ibrahima's capture by Mandingo warriors
1788—Ibrahima's arrival in Mississippi; Thomas Foster's purchase of Ibrahima to be his slave
—Ibrahima's second marriage
1807—meeting of Ibrahima and Dr. Cox in Mississippi
—Dr. Cox's attempts to secure Ibrahima's freedom
1816—death of Dr. Cox
—receipt by Moroccan government of Ibrahima's letter to the Fula people
1829—release of Ibrahima; voyage back to Africa; death in Liberia

Literary Analysis SkillBuilder, page 134

(Possible responses are provided.)

Primary Sources: birth certificates and other official documents; medical records; grades on report cards; letters to friends and family; journal entries; home videos; awards

Secondary Sources: letters from friends and family; interviews with friends and family; comments from teachers on report cards and papers

Sources of fact (circled sources): photographs, birth certificates, official documents, medical records, report cards, awards, home videos

Sources of insight (underlined sources): journal entries, letters, home videos, photographs

Words to Know SkillBuilder, page 135

A.
1. trek
2. chaos
3. reservation
4. premise
5. status
6. dynasty
7. procedure
8. inhabitant
9. bondage
10. prosper

Who captured Ibrahima? The Mandingo

B. Students' responses should accurately use at least four Words to Know.

from **The Story of My Life,** page 136

Connect to Your Life, page 136

Possible responses: touch—sandy beach, silk; smell—freshly cut grass, clean laundry; taste—chocolate, barbeque

Key to the Autobiography, page 136

Possible responses: Every child should know love and kindness. People should give you more of a chance.

English Learner Support, page 138

Possible responses: Words circled—tense, anxious, groped her way. Helen is like the ship. Both Helen and the ship are trying to find their way safely through the fog.

Pause & Reflect, page 139 (Plus)

1. Possible response: Before she met her teacher, Helen was bitter and angry, and she could communicate very little.
2. a ship in a fog

Pause & Reflect, page 139 (AS and EL)

a ship in a fog

Reader's Success Strategy, page 139

Students may highlight the following: Before: dumb, expectant (line 13); anger and bitterness preyed upon me (lines 22–23); languor (24); After: interested (line 51); flushed with childish pleasure and pride (lines 53–54); for the first time I felt repentance and sorrow (line 113); for the first time longed for a new day to come (lines 121–122)

Reading Check, page 140

Helen becomes impatient because Miss Sullivan keeps repeating her efforts to make Helen understand.

Pause & Reflect, page 141 (Plus)

1. spells words in Helen's hand
2. breaks her doll

Pause & Reflect, page 141 (AS and EL)

breaks her doll

Reading Check, page 141
Helen discovers that everything has a name.

Reader's Success Strategy, page 142
Possible response: She is able to communicate. She feels sorrow and repentance for the first time.

Reading Check, page 142
Possible response: For the first time, Helen feels repentance and sorrow. She becomes a happy child and looks forward to the future.

Pause & Reflect, page 142
1. As Helen felt the water running over one hand and her teacher spelling the word in the other hand, she realized that everything had a name.
2. Students may say that Helen's life will be different because she is learning new things and discovering the world around her.

Challenge, page 142
Possible response: It is extremely hard for a person to be both blind and deaf. With the right teachers and education, however, you can get beyond the darkness and learn to communicate. You must rely heavily on the other senses in order to succeed. Students might mark passages such as: "at sea in a dense fog" (line 26); "as if a tangible white darkness shut you in" (line 27); "every object which I touched seemed to quiver with life" (line 107).

Active Reading SkillBuilder, page 143
(Possible responses are provided.)
Important Events
Miss Sullivan teaches Helen the finger motions of sign language.
Questions/Answers
How does Miss Sullivan succeed? / She persists. She involves Helen's other senses, such as touch, to help her comprehend the connection.
Important Events
Helen has a temper tantrum and breaks her doll.
Questions/Answers
How will sign language help Helen? / It makes her a part of the communicating world and allows her to express her feelings and ideas.
Important Events
Helen understands the connection between the letters and the substance of water.
Questions/Answers
How will Helen's world change? / Helen feels repentance and sorrow as well as joy.

Literary Analysis SkillBuilder, page 144
(Possible responses are provided.)
Smell: "fragrance of the honeysuckle"
Touch: "fingers lingered . . . on the familiar leaves and blossoms"; "felt approaching footsteps"; "I felt the fragments of the broken doll"; "warm sunshine"; "cool stream gushed"; "misty consciousness"
Sight: "seizing the new doll, I dashed it upon the floor"; "at sea in a dense fog . . . the great ship, tense and anxious, groped her way to the shore"; "hop and skip with pleasure"; "words that were to make the world blossom"

Hearing: No sensory details that describe people's voices are given.

Words to Know SkillBuilder, page 145
1. succeed
2. impress
3. bitterness
4. reveal
5. persist
6. repentance
7. tangible
8. vainly
9. sentiment
10. prey

Lob's Girl, page 146
Connect to Your Life, page 146
Possible responses: keeps me company, alerts me to visitors, finds lost things
Reader's Success Strategy, page 148
Possible response: British Expression—Christmas puddings; What I Think It Means—holiday dessert
Pause and Reflect, page 149 (Plus)
1. older than the twins, named after a queen
2. Possible response: Sandy meets the German shepherd while sitting on the beach one day. From out of nowhere, the dog jumps on her and covers her with kisses.
Pause and Reflect, page 149 (AS and EL)
older than the twins, named after a queen
Reading Check, page 150
Lob must return to Liverpool with his owner, Mr. Dodsworth.
Reader's Success Strategy, page 150
Possible response: British Expression—scones; What I Think It Means—biscuit
English Learner Support, page 150
English
Pause & Reflect, page 151
1. Possible response: Sandy and Lob love each other the minute they meet.
2. Possible response: Lob is determined and intelligent.
Read Aloud, page 152
Possible response: I would feel sad watching the train leave the station, knowing Lob was on it.
Reading Check, page 152
Possible response: She feels sad and gloomy because she has just seen Lob leave on the train.
Reading Check, page 153
His feet are worn, dusty, and tarry.
Pause & Reflect, page 153
1. Possible response: Both times Lob comes to the Pengellys' house, he jumps through the window, knocking off food cooling on the sill.
2. Some students may say yes, because Lob keeps coming back, as if he lived there. Others may say no, because Mr. Pengelly seems very firm about sending Lob back to his owner.
Mark It Up, page 154
Students may circle the following words and phrases: "limping this time, with a torn ear and a patch missing out of his furry coat"; "as if he had met and tangled with an enemy or two"; "four-hundred-mile walk"

Reading Check, page 155

He has become a bit more slow and stiff and there is some gray hair on his nose. But he is still handsome.

Pause & Reflect, page 155 (Plus)

1. Possible response: Lob loves Sandy and her family because they show him love.
2. sleeps outside

Pause & Reflect, page 155 (AS and EL)

sleeps outside

Reading Check, page 156

Aunt Becky is lonesome.

Read Aloud, page 157

Most students will say that the injured girl might be Sandy.

Reading Check, page 157

A truck, speeding down a hill, crashed into the post office wall and hit Sandy.

Pause & Reflect, page 158 (Plus)

1. 2, 4, 3, 1
2. Possible responses: Yes, because this story seems to be about will and determination. No, because her condition seems very serious.

Pause & Reflect, page 158 (AS)

2, 4, 3, 1

Pause & Reflect, page 158 (EL)

Possible responses: Yes, because this story seems to be about will and determination. No, because her condition seems very serious.

Reread, page 159

Possible responses: Yes, because Lob always comes back. No, because without Sandy he won't want to come home.

Pause & Reflect, page 160 (Plus)

1. tries to walk
2. Most students will say they would be very worried, wondering if Sandy would live.

Pause & Reflect, page 160 (AS and EL)

Most students will say they would be very worried, wondering if Sandy would live.

Reading Check, page 160

He repeatedly tried a number of entrances and tried to get inside by following visitors.

Reading Check, page 161

She knows the dog is Lob and wants him to be allowed inside to be with Sandy.

Pause & Reflect, page 162

1. wants to see Sandy; seems weighted down; looks very wet
2. Possible response: Granny Pearce convinces the hospital to allow Lob to see Sandy.

Reader's Success Strategy, page 163

Students may circle the following clues: "She sighed and moved her head"; "Her eyes opened"; "'Lob?' she murmured"

Reading Check, page 163

Possible response: She wakes from the coma, recognizes Lob, and reaches her arm out to touch him.

Pause & Reflect, page 163 (Plus)

1. Possible response: Lob lets out a faint whine that causes Sandy to wake from the coma.
2. The doctors rely on skills to cure Sandy, while her dog gives her total love.

Pause & Reflect, page 163 (AS and EL)

Possible response: Lob lets out a faint whine that causes Sandy to wake from the coma.

Pause & Reflect, page 164 (Plus)

1. Possible response: Lob was killed by the truck and was buried at sea by Don.
2. Possible response: I was left wondering how Lob came back to help Sandy. It felt creepy that the dog could be in two places at once.

Pause & Reflect, page 164 (AS and EL)

1. Possible response: Lob was killed by the truck and was buried at sea by Don.
2. Possible response: I think it was Lob's spirit that returned to Sandy.
3. Possible response: I was left wondering how Lob came back to help Sandy. It felt creepy that the dog could be in two places at once.

Challenge, page 164

Possible response: The different settings help readers visualize the terrain and conditions Lob endures to find Sandy. As a result, they make the story more powerful. Accept all reasonable answers that show text comprehension with supporting evidence.

Active Reading SkillBuilder, page 165

(Possible responses are provided.)

Cause: Lob jumps on Sandy and licks her face.

Effect: Sandy falls in love with Lob.

Effect: The Pengelly family spends a day at the beach playing with Lob.

Cause: Lob walks from Liverpool to Cornwall.

Effect: Lob's feet are sore and dirty.

Effect: Sandy washes and cleans his feet.

Cause: Aunt Rebecca is lonely.

Effect: Sandy takes Lob and they go visit Rebecca.

Effect: A speeding truck runs into Sandy and Lob.

Cause: Granny Pearce finds Lob outside the hospital.

Effect: She convinces a guard to let Lob inside the hospital.

Effect: Sandy wakes up when she hears the dog's whine.

Literary Analysis SkillBuilder, page 166

(Possible responses are provided.)

Dialogue or Event: Sign reading "Steep Hill. Low Gear for 1 ½ miles"

Mood: anxiety, anticipation, dread

Foreshadowed Event: Someone didn't slow down on the hill, and a truck ran out of control and hit Sandy and Lob.

Dialogue or Event: Sandy is in a deep coma.

Mood: fear, sadness, anticipation

Foreshadowed Event: Sandy wakes up only when she thinks Lob is present.

Words to Know SkillBuilder, page 167

A. 1. melancholy
2. atone
3. draft
4. inquire
5. rivet
6. transfusion
7. assure
8. conceal
9. agitated
10. heartfelt

B. 1. C
2. E
3. D
4. B
5. A

from **The Phantom Tollbooth,** page 168

Connect to Your Life, page 168

Possible responses: (character) Babe, (from) *Babe: Pig in the City*, (goal) to save the farm; (character) Meg, (from) *A Wrinkle in Time,* (goal) to find her father; (character) Mako, (from) "Ghost of the Lagoon," (goal) to defeat Tupa

Key to the Drama, page 168

Possible responses: weigh, way; threw, through; tail, tale

Reader's Success Strategy or **Reading Tip,** page 171

Students should use five different colors to highlight the settings and details listed on page 171. Students may continue to highlight details and settings as they continue reading. Students may highlight details to describe the Road to Dictionopolis, the Land of Expectations, and the Doldrums, which are all along the road to the Land of Wisdom. Students may note that Dictionopolis and Digitopolis are cities in the Land of Wisdom. Students may highlight details to describe the World Market and the Royal Banquet located in Dictionopolis. Students may highlight details to describe the Mountains of Ignorance and the Castle-in-the-Air located in the Land of Ignorance.

Pause & Reflect, page 171

1. Possible response: The Humbug; it's such a funny name and it might be some kind of a bug.
2. Digitopolis: numbers shining everywhere
   The Land of Ignorance: gray and gloomy
   Dictionopolis: open-air stalls and letters

Pause & Reflect, page 173

1. What you do with time matters most.
2. likes reading books

Reading Check, page 174

Possible response: The package intrigues him, and he is bored and has nothing else to do.

Pause & Reflect, page 175 (Plus)

1. a map, coins, a turnpike tollbooth
2. Dictionopolis (line 99)
3. Possible response: I hope I will see new creatures and new lands.

Pause & Reflect, page 175 (AS and EL)

1. a map, coins, a turnpike tollbooth
2. Dictionopolis (line 99)

Reading Check, page 176

Possible response: The homophones *weather* and *whether* cause Milo to confuse the Whether Man with a weather man.

Reread, page 176

Possible response: Some people have expectations about things and never find out whether or not they are true. Milo will go beyond Expectations because he seems willing to try anything, hoping for something he won't find boring.

Pause & Reflect, page 177

1. Students should circle: "I do so hate to make up my mind about anything" (lines 157–158).
2. I do not know whether the weather will be sunny or rainy.

Reading Check, page 179

Thinking and laughing are against the law in the Doldrums.

Pause & Reflect, page 180

1. linger and loiter, daydream, waste time
2. The Lethargarians don't like the Watchdog because he's always checking to see that no one wastes time.

Reading Check, page 181

Milo's car gets stuck because Milo isn't thinking hard enough.

Pause & Reflect, page 182 (Plus)

1. The secret to escaping is thinking.
2. Possible response: my cat

Pause & Reflect, page 182 (AS and EL)

The secret to escaping is thinking.

Reading Check, page 182

Azaz is the king of Dictionopolis and the Mathemagician is the king of Digitopolis.

Reading Check, page 183

Azaz has a great stomach, a long gray beard, a small crown, and a long robe covered with the letters of the alphabet. The Mathemagician has a tall pointed hat, carries a long staff with a pencil point at one end and a large eraser at the other end, and wears a long robe covered with complex mathematical equations.

Reading Check, page 184

They decide that words and numbers are of equal value and that the kingdoms of Dictionopolis and Digitopolis should live in peace.

Pause & Reflect, page 185 (Plus)

1. They are arguing over which is more important, words or numbers.
2. Their job was to solve the differences between the two kings.
3. Possible responses: Will the princesses be rescued? Will the Kings solve their argument? Who sent Milo the tollbooth?

Pause & Reflect, page 185 (AS and EL)

They are arguing over which is more important, words or numbers.

Reading Check, page 186

words

Reading Check, page 187

individual letters

Pause & Reflect, page 187

1. Possible response: *where* and *happy;* (Why?) You could use them to ask directions and for greetings.

2. Students may underline: "noisy marketplace" (lines 430–431); "Hey-ya, hey-ya, hey-ya, step right up and take your pick" (lines 435–436).

Reread, page 189
Accept all appropriate drawings depicting the Humbug.

Reading Check, page 189
The Spelling Bee does not believe a word the Humbug says.

Reread, page 191
They are synonyms.

Reading Check, page 191
It isn't their job to make sense.

Pause & Reflect, page 192
1. Possible response: The name is appropriate because he pretends to be important by attending the Royal Banquet, even though he is not officially invited.
2. They invite him to the Royal Banquet. (Students should circle lines 609–610.)

Reread, page 194
Possible response: They take his words literally rather than as idiomatic expressions, serving a snack of light and a meal of squares.

Mark It Up, page 194 or 195
Students should circle lines 694–696: Milo. "I didn't know I was going to have to eat my words." / Azaz. "Of course, of course, everybody here does."

Read Aloud, page 195
synonym bun—cinnamon bun
somersault—salt
rigamarole—dinner roll
ragamuffin—muffin

Mark It Up, page 196
"They've gone to dinner" (line 733).

Reading Check, page 196
confused

Pause & Reflect, page 197 (Plus)
1. Possible response: It is not a very well thought-out idea because people would simply fall off when they got to the edge.
2. "They've gone to dinner" (line 733).

Pause & Reflect, page 197 (AS and EL)
Possible response: It is not a very well thought-out idea because people would simply fall off when they got to the edge.

Reader's Success Strategy or **Reading Tip,** page 198
1. cross the dangerous countryside to Digitopolis; 2. persuade the Mathemagician to release the princesses; 3. climb the Mountains of Ignorance to reach the Castle-in-the-Air; 4. travel back down through the crags with the princesses; 5. hold a triumphal parade

Reading Check, page 198
the dangerous, unknown countryside between Dictionopolis and Digitopolis; the Mountains of Ignorance; the frightening fiends in the chaotic crags

Pause & Reflect, page 199
1. Possible response: "the Mountains of Ignorance from where no one has ever returned alive . . . in a high wind at night" (lines 784–787)

2. Some students might say yes, because they will be protected by the letters given to them by Azaz. Others may say no, because there seem to be far too many dangers and obstacles along the way.

Challenge, page 199
Possible response: At the beginning of Act One, Milo always wants to be somewhere else, and isn't interested in anything. By the end, he is involved with the adventures going on around him. He has used his imagination to overcome boredom.

Mark It Up, page 200
Accept all appropriate drawings depicting a scene from the play. Be sure the scene number and character names correctly match the sketch.

Active Reading SkillBuilder, page 201
(Possible responses are provided.)
Setting: Word Market
Details from Text: It is a "noisy marketplace." "As some people buy and sell their wares, others hang a large banner . . ."
Mental Picture: a square crowded with people trying to get to the stalls set up with the entrance indicated by a large and colorful sign; vendors shouting and gesturing
Setting: The Doldrums
Details from Text: "where nothing ever happens and nothing ever changes"; "people come out of the scenery colored in the same colors of the trees or the road. They move very slowly and as soon as they move, they stop to rest again."
Mental Picture: a slow-moving place where there are no colors that stand out; everything is plain and nothing changes
Character: Tock
Details from Text: "large dog with the head, feet, and tail of a dog and the body of a clock"
Mental Picture: St. Bernard with a visible clock in its side
Character: King Azaz
Details from Text: "a great stomach, a gray beard reaching to his waist, a small crown and a long robe with the letters of the alphabet written all over it"
Mental Picture: a fat man with a long gray beard and a colorful robe that drapes over his body like a tent
Character: Mathemagician
Details from Text: "long flowing robe covered entirely with complex mathematical equations and a tall pointed hat"; "carries a long staff with a pencil point at one end and a large rubber eraser at the other"
Mental Picture: a wizard carrying an oversized pencil
Character: Humbug
Details from Text: "lavish coat, striped pants, checked vest, spats and a derby hat"
Mental Picture: grasshopper-type creature standing upright and dressed like someone going to a garden party or wedding

Literary Analysis SkillBuilder, page 202
(Possible responses are provided.)
Setting or Character: Milo
Fantastic Details: travels to Land of Wisdom in his toy car
Realistic Details: has feelings of boredom; is friendly; doesn't have a very high opinion of his verbal or mathematical skills
Setting or Character: Tock

Fantastic Details: has a clock in his stomach; can talk
Realistic Details: loyal; has the head, feet, and tail of a dog; relies on sense of smell
Setting or Character: Word Market
Fantastic Details: sells letters and words; letters and words are edible
Realistic Details: has stalls and vendors; customers mill around
Setting or Character: King Azaz's banquet
Fantastic Details: guests literally eat their words
Realistic Details: strict seating arrangement and order of events; pace set by the king

Words to Know SkillBuilder, page 203

A. 1. F
2. C
3. A
4. E
5. B
6. D

B. 1. ignorance
2. dejectedly
3. fanfare
4. leisurely
5. acknowledge
6. destination
Character: Reason

C. Students' responses should accurately use three Words to Know.

The Fun They Had, page 204
Connect to Your Life, page 204
Possible responses include: e-mail, satellite television, Internet
Key to the Story, page 204
Most students will probably say it would be less fun because students would have to stay home with their mechanical teachers and wouldn't get to interact with other kids.
Reader's Success Strategy or **Reading Tip,** page 206
Possible responses: Real—Margie and Tommy look at an old book; Fantasy—books have been completely replaced by telebooks.
Reading Check, page 207
Possible response: Her mechanical teacher keeps giving her test after test and she is doing poorly in geography.
Pause & Reflect, page 207 (Plus)
1. telebooks
2. Drawings should show details of the mechanical teacher described in the story, such as a big screen and a slot.
Pause & Reflect, page 207 (AS and EL)
Drawings should show details of the mechanical teacher described in the story, such as a big screen and a slot.
Reading Check, page 208
Possible response: She is doubtful. She doesn't believe that a human teacher could know as much as a mechanical teacher.
Reread, page 209
Possible response: Margie is curious about the way school used to be. She seems to think that those old schools might not have been as bad as she first thought.
Reading Check, page 209
Possible response: Margie's schoolroom is next to her bedroom. The screen of her mechanical teacher is lit up and on, waiting for her. She is the only student in her schoolroom, which feels lonely and cold.

Pause & Reflect, page 210
1. Possible responses: Margie goes to school in her home instead of in a separate building. She has to write her homework in punch code.
2. She thinks kids had more fun in school in the old days.
Challenge, page 210
Possible response: Asimov is giving a warning about relying on machines or computers too much. In the story, he suggests that kids learn better and are happier when they share the experience with other people.

Active Reading SkillBuilder, page 211
(Possible responses are provided.)
Clue from Text: "There was a time when all stories were printed on paper."
Inference: Books in the future are not printed on paper, like the ones we have today.
Clue from Text: "This is the old kind of school that they had hundreds and hundreds of years ago."
Inference: By 2157, the days of going to school in a building like today are long since past.
Clue from Text: "A man? How could a man be a teacher?"
Inference: All teachers in the future are machines, not real people.

Literary Analysis SkillBuilder, page 212
(Possible responses are provided.)
Present
- Most students go to school with others of their own age.
- Teachers are human.
- School involves learning to socialize.
- Books are a primary source of information.
- Many homework assignments are written out.

Future
- Parents oversee their children's education.
- County inspectors are called to fix the mechanical teachers.
- Each student is educated individually.
- Homework is done in punch code.
- School is at home.
- There is no human interaction during "school."

Both
- Students dislike some aspects of school, such as homework.
- Parents are anxious for their children to do well in school.
- People live in houses and visit each other.
- People keep old things in their attics.

Words to Know SkillBuilder, page 213

A. 1. nonchalantly
2. dispute
3. scornful
4. sector
5. loftily

B. 1. sector
2. dispute
3. nonchalantly
4. loftily
5. scornful

C. Students' diary entries should accurately use three Words to Know.

The Dog of Pompeii, page 214
Connect to Your Life, page 214
Possible responses: smell—books, cleaning fluid, an apple;
hear—voices, birds, footsteps
Key to the Story, page 214
Typical responses will include thoughts about what students
want to learn about the ancient city of Pompeii and what they
have learned about Pompeii after reading the story.
Reader's Success Strategy or **Reading Tip,** page 216
(Possible responses are provided.)
Fact: Glaucus Pansa lived in Pompeii; there were public baths;
the forum was the central square; an earthquake had rocked the
city twelve years before; Caesar's birthday was celebrated;
houses fell during the eruption; some people escaped in boats.
Fiction: Bimbo would put his paw on Tito's knee; Tito said,
"Glaucus Pansa is giving a grand dinner tonight"; a stranger
came to town and warned the bath master; Tito was excited by
the shouts and cheers; Tito kept crying for Bimbo.
Reading Check, page 217
He disappeared three times a day to find food.
Pause & Reflect, page 217
1. has wealthy parents
2. Most students will say no, because Tito has no one else to
   care for him. Bimbo watches over Tito and finds him food.
Read Aloud, page 218
Most students will stay he copes well with his blindness. His
senses of smell and hearing are very strong and help him "see."
Reading Check, page 218
through his keen senses of smell and hearing
Pause & Reflect, page 219 (Plus)
1. Possible response: Tito copes very well with his blindness,
   relying on his other senses to help him "see."
2. food cooking, spring cleaning, fresh fish market
Pause & Reflect, page 219 (AS and EL)
food cooking, spring cleaning, fresh fish market
Mark It Up, page 219
Students may circle three of the following details: "everything
happened here" (line 117); "the chief temples, the gold and red
bazaars, the silk shops, the town hall . . . the shrine of the
household gods" (lines 119–123); "everything glittered here"
(line 123); "the buildings looked as if they were new" (lines
123–124).
Reading Check, page 219
An earthquake twelve years earlier had destroyed all the old
buildings.
Pause & Reflect, page 220 (Plus)
1. Students may mark the following details: "everything
   happened here" (line 117); "the chief temples, the gold and
   red bazaars, the silk shops, the town hall . . . the shrine of
   the household gods" (lines 119–123); "everything glittered
   here" (line 123); "the buildings looked as if they were new"
   (lines 123–124).
2. city center
3. Priests get too many offerings.
Pause & Reflect, page 220 (AS and EL)
1. city center

2. Priests get too many offerings.
Pause & Reflect, page 222 (Plus and AS)
1. Possible response: The stranger warns the people to listen
   to warnings, and if the smoke tree is in the shape of an
   umbrella pine they will be in great danger.
2. to forecast weather
Pause & Reflect, page 222 (EL)
Possible response: The stranger warns the people to listen to
warnings, and if the smoke tree is in the shape of an umbrella
pine they will be in great danger.
Reading Check, page 223
Tito and Bimbo join the merrymakers, go to the open theater, and
then go to the city walls for a mock naval battle.
Pause & Reflect, page 223
1. Students may circle the following details: "holiday mood"
   (lines 222–223); "merrymakers" (line 224); "mock naval
   battle" (lines 239–240); "thousands of flaming arrows" (line
   241); "thrill of flaring ships and lighted skies" (lines
   243–244).
2. Possible response: The people of Pompeii might be faced
   with an earthquake the next day.
Reader's Success Strategy, page 224
Students may use five different colors to highlight the following:
Sight: "heavy mist in the air" (lines 259–260); "haze has spread
all over the bay" (lines 263–264); Sound: "Peculiar sounds. Like
animals under the earth. Hissings and groanings and muffling
cries that an animal might make dislodging the stones of his
underground cave." (lines 281–284); Smell: "to get a breath of
the sea" (lines 262–263); "even the salty air seemed smoky" (line
264); Touch: "a warm powder that stung his nostrils and burned
his sightless eyes" (lines 279–280); "He not only heard them—
he could feel them. The earth twitched; the twitching changed to
an uneven shrugging of the soil." (lines 286–288); Taste: "So
heavy that he could taste it." (lines 277–278)
Reading Check, page 224
Possible response: The air was hot and a warm powder stung the
nostrils and eyes.
Pause & Reflect, page 225
1. Students should star various details that help them picture
   Tito's situation. Accept all appropriate responses.
2. Possible responses: Will Tito and Bimbo survive? Is Tito a
   real person?
Pause & Reflect, page 226 (Plus and AS)
1. Possible response: I would run away from the buildings and
   try to get to the sea.
2. bitter cold
Pause & Reflect, page 226 (EL)
bitter cold
Read Aloud, page 227
Some students may say no, because Tito would not be able to
escape fast enough due to his blindness, or because of the state
of danger the city was in. Others may say yes, because Bimbo
will make sure Tito gets out.
Reading Check, page 227
falling buildings, heaving ground, trampling crowds

Reading Check, page 228
Bimbo wants to keep Tito moving.

Pause & Reflect, page 228 (Plus and AS)
1. Possible response: Bimbo pushes Tito to the sea where Tito is brought onto a boat by other people trying to escape.
2. Students may mark the following: "Bimbo had disappeared" (line 387); "frightened" (line 389); "calling for someone" (line 390); "wept continually" (line 394); "could not be comforted" (line 396).

Pause & Reflect, page 228 (EL)
Possible response: Bimbo pushes Tito to the sea where Tito is brought onto a boat by other people trying to escape.

Reading Check, page 229
They discover the skeleton of a dog.

Reading Check, page 230
Possible response: He went to the bakery to find food for Tito; in his mouth were the remains of a raisin cake.

Pause & Reflect, page 230 (Plus)
1. Possible response: Bimbo went to get the cake only after he knew that Tito was safe in the water.
2. Students may say they felt sad that Bimbo had to die, leaving Tito alone with no one to care for him. At the same time, they may express some positive feelings after reading about the loyalty and love between Tito and Bimbo.
3. Volcanic ash preserved artworks. The skeleton of a dog was dug up.

Pause & Reflect, page 230 (AS and EL)
1. Possible response: Bimbo went to get the cake only after he knew that Tito was safe in the water.
2. Volcanic ash preserved artworks. The skeleton of a dog was dug up.

Challenge, page 230
Students may mark the following as powerful scenes: the foreigner giving the warning about the earthquake, Tito and Bimbo at Caesar's birthday celebration, Bimbo and Tito running through the town trying to escape, Tito calling for Bimbo from the boat, the discovery of Bimbo's skeleton. Accept appropriate answers and words from the text that show how these passages stand out.

Active Reading SkillBuilder, page 231
(Possible responses are provided.)
Fact: Glaucus Pansa lived in Pompeii; there were public baths; the forum was the central square; an earthquake had rocked the city twelve years before; Caesar's birthday was celebrated; houses fell during the eruption; some people escaped in boats.
Nonfact: Bimbo would put his paw on Tito's knee; Tito said, "Glaucus Pansa is giving a grand dinner tonight"; a stranger came to town and warned the bath master; Tito was excited by the shouts and cheers; Tito kept crying for Bimbo.

Literary Analysis SkillBuilder, page 232
(Possible responses are provided.)
Main Characters: Bimbo and Tito
Events Leading to Climax: Tito knows there was an earlier destructive earthquake; he overhears the stranger's warnings; people are focusing on the celebration.

Climax: The eruption of Vesuvius
How Setting Is Important: The main conflict is between the characters and the natural events that occur at that time and place.
Possible Theme: People must respect nature's powers.
Follow Up: Possible response: There would be no dialogue; there might be more of an overall description of the city or what it contained; there would be more dates.

Words to Know SkillBuilder, page 233

A.	1. F		**B.**	1. dislodging
	2. D			2. restore
	3. E			3. vapor
	4. A			4. eruption
	5. B			5. shrine
	6. G			
	7. C			

C. Students' responses should use at least three Words to Know.

Tutankhamen *from* **Lost Worlds,** page 234
Connect to Your Life, page 234
Possible responses: pottery, jewelry, gemstones, gold, weapons
Reading Check, page 236
Howard Carter was a British archaeologist who was looking for the tomb of Pharoah Tutankhamen.

Pause & Reflect, page 237 (Plus)
1. A tomb containing figures of the king was too small. Two jars found at the center of the valley contained items from Tutankhamen's funeral.
2. careful, determined

Pause & Reflect, page 237 (AS and EL)
1. the discovery of two jars of items from Tutankhamen's funeral
2. careful, determined

Mark It Up, page 238
Students may circle the following: "upper edges of a stairway on all its four sides"; "twelve steps"; "upper part of a sealed and plastered doorway."

Reading Check, page 238
a stairway that led to a sealed doorway

Reading Check, page 238
He wanted to wait for Lord Carnarvon's arrival.

Pause & Reflect, page 239 (Plus)
1. Possible response: First, Carter was excited and ordered the diggers to dig out the staircase. Next, he realized he should wait for Carnarvon, so he ordered the diggers to fill in the stairway.
2. Some students will say yes, because he had been part of the dig since the beginning. Others will say no, because Carnarvon had gone to England while Carter remained working.

Pause & Reflect, page 239 (AS and EL)
Possible response: First, Carter was excited and ordered the diggers to dig out the staircase. Next, he realized he should wait for Carnarvon, so he ordered the diggers to fill in the stairway.

Reader's Success Strategy, page 237
Student's diagrams should show stairs leading to a doorway with a passage behind the door leading to another doorway. Behind the second door students should label the antechamber and its contents. Students should label the door between the two statues and the annex to the antechamber behind the couch.

Reading Check, page 240
Possible response: three gilt couches, alabaster vases

Pause & Reflect, page 241 (Plus)
1. 3, 4, 1, 2
2. Students may circle the following: "no coffin in the room" (lines 155–156); "two statues stood on either side of a sealed doorway" (lines 158–159); "guarded door" (line 162). Students should check "many doorways in the room."

Pause & Reflect, page 241 (AS and EL)
3, 4, 1, 2

Pause & Reflect, page 242 (Plus)
1. F, T, F, T
2. Some students may say the treasures should be shipped to the museum, where they will be safe and help visitors learn about the history of Egypt and King Tutankhamen. Others may say that the treasures should be left alone, since they were buried for a spiritual reason.

Pause & Reflect, page 242 (AS and EL)
F, T, F, T

Challenge, page 242
Possible response: The use of spatial order in lines 142–170 helps the reader visualize the details of the room as Carter and Carnarvon see it. The reader is able to create a mental picture of where the statues are positioned, how the room is filled with furniture and ornate objects, and where the two men see the doorway leading to the room beyond.

Active Reading SkillBuilder, page 243
(Possible responses are provided.)
Text Structure: chronological order
Transitional Words: autumn of 1917, in the years that followed, November first, 1922
Main Ideas:
1. Carter and Carnarvon decide to dig at the center of the valley for the tomb of Tutankhamen, even though most people believed it had already been found.
2. Although they had to remove past excavators' refuse piled on their site, they would go over every inch of the ground.
3. They found ruins of huts and moved on to another site with possibilities.
4. They would continue to dig until all areas had been explored.
Supporting Detail: They believed that the pit-tomb already found was too small and insignificant for a king's burial.
Information It Provides: There was a chance that Carter and Carnarvon would find the real tomb.

Literary Analysis SkillBuilder, page 244
(Possible responses are provided.)
1. letters/telegrams
2. newspaper articles, logs or journals

3. biographies, interviews
4. photographs
5. diaries, logs or journals, interviews
Follow Up: Primary sources are autobiographies, diaries, interviews, letters, telegrams, logs or journals, photographs, and speeches.

Words to Know SkillBuilder, page 245
A. dissuade
sentinel
systematically
tedious
intact

B. 1. tedious
2. sentinel
3. dissuade
4. systematically
5. intact

C. Students' lists of instructions should use at least three Words to Know.

Barbara Frietchie, page 246
Connect to Your Life, page 246
Possible responses: sailing the ocean; living with a disability; staying with someone who is in trouble
Definition: taking a risk, showing strength when you have fear or pain
Example: Anne Sullivan helping Helen Keller

Reader's Success Strategy or **Reading Tip,** page 249
Event 1: General Lee and his troops march into Frederick.
Event 2: The townspeople take down their flags.
Event 3: Barbara Frietchie hangs a Union flag in her window.
Event 4: Stonewall Jackson is moved by Frietchie's bravery.
Event 5: Both Jackson and Frietchie die, but Frietchie's flag waves on.

Reading Check, page 249
The poem takes place in Frederick, Maryland, during the Civil War.

Pause & Reflect, page 249 (Plus)
1. flat landscape
2. Possible response: They took the flags down because the rebel army was marching through town.

Pause & Reflect, page 249 (AS and EL)
Possible response: They took the flags down because the rebel army was marching through town.

Reading Check, page 251
She is proud of her country and of what the flag symbolizes.

Pause & Reflect, page 251 (Plus)
1. Students should circle "She took up the flag the men hauled down; / In her attic window the staff she set" (lines 20–21).
2. Possible response: First Frietchie hangs the flag from her window. Then Jackson sees the flag. Next Jackson fires upon the flag. Then Frietchie grabs it before it falls.

Pause & Reflect, page 251 (AS and EL)
Students should circle "She took up the flag the men hauled down; / In her attic window the staff she set" (lines 20–21).

Reading Check, page 253
He is moved by her bravery and loyalty and orders her not to be harmed.

Pause & Reflect, page 253 (Plus and AS)
1. Possible response: She leans out the window and shakes the flag at Jackson; she tells him if he's going to shoot, he should shoot her and not the flag.

2. Possible response: The lines reveal that he was proud of Frietchie's bravery.

Pause & Reflect, page 253 (EL)
Possible response: She leans out the window and shakes the flag at Jackson; she tells him if he's going to shoot, he should shoot her and not the flag.

Pause & Reflect, page 255
1. Stonewall Jackson takes it down.
2. determined, loyal, brave

Challenge, page 255
Possible response: They are both strong-willed and determined. Frietchie, however, will not compromise her stance on flying the flag, whereas Jackson changes his mind once he sees how brave and determined she is. Frietchie shows courage by standing up to Jackson, and Jackson shows courage by going against the beliefs of the army and allowing her to fly the flag. Students may mark "shook it forth with a royal will"; "Shoot if you must this gray old head / But spare your country's flag"; "A shade of sadness, a blush of shame"; "The nobler nature within him stirred"; "Who touches a hair of yon gray head / Dies like a dog!"

Active Reading SkillBuilder, page 256
(Possible responses are provided.)
- There were 40 flags flying in the morning, but by noon there were none. The people had apparently all brought them in because they were afraid.
- Barbara Frietchie saw what the townspeople had done, and she got her flag and flew it out her attic window.
- When Stonewall Jackson saw the flag, he ordered his men to shoot at it.
- They hit the window and tore the flag. Frietchie grabbed the ripped flag, held it up, and leaned out the window.
- She told them they could shoot her, but not to shoot the flag of their country.
- Jackson ordered his soldiers to leave her alone, and they marched on.
- All day long soldiers marched through the city, with Frietchie's torn flag flying over their heads.
- Later, when the war is over and Jackson is dead, honor is still bestowed on Barbara Frietchie and the town of Frederick.

Literary Analysis SkillBuilder, page 73
(Possible responses are provided.)
Original: "Up rose old Barbara Frietchie then, / Bowed with her fourscore years and ten"
New: Out in the yard there stood a hen, / Keeping her eye on the fox's den
Original: "A shade of sadness, a blush of shame, / Over the face of the leader came"
New: After our practice and before the big game, / I put on the jersey with my number and name

Academic and Informational Reading Answer Key

Reading a Magazine Article, page 260
Mark It Up
1. Students should circle the exclamation point in the title; exclamation point.
2. soccer
3. Students should circle the photo of the boy kicking a goal.
4. Students should underline the three bulleted statements below the title; soccer.
5. Students should underline *association football*. Students should double underline *assoc.*
6. Students should circle "It's a lot of fun."

Reading a Textbook, page 262
Mark It Up
1. 700–500 B.C.; Students should circle the time line at the top of the page.
2. "How did democracy develop and work in Athens?"
3. Students should circle *democracy, monarchy, oligarchy, tyrant, barter.*
4. ancient Greek tokens
5. Xenophon
6. Students should draw an arrow pointing to the paragraph beginning "Let everyone who finds the generals guilty. . . ." Students should circle "Xenophon, *Hellenica,* Book I, c. 400 B.C."

Reading a Chart, page 264
Mark It Up
1. nutritional value of various insects
2. Students should circle the first column going down; cricket.
3. A bowl of crickets because it contains 5.5g of fat

Reading a Map, page 265
Mark It Up
1. Umpqua National Forest Bulldog Rock Recreation Area
2. rock outcrop or highpoint
3. Students should underline geographic labels. See student pages.
4. Students should circle Bullpup Lake.
5. approximately 1 1/4 miles, or 1.25 miles

Reading a Diagram, p. 266
Mark It Up
1. An ecosystem is all the living and nonliving things in an area and the relationships among them. Students should circle the sentence in the top of caption, "*Ecosystem* is a scientific term for all the living and nonliving things in a given area and the relationships among them."
2. Students should draw a line between the sun and the tree (at letter C), then between the tree and the squirrel (at letter D), and finally between the squirrel and the marten (at the bottom right-hand corner).
3. The arrow shows that the marten eats the squirrel; or that energy is transferred from the squirrel to the marten.

4. Producers are trees that use sunlight to make food. Students might also write that all plants—not only trees—are producers. Students should circle the caption by letter C: "Trees are producers. They use sunlight to make food."

5. Students should circle the squirrel and the rabbit.

6. Primary consumers eat green plants, such as clover and grass, and nuts and seeds. Students might also write that primary consumers eat other plant products, such as fruits and roots.

7. Students should draw a box around the caption "Bacteria and fungi decompose plant and animal remains into the nutrients needed by growing plants."

Main Idea and Supporting Details, page 268
Mark It Up

1. Students should underline "As heaps of trash pile up in garbage dumps, communities are trying to cut back on the amount of trash that is thrown away."

2. Students should number the three sentences that follow the main idea sentence.

Problem and Solution, page 269
Mark It Up

1. Students should underline "The park district has proposed frequent ten-minute safety lessons along the path for the first three weekends of summer."

2. Students should circle either "These lessons would make people think about safe riding and skating," or "With a little help, both riders and skaters can easily build safe habits."

3. Possible responses: Yes, I think it's a good solution. I think that short safety lessons would be an easy way to raise people's safety awareness. No, I don't agree with the solution. I think that short lessons wouldn't have any impact on people's habits; people would take the lesson and then forget all about it.

Sequence, page 270
Mark It Up

1. Students should underline (1) *make up a folder;* (2)*Then comes the screenplay;* (3) *make up a shot list;* (4) *make a shooting schedule;* and (5) *Get the camera rolling!*

2. Students should circle *Before, First, Next, Then, first, then, When,* and *After.*

3. (Possible responses are provided.)
    1. Make a folder: Add a cover page; add a summary
    2. Write a screenplay: Write out ideas; put ideas in short story form; put it in screenplay format
    3. Make up a shot list
    4. Make a shooting schedule
    5. Get the camera rolling: Mark each scene at the start

Cause and Effect, page 272
Mark It Up

1. Students should circle *as a result, since, because, consequently, because.*

2. **Cause:** Melted rock is lighter than the solid rock around it.
   Effect: The melted rock rises, pushes through cracks in the earth, and erupts.
   Cause: Flowing lava moves slowly.
   Effect: People can get out of its way.
   Cause: Ash, gases, and hot lava blast from a volcano.
   Effect: Exploding lava can cause death and destruction.
   Cause: Winds carried the thick ash to a campsite twelve miles from Mount St. Helens.
   Effect: Two men suffocated and died from the ash.
   Cause: Winds carried ash to Yakima.
   Effect: Lights had to be turned on all day.

3. Students can use the last four causes and effects listed in #2 to fill in the three diagrams.

Comparison and Contrast, page 274
Mark It Up

1. *too, also, were much like, the same kind . . . as, also, Like*

2. *but, Unlike, The biggest difference . . . is, However, However*

3. (Possible responses are provided.)
   Old space suits: not strong enough to wear outside of spacecraft, stiff, made it hard to bend knees, difficult to pick up small objects, did not protect against micrometeoroids
   Both: give astronauts air, uncomfortable to wear, hard to move around in
   New space suits: can be worn on space walks, protect against micrometeoroids, not as uncomfortable, size is adjustable, gloves let astronauts hold small objects more easily

Argument, page 276
Mark It Up

1. *claim* and *believe*

2. *stop capturing dolphins just to display them for our entertainment*

3. *Talking to dolphin trainers is useless.*

4. **Opinion 1:** *Stop capturing dolphins to display them for entertainment*
   Reasons: dolphins suffer, unable to swim and dive freely, sometimes become ill and are not able to produce babies
   Opinion 2: *Dolphins are thrilled to entertain the public.*
   Reasons: dolphins like being around people; enjoy learning new tricks; like the attention and applause

Social Studies, page 278
Mark It Up

1. Students should put a star next to the Focus section.

2. ***polis:*** *independent communities composed of villages and surrounding farmland* or *a city-state;* **aristocracy:** *government by the nobility;* **sponsored:** *paid for;* **democracy:** *a system of government . . . all male citizens—not just nobles—were allowed to play an active role.*

3. The Greeks developed democracy; students should underline this point in the main text and the time line.

4. Greeks painted many scenes from everyday life; students should draw a box around this point in the caption.

5. Possible responses: *After the Trojan War, By the mid-900s B.C., By the 700s B.C.*

Science, page 280
Mark It Up

1. The lesson will cover water tables. I found this information at the very top of the page (by letter A).

2. The zone of saturation is the area of rock or soil where the pores are completely filled with groundwater.

3. Students should circle the second paragraph. They should underline the first sentence of that paragraph: "How does this model of groundwater relate to what happens inside Earth?"

4. Students should underline the sentence "Look at Figure 21-9, near letter D."

5. The zone of aeration is the top half of the circle and the zone of saturation is on the bottom half of the circle.

Mathematics, page 282
Mark It Up

1. Students should circle *Multiplying Fractions and Mixed Numbers.*

2. mixed numbers

3. Students should box *Solve problems involving multiplication of positive fractions* and *Explain the meaning of multiplication of fractions.*

4. words; algebra

5. a model; Students should put a star next to the study tip.

6. Students should underline *the product is $\frac{3}{10}$* and *You play soccer for $\frac{1}{2}$ hour.*

Reading an Application, page 284
Mark It Up

1. Students should put a number 1 next to the top third of the application, a number 2 next to the middle portion, and a number 3 next to the very bottom portion.

2. Students should cross out the bottom section, marked "for office use only."

3. Students should draw an arrow pointing at the section with a box around it, beginning "If applicant is 14 years old or under . . ."

4. The box draws special attention to that section, so people are less likely to overlook it. It also shows that the different items in that section belong together.

5. Students should circle "I agree to be responsible for all materials borrowed from the Millwood Public Library in my name."

6. B

7. Students should fill out every section but the work phone number, the parent information, and the sections at the top and bottom marked "for office use only."

Reading a Public Notice, page 286
Mark It Up

1. the resident at 11120 Elmwood Avenue

2. promptly fill out and mail the census form that will arrive in about a week

3. Kenneth Prewitt, Director, Bureau of the Census, U.S. Department of Commerce

4. a counting of all the people living in a country

5. Students should circle "The United States Constitution requires a census of the United States every ten years."

6. Students should put a star by "Official census counts are used to distribute government funds to communities and states for highways, schools, health facilities, and many other programs you and your neighbors need."

7. C

Reading Web Pages, page 288
Mark It Up

1. Students should circle the following URLs:
http://www.lookquick.com/search/+pyramids+Egypt
http://www.pbs.org/wgbh/nova/pyramid

2. Students should underline *12,099.*

3. Follow the Excavation

4. a bakery; Students should circle the paragraph at the bottom of the "Pyramids—The Inside Story" site.

5. D

Reading Technical Directions, page 290
Mark It Up

1. Slide the back cover release

2. a blower brush

3. The film leader should be lined up with the red mark.

4. The film is not properly loaded.

5. B

Product Information: Food Label, page 292
Mark It Up

1. 4; Students should circle *Serving Size 4 cookies (31g).*

2. Students should circle *Saturated Fat.*

3. carbohydrate; Students should draw a line connecting *Sugars* to *Total Carbohydrate.*

4. 2%; Students should underline *Iron 2%.*

5. 2,000; Students should underline the sentence following the asterisk.

6. Assessment Practice: C

Reading a Schedule, page 293
Mark It Up

1. to present the schedule of the large gym

2. a weekly schedule; Students should circle *Week of October 5, 2004.*

3. Students should find three Tae Kwon Do labels to underline.

4. Students should correctly circle the hours. They should put an "X" by the Tae Kwon Do class on Saturday.

5. Assessment Practice: B

Comprehension Mini-Lessons Answer Key

Main Idea and Details

Main Idea	Details
Paragraph 1: People did not always have the convenience of walking into a movie theater or renting a video to watch a movie at home.	• In the late 1800s, traveling projectionists would bring movies to small towns. • By 1905, stores were converted into theaters by adding folding chairs and screens.
Paragraph 2: Exhibitors in these new locations looked for creative ways to make up for the lack of sound in film.	• Movie theaters often provided a pianist who would vary the music according to the action of the film. • Lecturers would give their own commentary or describe the action. • Sometimes off-screen actors would be hired to provide the dialogue.

Sequence

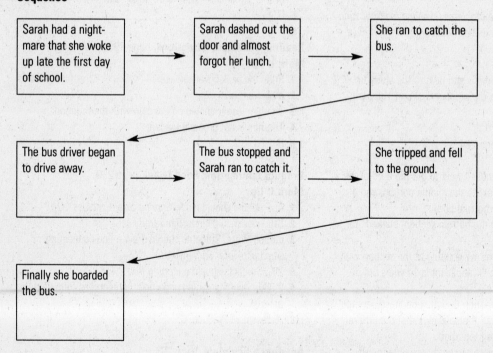

Cause and Effect

Cause	→	Effect(s)
Anna's dad changed jobs.	→	Anna's family moved to another state. Anna left her old friends. Anna started sixth grade at a new school.
A girl smiled at Anna and began talking to her	→	Anna and the girl became best friends.

Compare and Contrast

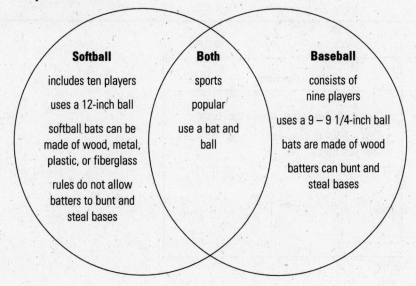

Softball

includes ten players

uses a 12-inch ball

softball bats can be made of wood, metal, plastic, or fiberglass

rules do not allow batters to bunt and steal bases

Both

sports

popular

use a bat and ball

Baseball

consists of nine players

uses a 9 – 9 1/4-inch ball

bats are made of wood

batters can bunt and steal bases

Making Inferences

Selection Information	+	What I Know	=	My Inference
Principal Sanchez is preparing to address the audience.	+	The principal of a school often introduces school events.	=	Josh is acting in a school play.
Five people in the front row have Josh's red hair and freckles.	+	Family members often resemble each other or share some of the same physical traits.	=	Five members of Josh's family have come to see him in the play.
Josh speaks his lines clearly and confidently.	+	Actors suffering from stagefright do not speak their lines clearly and confidently.	=	Josh is going to overcome his nervousness and do well.

Answer Key (continued)

Predicting

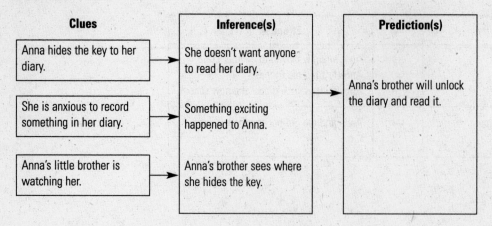

Clues	Inference(s)	Prediction(s)
Anna hides the key to her diary.	She doesn't want anyone to read her diary.	Anna's brother will unlock the diary and read it.
She is anxious to record something in her diary.	Something exciting happened to Anna.	
Anna's little brother is watching her.	Anna's brother sees where she hides the key.	

Fact and Opinion

Fact	Opinion
• Dogs can be trained to protect their owners. • Dogs can be trained to provide special services. • There are guide dogs specially trained to guide a blind person and hearing dogs trained to alert a person who can't hear.	• Dogs make better companions than cats. • Cats are lazy animals that run when strangers approach them.

Narrative Elements

Setting: a crowded city park at sundown, shortly before a fireworks show	**Characters:** Mai and Peter, their parents, and strangers at the park

Plot

Problem: Mai has a twisted ankle and gets lost in a crowd.

Events:
1. Mai chases Peter through the park.
2. She falls and twists her ankle, losing track of Peter.
3. She limps through the park, looking for her family as darkness falls.
4. She sees a red flashlight at the edge of the park and thinks it might be Peter's.

Resolution: Peter finds her, and her ankle begins to hurt less. She acts as if "losing track" of him did not worry her.